TELLING IT

Writing for Film and Television in Canada

Other books in this series

Making It: The Business of Film and Television Production in Canada

Selling It: The Marketing of Canadian Feature Films

TELLING IT

Writing for Film and Television in Canada

Anne Frank, Editor

The Academy of Canadian Cinema and Television

Doubleday Canada Limited

Canadian Cataloguing in Publication Data
Main entry under title:
Telling it: writing for film and television in Canada
Co-published by the Academy of Canadian Cinema and Television
ISBN 0-385-25584-5
1. Television authorship. 2. Motion picture authorship.
1. Frank, Anne. II. Academy of Canadian Cinema and Television.
PN1996. T43 1996 808.2'3 C96-930562-1

Cover design by Avril Orloff
Cover illustration by Pol Turgeon
Text design by Heidy Lawrance Associates
Printed and bound in Canada

Published in Canada by
Doubleday Canada Limited
105 Bond Street
Toronto, Ontario
M5B 1Y3

CONTENTS

Preface

Telling It is the third in a unique series of professional "how to" books produced by the Academy of Canadian Cinema and Television. Like its predecessors, *Making It: The Business of Film and Television Production in Canada* and *Selling It: The Marketing of Canadian Feature Films*, *Telling It* offers readers an invaluable collection of personal "essays" written by a talented and eclectic group of seasoned professionals at the peak of their respective careers. What makes this latest "It" book especially intriguing is that it is a book *about* writing written *by* writers. And rather than focusing on the *craft* of writing for film and television as so many other books do, our writers forge into more challenging territory and focus on the writing *process*.

As you will read in the Introduction, the genesis of *Telling It* was rooted in a series of tremendously successful and popular professional development workshops for writers, story editors and subsequently producers that was developed by the Academy and held in production centres across Canada over the past three years. The Academy of Canadian Cinema and Television, a professional association representing over 2,500 film and television craftspeople and artists, has played a key role over the course of its seventeen-year history in developing and undertaking unique training programs for our industry. The challenge of developing a hands-on workshop that focused on the writer, the writing process, the story and communicating that story, was unquestionably an exciting new training area for the Academy to explore. Together with our writers, branch members and our keen funding partners, we plunged right in.

From the initial stage, the concept was championed and supported by our founding program partners: the Maclean Hunter Television Fund; CBC's National Training and Development Department; FUND, the Foundation to Underwrite New Drama; and Telefilm Canada. Many individuals deserve thanks for their time, commitment and considerable effort in developing these workshops, but I particularly wish to acknowledge and thank Andra Sheffer, Executive Director of the Maclean Hunter Television Fund and Richard Rogers, coordinator of CBC's National Training and Development Department, for their determination and enthusiasm in developing the program and then ensuring their financial resources. As well, sincere thanks to Academy Board member and workshop coordinator, Donald Martin, for his patience and keen skills and to all our facilitators and staff for their hard work. I offer a personal thank you and much appreciation to Anne Frank who served as a facilitator of the workshop over the course of the entire program and then accepted and met the formidable challenge of translating the spirit of the workshop and its concept into this book. No one else could have done it.

Thank you again to our publishing partner Doubleday Canada, and particularly Alison Maclean, for their support and commitment to the publication of books like *Telling It, Selling It,* and *Making It.* And finally, my utmost respect and admiration to all of our writers who were willing to "Tell It" from their own perspectives, experiences and hearts. Your efforts, I am certain, will have far-reaching results.

Maria Topalovich
Chief Executive Officer
Academy of Canadian Cinema and Television

A Note from the Editor

Anne Frank is an independent producer and script consultant. She has been executive story consultant for Atlantis Films on such television movies as The Diviners, the Emmy Award winning Lost in The Barrens, Tom Alone and Race to Freedom. She has won numerous awards as producer of such CBC films as A Change of Heart, Harvest, Seer was Here, A Matter of Choice and the MOW, A Far Cry From Home, Moving Targets. She has been consulting executive producer for the National Screen Institute and was a member of the National Advisory Committee (Academy of Canadian Cinema and Television), that led to the design of the Academy's "National Story Editor Training Program" and the popular "Understanding Story" workshop.

Several years ago the Academy of Canadian Cinema and Television approached me to help develop and design an innovative professional training program for story editors. "It's a new idea," they said, "we've not done anything like it before." I joined an assembled group of senior film and television writers and story editors, and together we began the task of defining the content of the workshop. There was an almost immediate consensus within the group to stay away from teaching easy formulae, offering paradigms or handy recipes for writing screenplays. So if it wasn't about teaching how a good screenplay is written, then what was it about?

The "innovation" that the Academy was hoping for lay in the creation of a workshop which focused on establishing respect for the writing process, respect for the writer and an appreciation for all aspects of developing a screenplay. The session proved to be so successful that the mandate was expanded to include producers, directors and development executives.

The popularity of this program demonstrated that there was an appetite in our industry for learning about writing for film and television which went beyond the fundamental basics of screenwriting. When the mandate was broadened to include producers and development executives, it confirmed that there was a strong interest on all levels to develop and improve the skills which were needed to make their work with writers more effective and meaningful. They wanted to know how to recognize a good story, how to understand the writer's intention and how to communicate, in a positive and constructive way, their understanding and concerns about the story. They wanted to hone the fundamentals of creative collaboration so that the story, screenplay and, ultimately, the film had the strength and integrity they first envisioned.

When Maria Topalovich, chief executive officer of the Academy, and Donald Martin, a member of the Board of Directors representing screenwriters, approached me to ask if I would be interested in editing a book that would synthesize ideas about the writing process, I was enthusiastic about their proposal. The Academy and Doubleday wanted a book which would take the reader from understanding the critical importance of knowing the heart of a story to where to set the margins on the page. They wanted a book with an overview on how the film and television industry works within Canada; how the writer is placed within that industry; how programs get made, who creates them and who gets to work on them and advice on how to pitch a story or story idea to a story editor or industry executive. The book was to touch on the different forms of writing and it was to reach into the future and deal with new technologies and the consequent writing opportunities created in interactive media.

Each and every writer with whom I spoke greeted the idea with excitement and enthusiasm. They gave their creative energies freely, not only in respect to their specific contribution, but often to the book as a whole. As a result, *Telling It* is a book about writing which is written by writers. It focuses on the writing process rather than on the craft of writing for film and television. It is about how writers approach story and what they need to know in order to tell the story. It takes you on a journey of understanding into how writers feel, think and work. Each chapter reflects an individual approach to writing — the results are sometimes wise, sometimes serious, sometimes witty and acerbic but always informative and candid. The writers make it abundantly clear that there are no fail-safe methods. There is no single way to approach writing. There is craft and there are techniques, but beyond that, each writer uses different methods of getting to story — devising and refining the way which is right for them.

An enormous amount of enthusiasm and commitment has been given to this project, and I am grateful to the writers for their support, their patience, their tolerance for doing "yet another rewrite" and for rising to meet those occasionally impossible deadlines. I wish to thank each one of them for making my job so rewarding.

There are a few people to whom I would like to extend a special thank you. Donald Martin for his invaluable input into the project early on, Pete White for his excellent feedback and my initial idea, David Barlow for his generosity, Nancy Botkin for her critical eye and her passion, Ann Medina, Rob Forsyth, Gail Carr and Paul Quarrington for their support, Steve Lucas for going the extra mile, and Anne Hooper for her help in countless logistical ways. A personal thank you to Maria Topalovich for giving me the opportunity to put this book together and through that experience to connect with so many extraordinary individuals in our film and television writing community. Thanks to Alison Maclean at Doubleday for her quiet confidence that it would all somehow come together.

The book is winding down. The final revisions are in. It is time for me to write this introduction. I sit in front of my computer staring at the blank screen, panic gradually rising in my throat. *It's such a simple task,* I say to myself, *why can't I do it?* I hear dim echoes of all the writers I've worked with over the years and, for the first time, I understand. I can only imagine that in the deepest, darkest night of every single writer there must be a moment like this, when that blank page stares back to challenge everything you know.

The writers who meet that challenge and have the courage to struggle through that moment without turning to easy solutions can create a screenplay or a film which is true and which resonates with all of our feelings and lives. I have nothing but respect and admiration for our writers. Without them we would not have the films and television programs which entertain, inform and delight us year after year.

Anne Frank

1

WHAT IT MEANS
TO BE A WRITER

by SHARON Riis

Sharon Riis is a novelist who wrote The True Story of Ida Johnson, *and* Midnight Twilight Tourist Zone. *She wrote the feature screenplays for* Latitude 55 *and* Loyalties; *and MOW,* The Wake, *and a television drama* Change of Heart. *She works with novice screenwriters through Praxis and is occasionally brought in to the Canadian Film Centre to lower the tone. She has a miniseries, a television movie, a feature film and three half-hour cinematic monologues in development. She lives in Saskatoon ... just because.*

> *I am a country and western song*
> *splayed and obvious*
> *my breast bone cracked in two.*

Or, I can forego the metaphor and simply say: I am a writer. The currency of writing, *good* writing, whatever the form, is your own life; your own visceral experience. I'm not referring to circumstances: class education, age, gender, genetics; but to deep, often buried, sometimes unpalatable, occasionally terrifying emotion. Loneliness, dread, joy, grief, despair, delight, torpor, desire, shame ... When people say "write what you know" they're not talking about place but about emotional experience. David Adams Richards needn't be restricted in his writing to the Miramichi nor Suzette Couture to Franco-Ontario. They are *good* writers. Give them a subject (marriage) and an unusual setting (fourteenth-century Cambodia) and, with a little research regarding time and place, and perhaps a brief sojourn in Phnom Phen to experience the unholy humidity, they could deliver a fabulous story, each utterly different from the other. The point is: there's no such thing as generic life; every life is peculiar. When you tell the truth, you can hang any story, any idea on it, in whatever genre you like, comedy, satire, drama or adventure. The truth will be recognizable by everyone, everywhere. You may even have a hit on your hands.

Of course, unhinged emotion like an unhinged idea means less than nothing. It just means that you're unhinged. Writers are first and foremost storytellers. Ideas are a dime a dozen; a good story is a rare and wondrous thing. But a good story isn't simply narrative. It's narrative driven by emotional truth, honed by a distinct point of view. The point of view might make us uneasy, but if the emotion supporting it is honest, then that's reason enough to accept the point of view as authentic and therefore worthy of our attention. *The Night Porter* comes to mind. Or, closer to home, *Leolo*. But I don't mean to single out already celebrated films as examples of what I'm on about. A television series like "Straight Up" both entertains *and* cuts close to the bone with its eerily real and disjointed depiction of late adolescence. And "Traders" has found an audience not only because of its tight, flashy style but because the characters are genuine enough that we can believe in their authenticity. Their machinations are motivated. It's not *simply* about greed. The writers are doing their job. Just because we suck on our own bone marrow for sustenance doesn't mean our stories have to be earnest or dead serious. The greatest comic writers in the world expose their nerve endings in their work.

Writers are isolated, obdurate, antisocial individuals with enormous egos, and sometimes no ego at all. We sit in our rooms and ruminate; occasionally we write something down. How then does such a lonesome charlie survive in the endlessly social, often glib world of film and television production? The short answer is that many don't. They don't have the temperament nor the stamina. Those who do have discovered the very real excitement of collaboration; of having a producer or director *almost* as interested in your writing as you are; of having half a dozen individuals enter into your peculiar world-view to try to make it better — clearer, more dramatic, more interesting — *with* you. And all this buoyant support is before production. If your script actually gets shot there are dozens, maybe hundreds, of people whose business it is to make your work sing. Not all collaborative efforts are charmed. But I've been writing scripts for sixteen years and only twice have the collaborations been a nightmare. Partly because of the banality of the producers in question, but mostly because we were approaching the material from different planets. The only thing to do in a situation like that is to bail out as quickly as possible. In order to be able to do so, it's important to steer clear of a big mortgage. It's also vital to have a life, tricky as that may sound ...

Screenwriting is the most difficult form of writing there is. It's as succinct a medium as poetry and yet it must often do the narrative job of *War and Peace*. It requires us to write in images, to create meaning visually. The interior authoritative voice of prose is anathema to screenplays. Nonetheless we, as screenwriters, must have something to say. But we must show it, not tell it. And we must do so in 22 or 48 or 95 pages wherein we *never* repeat ourselves, for our worldwide audience is astonishingly literate.

A brilliant screenplay, like a brilliant play, poem or novel, is a work of art. But only potentially. A screenplay is not something in itself, but a map, a blueprint for something else entirely. That something else is dependent on a host of people. Those of us who've languished in development hell for any period of time, and that would be *all* of us, know this only too well. This may be especially true of long-form screenwriting. When a script stays unproduced, as most do, it doesn't quietly fold its tent and steal away; it treads water in the "slough of despond" inside your head, and clamours for release. The characters, central and secondary, harangue you for their day in the sun and there's little you can do about it. Well, you can always drink. And commiserate with their predicament because their predicament is *your* predicament.

Not only is screenwriting the most difficult form of writing, it's also the least respected. This is partly the result of a cavalier attitude among producers, agency drones and occasionally directors who think one writer is much like another. This is not so, though often I suspect we do end up *seeming* remarkably the same. This is probably rooted in the high costs of film-making and the bone-headed notion that the only way to make money is to produce a film that appeals to everyone. So terrific scripts are bled of all that makes them terrific. And terrific writers suddenly all seem the same. But good stories are always peculiar. They always have a strong central point of view. And if there's anywhere we should stamp our dainty foot and draw the line in all those story meetings, it's here. "Let me have my say. Help me say it better, clearer, but let me have my say!" When I started writing scripts way back when, I regarded almost everyone as an enemy. The producer, the networks, the agencies, the distributor, the script editor and sometimes even the director. But now I know better. *None* of these are enemies. We're all in it together. And these days, when I feel I'm crying in the wilderness, I realize that I simply haven't done by job yet. My first job being to include all the assembled players in my world-view. And I've come to understand that sometimes my world-view is enhanced and expanded when I take into consideration the peculiar slant of those around me. Lucky for me I'm a socialist.

So with the difficult form and the lack of respect, why on earth do we do it? Are we peculiarly masochistic, greedier than most or simply more sociable? There *is* money to be made. And the parties are a lot better than what the literary world offers up. Film and television are remarkably democratic mediums. If you've got talent *and* an obsessive, driven nature, you'll do fine. But I think the real reason we are drawn to the medium, as writers, is that the medium is *the* art form of our time. Believe it or not. We can all scorn that notion and list endless examples of bad TV and bad film. But there are lots of bad books and bad plays and bad poems too. The truth is that when our work is produced it is seen by hundreds of thousands more people than those reading a best-selling novel in this country. And that, fellow travellers, is power. We have the power to enlighten, unnerve, educate, expose, exhort, dismiss, *astonish*. We are a force to be reckoned with. Without the writer, there's no industry.

What every writer wants is to be brave in their work. What this requires in a collaborative medium is a brave producer, a brave director. And God knows ... brave actors. Then the astonishing is possible. I wish you all, every one, courage.

2

LONG-FORM DRAMATIC WRITING

by JOHN HUNTER

Writer-producer John Hunter has been active in Canadian films and television since 1969. He has been involved in twelve Canadian feature films as a writer and/or producer, including The Grey Fox, *for which his screenplay won a Genie Award in 1983. He has also written ten television dramas and has taught screenwriting at the Canadian Film Centre, Algonquin College and Praxis. John currently lives in Vancouver.*

"Long-form," which encompasses all dramatic films over one hour in playing time, is the El Dorado towards which almost all screenwriters trudge. This makes some sense for anyone who aspires to win more glory than all those anonymous people who write TV episodics. The fact is, one credit on a decent long-form will do more for a screenwriter's reputation than 30 credits on "Road to Avonlea" or "Due South" because a long-form film, be it a feature, a TV movie or a miniseries, is something of an event. It's anticipated more eagerly and scrutinized more closely than an episode of any series, except when a rare series like "Twin Peaks" becomes a cult hit. Writing long-form does not necessarily make financial sense. It customarily takes a year or longer before your idea becomes images on positive-print film, a length of time during which you could have churned out and pocketed the money for ten or twelve episodics. If money is your objective, then write episodics.

Writing long-form also entails a willingness to tote heavier burdens of risk, frustration, failure and humiliation because the long-form writer must run a long gauntlet comprised of worried, picky, egomaniacal and sometimes devious people, all of whom might do harm to you and your work. Writing long-form is mostly about rewriting in order to satisfy the whims, suggestions and demands of everybody who has some clout. "Everybody" includes the producers, the director, network executives, the distributor, funding agency bureaucrats and (when applicable) stars. In long-form production, because the film is going to cost a lot of money and will be, for better or worse, "something of an event," the principals often become infected by a virus I call "Only My Way is the Right Way." If it goes unchecked, this virus invariably damages the outcome of the film. An example of this is painfully described in Robert Geoffrion's mordantly funny piece later in this chapter. Long-form? One could ask why any right-thinking screenwriter would want to do this work. My answer is when you are lucky enough to work with a team of really good professionals, it's more than worth the struggle. In this section you will read six pieces by talented, experienced writers of long-form who bring their own perspectives to the subject.

Pete White *(The Ruby Silver)* shares his experience of writing and bringing to production an original TV movie, or MOW, as we like to call them even though Canada produces only five or six per year. Keith Leckie *(Where the Spirit Lives)* discusses the writing of an MOW which he adapted from a Farley Mowat novel and offers some excellent, wise advice on the necessity of working from a detailed outline. Pay attention. The wonderful Suzette Couture *(Love and Hate, Conspiracy of Silence)* offers her moral raison d'être for writing long-forms based on events that happened to real people, a dramatic form in which she must weave her way between illumination and exploitation. Jefferson Lewis *Les Noces de Papier, (Paper Wedding)* describes the usual creative agonies he experiences when trying to develop an original feature film screenplay, while Robert Geoffrion *(Scream of Stone)* gives us chapter and verse on the travails of a rewrite man on a feature film co-production where each of the principals seems to have his own agenda. Novelist and screenwriter Paul Quarrington *(Perfectly Normal, Whale Music)* offers his take on the problems of adapting novels to the screen and expresses his opinion of the writer-director relationship.

All the contributors to this chapter confront the various kinds of difficulties that go with the territory when you are writing long-form, yet all the pieces are fundamentally optimistic, which I believe to be a necessary trait of long-form screenwriters. Deep down, we all hope to write a film that might make a difference and be remembered fondly over a period of time. We soon realize that the high cost of long-form production puts an undue emphasis on business considerations that often force us to soften what should be sharp and sentimentalize what should be tough. These are the standard commercial pressures and they usually drive screenplays to a lower common denominator. They are a fact of screenwriting life. In spite of them, we also know that it's still possible to author a *Boys of St. Vincent,* a *Prime Suspect,* a *Crying Game,* a *Pulp Fiction* or a *Leaving Las Vegas,* the kinds of films that knock us all over without ever asking for our approval. It's those kinds of possibilities, however remote, that keep all long-form screenwriters trudging down that road towards El Dorado.

Because movies and television dramas occupy such a central role in people's lives, we forget that screenwriting, as a writing art, is only 70 years old, whereas novels have been around for 400 years and stage plays, even longer. Screenwriters have accomplished a lot in a short period of time and I'm proud to ply the same craft as people like Preston Sturges, Robert Bolt, Reginald Rose, Paddy Chayevsky, Joan Tewkesbury, Frederic Raphael, Horton Foote and Woody Allen, to name just a few of the great ones. I also like screenwriters as people, which is the reason they are prominent among my list of friends. Sure, our work often falls short of greatness because dramatic writing is a perilous activity, but just as often the exigencies of the business fall short of us. That is to say what we write gets interfered with in a hundred ways, sometimes to the detriment of what was written on the page. It goes with the territory of writing for the screen.

My small advice to writers who aspire to long-form is: (1) Try to work with and for good professionals who can actually read and respond to what is written; (2) Always start with the pick-and-shovel work of a detailed outline; (3) Aim for creative excellence every time out, otherwise you're already settling for a second- or third-place finish; (4) Don't write too much trash-for-cash or you'll start relying on tricks instead of your imagination. A good screenplay is not like a recipe for chili.

Writing An Original Screenplay

by Jefferson Lewis

A former journalist and professional musician, Jefferson Lewis wrote and directed documentary films before giving up all hope of making an honest living and turned to screenwriting. His first feature-length screenplay, Les Noces de Papier *(Paper Wedding), was a Canadian hit and is still playing deep in the pampas of South America as* Bodas de Papel. *He is the author of more than a dozen screenplays, including* Mon amie Max *with Geneviève Bujold and* Ordinary Magic *with Paul Anka and Glenne Headley. Lewis lives in Montreal and commutes to Los Angeles.*

I write original screenplays because I have to. They come up and tap me on the shoulder, and when I try to ignore them they cuff me upside the head. I give them my standard arguments: I'm too busy adapting a novel, I'm having (another) mid-life crisis, no one wants original screenplays anymore and so on. But in the end, if the idea is *really* good, I give in. After all, it is my story, acne, braces, smile and all. And hope springs eternal. Maybe *this* time everything will go smoothly.

From conception to screen, the life cycle of an original screenplay that actually gets produced — and it doesn't seem to make a huge difference whether you are trying to get it produced in Montreal or Los Angeles or Toronto or Paris — is about five years. There are always exceptions, thank the Buddha. But for each one that takes less, there is one that takes ten years to get to the screen. Of course this depends on what you're writing — I suppose if you wrote the perfect vehicle piece for Sylvester Stallone and actually got it into his hands in less than a year, you might be able to beat the odds, but I wouldn't hold my breath.

The fact is I could work steadily just doing adaptations of books or plays or short stories. It is very appealing for producers to buy a book they enjoy reading and are convinced will make a great movie, and there is a never-ending supply of books to be adapted. And often they do make great movies — 85 per cent of all the movies that have ever won an Oscar for Best Picture are adaptations. Scary.

But then I glance at the shelves where I pile up the notebooks and file cards, outlines, treatments, drafts (and drafts) for each finished screenplay, and I realize that I am basically writing novels, and cutting them into screenplays. So maybe I am beating the odds that way.

There is not, in fact, a huge difference in the amount of "creation" that goes into an original screenplay versus an adaptation: when you adapt a book you usually end up cutting huge amounts, changing characters, inventing new ones, rewriting dialogue until much of the screenplay is original to the screenwriter. And with a so-called original screenplay I am stealing ideas, context, characters and dialogue all the time from the world around me. Well, maybe not stealing, borrowing.

So it's not that adaptations don't satisfy my creative urge that makes me continue to write original screenplays, and it's not that they are easier to get produced (they aren't). It's just that when a great idea comes along and I can *see* the movie on the screen and hear the dialogue, it's impossible for me to resist.

Where It Begins

The right story for me is something that I find interesting. This may seem absurdly obvious — but it isn't. Writers whose primary goal is commercial success usually start off by saying, "What will sell?" which is another way of saying, "What will other people find interesting?"

Don't get me wrong. I think commercial success is great when it means that all of the pieces came together by brilliant planning or serendipity — script, director, cast, producer, timing and an audience that responded enthusiastically. More frequently, though, commercial success has to do more with tens of millions of dollars spent relentlessly promoting some tired piece of dreck. I come out of movies like that knowing why the producer made the movie; what I don't get is why the writer wrote it. Or would want to.

I can't do that. I've tried. It doesn't work — I get bored and stop writing. Since I know I am going to have to spend a long time spinning this yarn, through pitches and outlines and draft after draft, I'd better start off by finding it riveting or I will end up hating the story, hating myself, and hating writing.

A story that works for me has appealing characters who get into trouble, and struggle like hell to get out. It has characters who are transformed by the story, whose lives are changed drastically by the events that unfold on the screen. I like a story that makes me laugh. I love surprises. Unexpected villainy. Unexpected heroism. I like to see people struggling to be better than they are instinctively — more heroic, more generous, more open — but I like endings that are ambiguous, that return the audience to real life and have a way of saying that you can take a piece of it back with you into your own lives, but it is just a movie.

This is all a matter of personal taste, so let me give you an example of mine, and how this process unfolds. I am visiting my sister one day and she tells me she needs a new roommate — her former room-mate got married. Actually it's a strange story. Her room-mate was asked out of the blue if she would marry a French man, a friend of a friend, so that he wouldn't have to go back to France and do his compulsory military service. And she said, "Why not?" So on the chosen day she put on a dress and went to city hall and met her husband to be — and married him. Their friends had a little party, they talked and danced — a fairly unlikely pair: he was tall and quite strait-laced, she was tiny with a huge head of red hair and wildly impulsive (witness her willingness to enter into this marriage).

And — you guessed it — they fell in love. They ended up emigrating together to Australia, husband and wife, to raise sheep and children.

As my sister was telling me this story, I started to get a creepy-crawly feeling, which I have since learned to recognize. It is as though a part of my consciousness suddenly woke up, looked around, sniffed the air, and said, "time to boogie." That is pretty much the way it works: I want to see that movie. I want to see what happens to those characters — I want to *know*.

However, I didn't want to write about my sister's room-mate. I hardly knew her, and besides, that was her story. I wanted to tell my own. Meanwhile, an instinct was saying "something is missing." I didn't like the guy being French — dodging military service — I had French friends doing that a dozen different ways. Not enough risk involved. Should be something worse that happens if she doesn't marry him. At that time in Montreal I kept running into Chileans who were living here illegally because the Canadian government hadn't yet decided that torture and death in Pinochet's jails was a good enough reason to declare Chileans legitimate political refugees. So here they were, journalists, doctors, teachers, washing dishes and running from the *migras* — the immigration police.

So my story would have a Chilean who needed a Canadian wife to save him from being sent back home to prison and, possibly, death. An arranged marriage that turned into love *after* the ceremony — that is what the story was about, in the beginning. And that's what it was about in the end when it was made into a movie called *Les Noces de Papier* (*Paper Wedding*) with Geneviève Bujold and an unknown Chilean actor and writer named Manuel Aranguiz.

From Idea To Pitch

Once my curiosity and interest are aroused by a story, I scribble down a short summary and stuff it into my bulging "Ideas" file, and let my subconscious take over again. A process of elimination begins: How often does it drift into my dreams, or my day-dreams? How does the story evolve as I run it back and forward in my mind? Does it still give me a twinge? Essentially I am a lazy bugger and I'm not going to tell any story I don't *have* to tell.

But if I'm still hot to take a crack at it a couple of months later, if it's kept me awake a couple of nights figuring out how it would fit together, who would that character be, I begin the ritual. I buy a notebook, something appropriate if possible, like Donald Duck or Star Wars or a Chinese scribbler, or if I'm feeling flush, one of those $30 leather-bound beauties you can buy in fancier stationery shops. I think up a working title and start the process of filling the book with notes as they occur. Notes about characters, locations, twists in the plot, scraps of dialogue, whatever comes out.

Meanwhile, I take every occasion to *tell* the story out loud. From now on every time some unwitting friend says, "So what are you working on?" my answer is, "Well, it's a story about ..." and I'm off. As I'm telling the story I watch the victim closely, looking for clues; where do their eyes start to glaze over, when do they start to take a great interest in their watch? What parts make them perk up, smile, laugh, ask questions? I use these clues to make changes in the story — and try out the revised version on the next person foolhardy enough to ask me what I'm working on.

Eventually I find I've got a one-sentence teaser that will make a majority of listeners prick up their ears and ask for more, a one- to two-minute version of the story with, if not a belly laugh, then a genuine grin in it, and a slightly offbeat run at the deeper elements in the story. And if they're *still* interested, I throw caution to the wind and start in on describing the characters and their lives, alternating that with carefully measured doses of plot.

In short, I've got a pitch. And I've got a notebook slowly filling up with story ideas and, in general, the project seems to be moving forward. Time for a major decision. Do I go out and find a producer and sell him or her on it now, or do I write it down — outline, treatment, draft — and try to sell it later?

I described myself earlier as "lazy." I'd like to upgrade that to "efficient," which I suspect is somehow the same thing, or if not, then related. In something like twenty years of professional writing I have never written on spec. I have written for free, to please myself or because the project was worth it and no one else was getting paid anyway. But spec writing is against my religion, or would be if I had one. The truth is that one of the main reasons I continue to write screenplays is that I like the public aspects of the work as an antidote to the long, solitary stretches of writing. In particular, I enjoy the relationship I have with producers. I like the seduction, the sparring, the enthusiasm, the goading, the encouragement, and I like getting paid.

Aside from all of those good reasons, if I am going to ask a producer to take my screenplay and go to war — and make no mistake, that's what it is — to get the movie made, then I want this producer to be totally committed to my screenplay. I want him or her to feel "this is my screenplay," and to be willing to fight for it on that kind of personal level. Nothing less will suffice to get it made. And the best way for a producer to come to feel that way is to have been a part of the whole process of creation.

So at this point I pick up the phone and call the producer I think most likely to be interested in a story like the one I want to write, and invite him or her to lunch. The shock of a writer proposing to buy lunch can be dangerous if the producer is in fragile health, so I don't always mention that part of it on the phone. But if the lunch goes well, I insist on picking up the tab, the result of another theory of mine about priming the pump, which I will spare you.

Usually I consult with my agent first and ask for advice. But in the end I rely on my own instinct. After all, I am the one who is going to have to spend the time with this producer listening to his yarn and boring him with mine, so if I don't like him or her at the outset, I'm in trouble.

So — lunch. Time for the Pitch. Now the ups and downs of a screen-play's progress from idea to screen release look like a cardiogram — of someone with a heart flutter. Up. Down. Way down. Way up. Down. I have come to recognize my own heartbeat, as a screenwriter, and it goes like this:

Idea born — way up. Panic sets in — back down (Oh God, another screenplay coming!). Germination and uncertainty follow, pit-a-pat, pit-a-pat, leading to a steadily rising beat as the ideas start coming and the note-book fills and I rehearse my story and I'm really thumping by the time I get to the pitch. I like this part — I like telling stories, I like the tension, the slightly sick feeling I get before, the rush I get when they laugh, eyes light up, get into it, start in on the suggestions. Get hooked. That's a big up — especially when the lunch ends with a handshake — let's do it!

This is an important peak for me because what follows tends to be a big down. First, I have to go and put the idea into five or so pages (hereinafter to be known as "the concept") which I hate doing because by this time I know too damn much, and second, the producer has begun to negotiate with my agent and the howls of outrage can be heard echoing across the tundra.

Still, most of the time everyone calms down, reason prevails, peace returns to the valley, a contract is drawn up and signed. Only now panic has well and truly set in — now I've got to write the damn thing.

Getting Started

On the cardiogram of my screenplay, this is the lowest point. My instinct, once the first cheque is deposited and a deadline established, is to go to bed for about a year, taking the phone off the hook first. Post-creative letdown, I guess or, pre-creative terror. This is a very fragile state, and it makes no sense to pretend it isn't, though I do pretend all the time that this is rational and logical and a simple matter of exerting discipline and taking cold showers.

The worst thing I can do at this point is start to pull back from my original idea and play it safe, take less risks. And yet it is always my first impulse. So I try to recognize what is going on, accept that I am panicking (again), let it go, and start with something simple. Tackle a small job and ignore the big one looming like a melting iceberg over my head.

I take a three- by five-inch card and write ACT ONE in big letters. I pin the card to my board, and go for lunch. Or if it is still 8:25 a.m. and a trifle early for the kind of four-martini lunch this resolve deserves — Script underway, by jove! Back in the saddle! — I go off to the nearest café for a double espresso. And there I open my notebook and start on another manageable and unthreatening task — writing down what I know about my characters. It's always remarkable to me how little I do actually know about my characters at this point. I have a sense of them — a sniff of them, I know them by a look or a laugh or a gesture, but I know *that ain't going to be enough*. I start with the simple stuff and work up from there. How tall is this character? What colour hair? Brothers and sisters? Left-handed or right? Parents — what about them? First sexual experience — who with? Good or awful? Does the character lie about it now? Lie in general — to him- or herself, or to others as well? When I've exhausted everything intelligent I have to say about a character, I move onto the next one.

There are two reasons I've found for doing the character work at this point. First of all, it is relatively painless, though it can feel like drudgery at first, especially when you are actually dying to plunge into the story and what happens to whom. Second, I know I am going to have to do it sooner or later, and if I do it at the outset, I'll have less corrections to make later. And the writing, when I get to it, will flow in a burst. Having said that, I often start in on plotting the story before I'm ready in terms of the characters, and then come back later when I discover I'm stumped. Knowing something was smart and actually doing it has never been my strong suit.

Besides, the character work always leads to scenes, or parts of scenes, so by now I am hot to write. Back to the board. I have finally settled on a giant one — four feet by six, nailed to the wall facing my desk, with room to pace in between. Up go the filecards — one per scene. INT. DAY — music to my ears. Back to my notebook, scribble another scene, up on the board. Next. In no time at all you have introduced the principle characters and set up the story and all of the subplots and — you're at the end of Act One. Time for another big card — ACT TWO. Only this time you don't want to stop for lunch, or even for dinner. You're on a roll. Don't look back — there'll be time for that later, when you're tired. And so it goes until you've rolled through the story with all of the twists and turns and reached the climax and ACT THREE and the resolution. The last card in ROLL CREDITS. Done.

Okay, it isn't perfect. For now that doesn't matter — go out and celebrate. You did it.

Characters Versus Structure

I have leaped over one of the burning issues of our time — character versus structure. The battle of the Titans. For some reason, these two are frequently considered to be alternatives, either you concentrate on character, or you concentrate on structure. But they aren't alternatives. They are interrelated, and in my humble view, the characters in a screenplay should be as complex as you can make them, and the structure should be as simple and watertight as possible.

Structure essentially means set-up, conflict, resolution — and the 60 million variations possible within that form. The same structure applies to a scene, a sequence of scenes or the screenplay as a whole.

There is no huge mystery to screenplay structure. It's like telling a joke. Can you tell a joke and make people laugh? Or do they roll their eyes and look away? My theory — and I'm sticking to it — is that if you can tell a joke well, you have the basic talent to write a screenplay. Think I'm nuts? Look what's involved in telling a joke well:

Selection — knowing the difference between a joke that is funny and one that isn't. More selection — knowing which joke *not* to tell your grandmother or an Alabama State Trooper. Character — a joke is something that happens to someone with whom we identify — like 'em or not. No character, no joke. Structure — a good joke has a set-up, conflict and a resolution, or punchline.

Most of all, a joke that makes someone laugh is a little gift that connects the teller and the listener, however briefly. It is what makes people tell jokes in the first place, and it is also what makes people write.

Creating character and establishing structure are inextricably entwined, much of the time, part of the big "what-if?" game of writing a screenplay. To go back to the example of *Paper Wedding*, the first what-if goes like this: What if a Canadian woman decided to marry a Chilean refugee so he would not be deported back to jail and torture in his own country? The second what-if is: What if after they got married, circumstances threw them together and they started to fall in love? Well, what kind of woman would agree to such a marriage? We have to figure that out first — is she doing it reluctantly or with conviction? You have to pick one, and then figure out scenes, bits of stage business, to convey that attitude. Does that attitude change? If so, how do you convey that? And so on — this is how you build a story, but the answer to each of these what-ifs has implications both for character *and* for structure.

What unites character and structure is conflict. We should all have the words *"Let them suffer!"* carved into our computers. This is a battle I have to fight all of the way through writing a screenplay, and I have seen many, many other writers in the same situation. You create these wonderful, rich, sympathetic characters and then you deliberately create scenes where they are in deep trouble, emotional or physical. So far so good.

But then instead of letting them suffer and grow and live, you rush in and — fix things. You go Parent. Crises get sidestepped, enemies back down, the hand of the Creator is everywhere. You've taken an exciting premise and made it tame and boring. The drama is gone.

There is an expression in French that I love — something that gets conveniently taken care of in a movie has been *"arrangé avec le gars des vues"* — an arrangement has been made with the guy behind the movies. If you're the writer, that's the kiss of death.

The Treatment

So with any luck, what I have up there on the board scribbled on those cards is a story rich in character and full of surprises.

Then I like to spend a few days, or weeks, not thinking about the script, but just eyeing the board from time to time, maybe changing a card around or adding a new one or scrapping another. But inevitably I am running late so it's time to get the treatment out.

The thing I try to remind myself about treatments is to be nice to the reader. Make the treatment as much like watching the movie as possible. Which doesn't mean endless camera movements and polished dialogue. It means get the reader inside the characters and inside the story as quickly and simply as possible. Don't make promises, as in "this scene will be about …" Deliver the goods. Do it for yourself — you will know your characters and your story that much better. Do it also for all of the people who are going to read the treatment and, unfortunately, judge you and the script by what is there.

By the time I have finished the treatment and polished it, the first draft is very close. The structure is in place, the characters revealed. All that is missing is dialogue and fiddling with the pacing, and often much of that is in the treatment.

Dealing With Criticism

Aside from being your first run at the story, on paper, a major function of this treatment is to keep everyone on board and excited. If you're lucky, that just means the producer and whoever he or she relies on to read scripts. If not, it means an ungodly host of agencies, distributors, network execs and their anonymous "readers" — some of whose comments will be generous and perceptive, while others will be mean spirited, dimwitted and vicious. This is where duck farming starts to look like a fine way to make a living. Many of these anonymous people want to write screenplays, but can't, for whatever reason. The most dangerous ones want to write *your* screenplay, only, of course, write it better. So it is a good idea to make your treatment as foolproof as possible. I seriously recommend Buddhist meditation, and its emphasis on letting go.

Which is not to say for one second that I don't listen to comments on my writing, whether it's a treatment or a final draft. On the contrary, I take these comments very seriously — after all, this is my first audience speaking. But I refuse to read anonymous comments. How else can I weigh the merits of what is being said if I know nothing about the author? I can't, so I don't.

On the other hand, I try to get as many careful and critical readings as I can at each stage — from friends, family, other writers, my agent. Some producers are terrific at reading treatments and drafts, thoughtful and clear in their criticisms, supportive and confident in your ability to make the screenplay better in the stage ahead. Other producers don't know what they think until their hired readers have told them what *they* think. When I find myself working with a producer like that, I usually suggest bringing in a story editor or consultant. Someone who understands that what I need is to have what I've done reflected back to me without fear or favour, and who can suggest solutions without pushing them.

One way or another, I gather my notes and distilled suggestions and advice, and write the draft, add dialogue and stir. In most cases I have dawdled as long as possible, and writing the first draft is invariably a pedal-to-the-metal kind of experience. My struggle is never really with the screenplay or the characters; it is against the depressing, lurking suspicion that this time I am truly writing total garbage, and that the producer will ask for his money back and I will never work again, ever, at anything. It doesn't matter how many times I do this, I always feel the same.

Rewriting

After years of rewriting my own scripts and working as a script consultant or editor or reader, with dozens of writers and directors, I have come to the conclusion that the ability to rewrite — maybe I should make that rewrite and *improve* the script — is the one factor more than all others that marks the difference between a professional and an amateur screenwriter, however inspired. Rewriting and improving is painstaking and difficult work. It is not done with the kind of raw inspiration that can get you through the first stages — pitch, outline, treatment. Rewriting needs patience, above all.

You have to start with the question — should this scene be here at all? If the answer is yes, then you have to sit down and take the scene apart piece by piece and figure out what isn't working: set-up, conflict or resolution. I find myself asking incredibly obvious questions over and over: What is this scene *for*? What is it doing to advance the story? What does it say about the character(s)? I have a category of scenes which don't satisfactorily answer any of those questions but which I will defend passionately to the bitter end because they ... they ... because I like them. I like the mood or the tone or some damn thing. Sometimes they're the best thing in a movie. Sometimes not.

But one way or another, by this point in the life of a script, the kind of work involved has fundamentally changed. You are probably in Year 1 still at the end of the first draft — which means you have four years to go to see the movie get made, if it actually ever does. Four years of rewrites and reader's reports, trying to deal with criticism without getting mad or hopelessly depressed, four years of highs and lows. Somewhere fairly soon after the first draft the director enters, and from being a duo of writer and producer, you are now a trio. Often the director injects energy into the project at a time when your own is starting to flag, and in general I am relieved to have the director as the principal audience for what I'm writing, and rewriting, and rewriting …

The fact is, in this long relay race of making a movie, it is getting to be time to hand your script on to the person who is going to have to make it happen. I usually feel mixed emotions at this point: I have lost all sense of perspective so I can't tell if it is good or awful, I'm sick to death of the screenplay and want to go on to something else. And then I see the director and producer huddling and talking about "their" movie and I feel a sharp pang of loss. Then they ask for my opinion and I get aggrieved and wonder — can't you make the damn movie without bothering me? Reasonable it is not.

In the long run I would prefer to have a director take the script I have written and make it thoroughly his or her own, rather than see on the screen the same movie I have been spooling and unspooling in my mind for the last four or five years. I'll take credit for the parts I like and shuck the blame for the parts that don't work anyway. I figure that's the writer's prerogative.

Writing screenplays is like throwing dice. So much of what happens is beyond your control, and if the idea of that makes you shudder, you should pick another line of work. At least it's rarely boring. As for the creative process, we pretend that it is rational and something we can control, but we can't. All of the courses and seminars and how-to books are only comfort food for the long journey, solace in moments of confusion. You've got to be on the road already.

The best advice I ever got was from someone I've never met — a writer named Natalie Goldberg who wrote a book called *Writing Down the Bones*. When I was teaching a course in screenwriting it was the only book I made compulsory reading for my students. In it she said, "Trust in what you love, continue to do it, and it will take you where you need to go."

Legend of the Ruby Silver: A Writer Looks Over His Shoulder

by Pete White

Pete White is a long-form screenwriter, story consultant and producer/co-producer of his own work. His chosen areas of specialty are action/adventure and period drama. Produced screenplays include Striker's Mountain, Legend of the Ruby Silver *and* Peacekeepers, *an MOW about to go into production with CBC about a platoon of Canadian peacekeepers on a tour of duty in Croatia. Besides his long-form work, White has written episodes for such series as "Beachcombers," "Campbells," "Danger Bay," and "Northwood." A songwriter, he has four albums of material recorded by folksinger Paul Hann. White lives in a house he designed on the shores of Kootenay Lake outside him home town of Kaslo, B.C., the setting for* Legend of the Ruby Silver, *the ABC MOW based on White's experiences as a teenager working in the silver mines. White is the current president of the Writers' Guild of Canada.*

"If you're a workaholic with no personal life to speak of who thrives on critical abuse, loves to argue even when wrong and doesn't mind compromising principles for money — this one's for you! A two-day introduction to storytelling for film and television. Not for the easily offended or faint of heart."

So read the advertisement for my screenwriting course taught one sunny weekend at Kaslo-on-the Lake Summer School of the Arts. If it seeped with a tinge of cynicism, it was inspired by the realities of twenty years of being constantly employed in the film and television industry in Canada.

Screenwriting is a much misunderstood profession. People think actors make up the words and directors create the action. In an industry that seems to value both above the author of the work, the writer is virtually invisible. But the industry is driven by stories and to the screenwriter they all must ultimately come.

In return for his founding contribution, the screenwriter gets to be the scapegoat. There are no good writers. There are no good scripts. Being told your stuff is crap is but the daily expectation. Your craft is reviled by playwrights and novelists as shallow hackism. People routinely try to steal your ideas, your credits and your money. Which ultimately is the one thing that makes it worthwhile. The money. If you work *all* the time — you can make a good living.

Given this general state of affairs, American screenwriter William Goldman's famous quote "Nobody knows anything" is fair comment. The view of the small-time Canadian screenwriter is slightly more charitable. "Everybody knows something." Otherwise they wouldn't be where they are. The trick is to get it out of them without getting replaced, rewritten or robbed in the process.

In that pursuit, I've written 65 television episodes, a six-hour miniseries and I'm starting my tenth screenplay. Though I've been paid for every screenplay, only two have so far been produced. The first was *Strikers*

Mountain (a gig for hire) and the second was *Legend of the Ruby Silver* — an original story. One in ten almost ten years apart. Which isn't to say a good screenplay doesn't have shelf life — only that the lag time between investment and return can be considerable.

For all my cynicism, the five years of development of *Legend of the Ruby Silver* was a positive experience which I enjoyed immensely. I got to research, write and co-produce one of my own stories and was paid for doing it. The basis of that positive experience lies first in working on something you believe in and working with people you like and trust.

Legend of the Ruby Silver is the story of a fast-talking mining promoter from Spokane named Tommy Town who arrives in the West Kootenay Valley in south-eastern B.C. in the midst of a modern-day silver boom to reopen an old mine "The Ruby Silver." In his quest, he enlists the aid of Bill McLean, an old burned-out, drunken miner; Kay Rainie, a cook and miner's widow determined that her son Matt will avoid the fate of his father; and fifteen-year-old Matt — a day-dreamer, get-rich-quick kid out to prove himself — initially drawn to Tommy's flash but opting ultimately for McLean's work ethic. For Matt, "Legend of the Ruby Silver" is a coming-of-age story in which he chooses the kind of man he will become; for his mother Kay, it's a growth to independence and control over her destiny; for hustler Tommy Town, it's a face-to-face confrontation with his own ever-adjustable bottom line; and for Bill McLean, it's a story of redemption as he rises from the ruin of his life to become the legend he once was.

The idea grew out of my experiences as a teenager working in the hardrock mines in the Kootenay and Slocan Valley of south-eastern B.C. The characters, environment, experiences and particularly the stories I heard, stuck with me and made me want to combine them into a movie. As well as being the name of the mine, "Ruby Silver" is the name of a blood-red silver stain that disappears when exposed to the light of day.

I wanted to tell a story rooted in time and place and history. I loved the poetry of the mine names: "The Noble Five," "The Slocan Star," "The Lucky Jim," "The Ruby Silver." I wanted to tell people that what happened in the Kootenays during the original mining boom at the turn of the century (and the ones that came after), was a classic tale of adventure.

Legend of the Ruby Silver was to be an old-fashioned story about mentors — about imparting values and building character — about the telling of stories and the growth of legends. I came to realize what I remembered from my youth were the stories, or fragments of them, told around the kitchen table over tall-necked beer bottles. The characters in the *Legend of the Ruby Silver* learn the fate of those who came before only to discover themselves condemned to repeat it.

My influences were *The Treasure of the Sierra Madre* and *Treasure Island* (particularly Fraser Heston's MOW version). I wanted to impose the structure of a classic tale of adventure over the history of the Kootenays and the experiences of my boyhood. In going for the classic, the risk is to end up with the formula as the two differ only in execution. Stylistically, I modeled it after the fifties action-adventure movies that I'd watched as a boy. I wanted a good piece of American-style entertainment combining action, comedy and romance.

I also wanted to participate as a producer, so I wanted the project small and containable. Four characters. Few locations. Not that it would be without challenge. It was outdoor adventure on mountain roads with old trucks. One of the sets called for an aerial tramway, the engineering marvel and forerunner of the ski lift that made it possible to transport ore down the steep mountain slopes. The fact that the characters were isolated for more than half the movie in a remote mining camp made it (I believed) an affordable period piece.

The first stage was the research. For me, even if it's contemporary, every story is a period piece that requires research. It's the unique details and fresh images that you unearth that will make your story different. In the case of *Legend of the Ruby Silver,* it was more checking and confirming what I already knew and filling in gaps in geology. As former archivist of the Kootenay Lake Archives, I was already familiar with the mining history of the area.

Writing for me is narrowing down your options to specifics. There's never a shortage of things to say or do, there's an over-abundance. The decisions made at the beginning of a project are basic and ones you will want to be able to live with throughout subsequent drafts. For *Legend of the Ruby Silver,* the big thing was deciding on the cast of four characters, making sure each was different enough from the others to interact effectively. And I wanted to keep it simple. I had just finished a Movie of the Week (MOW) for CBC in which I had six main characters (three of my own and three of the producer's) which meant working out a lot of relationships. I decided that though there would be a love interest, I did not want it to be a triangle between two men and a woman. I decided the period was to be 1956.

Characters are a combination of the physical, psychological and socio-logical. Each of these dimensions has to be filled in, if only in the writer's mind. As a development-type I know is fond of saying, "These characters should be interesting even if this stuff never happened to them."

For me, character is a process between two poles of contradiction. The greater the spread without losing credibility, the more interesting the character. In screenplays, characters are expected to change whether it's good for them or not. The character at the end of the story is a different person from the one at the beginning. These changes are the character's arc, be that growth, decay or revelation.

The main character was the drunken old miner Bill McLean. He was the easiest because I knew him so well. He was a composite of three different people but they were all mixed together in my mind. I pretty well just let him run.

Kay Rainie was harder because she was a woman and because of the interweaving of fact and fiction. She was inspired by my mother but I made her British like my wife so I could play her off against the primitive mining camp. She worked best when she was cranked up on righteous indignation. In the end I came to care for her because of her honesty and her stamina.

Tommy Town was the hardest character. People either wanted to redeem him (I actually wrote a pretty good scene where he returned) or write him off as a sleazebag. Somebody said I needed to love him and I finally came to a point which allowed me to open him up fully. Tommy really does believe his own bullshit. In the script, he was the best character.

Though it comes slightly after the characters (because story and character are happening simultaneously in my mind), story structure is the most important thing for me. Perhaps it comes out of working in story-driven series television but until I have some workable story beats structured (even if they're going to change), I feel uneasy. At the same time, the story must clearly come out of the characters and not be imposed upon them.

I generally work in four acts or quarters. To those acts I try to bring a particular sweep that ends in a major climax. The arrival at the Ruby Silver camp. The discovery of Tommy's dishonesty. The discovery of the Ruby Silver. Bill McLean's final departure. Which scene becomes the climax of the act is flexible in that every scene should in theory be strong enough to serve as the climax. However, some story beats are obviously more important than others and you need to spread them over the course of your screenplay to keep people interested and to advance the story.

For series episodes, act structure is more rigid, more of a format. For long-form, unless it's dictated beforehand, act structure is a template you use for convenience to be removed when the script is either complete or restructured for whatever medium it finally ends up in.

The acts then break down into scenes — each scene advancing the story as the scene itself advances to its own climax. Ultimately the scenes break down into moments and lines of dialogue, each of which must be interesting of themselves while advancing the story and developing the characters. In theory, as with good sex, a good story should break down into a series of moments that hold your interest as they advance you towards a climax, leaving you satisfied afterwards.

The weakness of the *Legend of the Ruby Silver* story was its predictability in that it was a classic/formula adventure tale about finding treasure. But the way around that was to use fresh images and to tell everybody what happened before (the legend) and then have it happen to the characters so that each predictable step became instead the pay-off to a set-up. (In retrospect, there were probably too many story beats for the 92 minutes that the ABC MOW format demanded, but I couldn't seem to simplify the story any more and still pay everything off.)

The dialogue was refined throughout the drafts, some lines ultimately taking to the final polish to ring true. It's been suggested that dialogue doesn't carry story but that doesn't make sense to me, particularly in television. To what degree it carries story becomes more evident as you move through pre-production, production and post-production — whittling down which moments and lines are going to stay and which are going to go and what the costs to the storytelling are going to be as a result.

The first written manifestation of all this was the treatment. In some ways the treatment is the most literary stage of the writing. It's pure storytelling in narrative present tense. (Keeping in mind, all drafts but the final are meant to be read.) It's where most of the story work gets done or should get done. Though normally I would do a ten-page spec outline, for *Legend of the Ruby Silver* I wrote a 25-page treatment which was essentially a scene-by-scene breakdown without scene heads with unformatted dialogue throughout. Unfortunately it took a year to complete as I was a week away from finishing it when I had to take some episodic work and I didn't get back to it for eleven months.

I didn't go beyond a treatment on spec because I figured if they didn't get it in 25 pages, they weren't going to get it in 100. And I wanted to get paid for the subsequent three drafts which at a minimum would be spread over the next year or two. With the finished treatment in hand, I went looking for a partner. I wanted somebody I could trust, somebody who trusted me, somebody who would be into it for the long haul.

While attending the Banff Television Festival, I ran into my ex-partner from Kicking Horse Productions, writer, director but mostly producer, Arvi Liimatainen. We hadn't worked together or seen each other in several years. I approached Arvi as a writer-co-producer looking for a senior producer-partner. I wanted to be one of the guys in the room when the final creative decisions were made. Arvi liked the story and we formed a company to develop it.

The first development decision to be made was whether to go for a theatrical feature or MOW. One can find differences between the two in respect to subject matter, language, opening sequence and budget but ultimately it's a subjective judgement that's made by the market place. Arvi figured we should go for the gold and so we went for theatrical with the intention of falling back to MOW if we had to. I still think it was the right strategy. The practical distinction between the two was the line-up of partners. For instance, a MOW would have a broadcaster, a feature, a theatrical distributor. Telefilm needed to know whether it was the feature fund or the broadcast fund. Ultimately, at $3.5 to $5.0 million, it would be too expensive to be a MOW in Canada.

Subsequent to the spec work of creating the treatment, the first formal step of development was the one-sheet. It's a corporate summary, an abbreviated pitch that sets out the territory — market, genre, story idea. With one-sheet and treatment we approached potential development partners. In the end, they were Calgary Television, Superchannel, Telefilm Canada, FUND and AMPDC. Whatever the criticisms levelled at the Public Agencies, we couldn't have done it without them.

I chose my own story editor, a good guy named John McAndrew whom I had worked with on two CBC MOW scripts. John story-edited the first two drafts but after that, I didn't use a story editor. Unlike series' story editors, one-off story editors don't rewrite. They prepare story notes and meet with the writer after each draft is delivered to challenge his ideas and storytelling without (hopefully) imposing their own agenda on the story. Their job is not to enforce solutions but to flag problems.

Probably the most important thing about working with a story editor is being able to recognize a better idea when you hear it. *Legend of the Ruby Silver* was slightly different in that the story editor was imposed by me and I outranked him. That doesn't mean, however, that I didn't listen to him.

We hired him for his expertise. In series, when the story editor gives you the changes, you go away and do them. In long-form, you don't ignore the changes but you ultimately have to go away and make it work for yourself. If it doesn't work for the writer, it won't work for anybody.

Through three drafts, the story remained pretty well the same structurally, becoming with input more focused and refined. Many potential partners passed through periods of interest but never enough of them at once to put together enough budget. The story was either too soft, too hard, too Canadian, not Canadian enough, too commercial, not commercial enough, too big, too small. There were occasions when Arvi and I looked at each other and wondered whether we were the only people in the universe who could see this was a good story. The movie people thought it was an MOW and the television people thought it was a feature. If I once wondered why they call it "development hell" (instead of "development purgatory" which would seem more apt) I now knew. In Canada, development doesn't end. I could hear the not unfamiliar sound of the toilet flushing when ABC bit.

Besides riding *Legend of the Ruby Silver* to its knees, Arvi had line-produced an American MOW in Canada for Los Angeles-based Green/Epstein productions. Arvi gave Jim Green a copy of the script and he liked it a lot. At Banff a year earlier, Jim had told me that *Legend of the Ruby Silver* would get made by an American network — it was just a matter of time. And it was. He and partner Alan Epstein watched for a niche and found it on the Saturday night family adventure movie slot on ABC.

A story meeting was called by ABC in Los Angeles. Arvi was too involved in prep to attend and so I went alone. It was unstated but we both knew whatever they asked for, we were probably going to go along with. It was time to get the sucker made. That said, we were also prepared to negotiate, manoeuvre and fight to keep it good. Fortunately, those things were not mutually exclusive.

A story meeting can go one of two ways. It can be a pleasant and productive experience in which writer, story people and producers focus on strengthening the work. Or it can be a knife fight in a clothes closet in which power, ego, ideology, career advancement and monetary gain motivate the combatants. I've been to both and generally prefer the former. I approached this one with low-grade apprehension. Lurking in the back of every writer's mind is the spectre of "imposed assistance" from another writer — particularly one resident in Los Angeles.

The meeting took 90 minutes. People were friendly and congratulatory. They liked the script very much and the changes were minimal. No one asked if I was "network approved."

Specifically, they wanted to focus the story from the point of view of the boy. They wanted more about the relationship between the dead father and son and wanted to some degree to make the dead father less of a loser than I had portrayed. They also needed it structured to accommodate seven acts and suggested the act breaks. I was going to have to clean up the language ("We don't say shit in the family hour, Pete.") and the "pissing off the back of the truck scene" was not going to fit there either.

The most serious change was moving the story up to the present — a consistent suggestion I had resisted throughout development. However, in the end it turned out to have a markedly small influence on the piece and ABC were pleased with the transition. The one thing I did not do was make more of the relationship between dead father and son. Instead, I strengthened the through-line of Mclean redeeming the dead father by redeeming himself as Matt's mentor. I delivered the new draft in two weeks and it was pronounced a success. There was a further half-page of six minor notes and that was almost the last that came down from the ABC story department.

The first big disappointment for me was not being able to shoot in the Kootenays where the story was set. In the end though, the location at the foot of Mount Yamnuska outside Exshaw, Alberta, was incredible and with the exception of B.C. mountain roads, totally lived up to the original.

Charles Wilkinson was hired as director. He was a Canadian who came recommended by ABC as a good action director. He liked the script very much and expressed that. I told him I wouldn't be looking over his shoulder and I didn't. At the same time, there was a clear tug-of-war between us over numerous minor details — dialogue, moments, a couple of the scenes. It was friendly but it was there. I thought he brought something to the picture and was pleased with what he accomplished.

Emmy winner Jonathan Jackson ("General Hospital") was cast as the boy Matt, John Schneider ("Dukes of Hazzard") as hustler Tommy Town, Rebecca Jenkins ("Bye Bye Blues") as Kay and Emmy winner Bruce Weitz ("Hill Street Blues") as Bill McLean the old miner. When I saw Bruce Weitz dressed as Bill McLean I knew we had a winner. All the actors delivered credible performances but Bruce in particular brought his character to life. He worked hard, knew the script, asked questions.

There were four weeks of prep and it was tight and busy. It was like gearing up to series pace with quick changes and bits of rewrite to accommodate everybody's notes: ABC, executive producer, Broadcast Standards & Practices, product clearances and director.

Towards the end of prep, the final budget was locked and the final trade-offs were made. Under ideal circumstances, this would have been at the smallest, a $5 million Canadian feature. It now had to downsize to a $3.5 million Canadian MOW. Something major was going to have to go. On the table were the special effects known as "the blowholes," the final out of control run down the twisting mountain road in the Dodge Power Wagon, and the whole concept of the aerial tramway.

I fought to retain the tramway because the Victorian engineering was a romantic thing with me (like the Dodge Power Wagon), because it had the effect of opening up the picture like an outdoor adventure movie, and most importantly, because it was integral to the story. It looked like the blowholes were already toast so I argued to cut the ride down the mountain. Fortunately, that's the way it went. To everyone's surprise (including my own), cutting the sequence (which brought us down to 94 pages) actually improved the script. And the tramway looked great. Artistic Director Rick Roberts' recreation of the Ruby Silver camp house, mine site, and tramway was beyond what any of us could have envisioned on our limited budget. Rick had just finished *Legends of the Fall* and *The Unforgiven* (both shot near Calgary) and it showed. Walking through empty sets that were identical to what I remembered proved an eerie experience.

One of the final hurdles was Broadcast Standards & Practices. I thought we had finished with them as I had made a pass on the language, excising the obvious things but retaining the rhythm of the speech so that you almost knew what the word would have been. But it wasn't enough to contain the language to "damns" and "hells" — there would only be a limited number of them and we were over, considerably. We negotiated through Green-Epstein production executive Mark Bacino, winning ultimately three hells and a damn and some big things like retaining McLean as a falling-down, puking-in-the-street, cigarette-smoking drunk.

At this point, I felt I'd won. We'd made trade-offs and compromises all through development and prep but I had been the person who made the changes, incorporating each new wrinkle into the story with minimal disruption and no loose ends. Everything was set up and paid off and it was still the same story I'd started with. Unfortunately I had to go to England during the first two weeks of production. Small changes are inevitable and small changes took place for a variety of reasons. Had I been there, I would have been able to steer some of them differently but others would have simply happened as a matter of course.

Lost were small details of the characters' pasts and motivations. Not that they weren't considered important but that they weren't as important as other considerations. A technical problem. Basic time constraints. A particular take by an actor. The greater importance of story over back story. A judgement as to the necessity of a particular line or moment to the effective telling of the story. Small scenes rolled into bigger scenes to cut down on locations in the hectic schedule of the nineteen-day shoot.

In post-production, the story gets retold yet again. Relative to the footage shot, director, editor and producers can (and do) reslant the story as they choose. But there are important input points. Rough cut. Final cut. Additional Dialogue Recording. Final mix. As a co-producer I had my say at these points but it's worth noting that I would not have "merely" as the writer.

Ultimately, ABC paid for the whole picture. Assumptions will be made about Canadianization trade-offs. There was no attempt by ABC to reset the story in the United States. In the tradition of the mining boom that had invaded the Kootenays, Tommy Town the mining promoter was always from Spokane. Kay was originally British and ABC wanted her to be American for casting purposes. Though we ended up with three American leads and one Canadian, the McLean and Tommy Town roles were first offered to high-profile Canadian actors who declined. Unexpectedly, the RCMP objected to the portrayal of the Mountie and refused to let us use him. He became a "Ranger."

The *Legend of the Ruby Silver* was broadcast Saturday evening, 13 January 1996 to 6.5 million viewers in the United States, earning the number two spot in the Neilson ratings for the evening. It had been six years from the time I started writing the treatment. All the debts I accumulated over that period were paid off and I now enjoyed the luxury of merely being broke again. But the picture got made and pretty well the way I wrote it.

The lessons of *the Ruby Silver* for me are simple. Enjoy the process because it may take some time. Work on things you care about. Work with people you like and trust. The way to be international is to be rooted and specific. There is an audience in the global village for Canadian stories.

Dramatic Long-Form Writing Based on a True Story
by Suzette Couture

Suzette Couture has been a journalist, an actor, one-half of a comedy team and, finally, a writer. Her first miniseries Love and Hate, *based on the true story of JoAnn and Colin Thatcher, was the first Canadian drama to air on a U.S. network in prime time. The miniseries placed number one in the ratings for that week and represented an opening up of opportunities for Canadian television production in the United States. Ms. Couture has since written the miniseries* Conspiracy of Silence *and* Million Dollar Babies *as well as the Canadian feature film* La Florida. *Her movie-for-television* She Stood Alone, *the story of the Tailhook scandal that changed the U.S. Navy, aired on ABC in 1995. The* Washington Post *praised the movie, calling Ms. Couture one of the best writers working in television today. Ms. Couture is a frequent flyer to Los Angeles but continues to live in Canada.*

A Canadian television producer once called me to say he had several ideas for movies based on true stories he wanted me to consider. He then faxed me a list. A family found murdered in a trailer park. A woman bludgeoned to death at a health club. A husband kills his family then turns the gun on himself. These weren't stories, this was a body count.

Yes, I have written a number of movies and miniseries for television based on true stories, some of them having to do with murders. But a murder does not a story make.

Mostly I say no thank you to these offers. When I do say yes it's because I've answered a series of questions I always ask myself.

Why Do This?
My first question is why. Why write this? Terrible things happen every day. What is there in this story that should be dramatized? What is there in it that a dramatization can say more powerfully than a documentary? What would compel me to watch this, let alone write it?

If there is no insight, there are only facts. And a mere retelling of the facts isn't good enough. In some cases it is simply voyeuristic. Perhaps this is why some movies of the week get such bad reviews.

But if there is something in the story that moves me, makes me angry, arouses my passion, my sense of justice (I should confess I get angry with great regularity), I know I am on my way to discovering a point of view that will justify a dramatization.

For me, point of view is crucial. It should be personal, deeply felt. After all, someone is telling this story.

Point Of View Is Crucial

Some people think writing for television and the concept of authorship are contradictory. Television writing is done by committee, isn't it? In my case that's not true. Maybe I've been lucky to work with talented people who respect writers, who understand that somebody is taking responsibility for telling the story. Good producers and network executives will support the writer's vision. If they like it. And they'll like it a lot more if the writer cares about the story because that passion will lead to a distinct and unique point of view.

Point of view, once you feel it, once you know it, is the way into that maze of facts, interviews, tapes, transcripts, news articles and documentaries, the mountain of research that faces the writer. Point of view will help you make choices and will solve problems.

A case in point: *Love and Hate*, a four-hour miniseries for the Canadian Broadcasting Corporation. The producer, Bernard Zukerman, had given me a copy of Maggie Siggins' book, *A Canadian Tragedy, The Story of Colin and JoAnn Thatcher, A Story of Love and Hate*. Maggie Siggins is a master at research and a gifted writer. Reading her book was an emotional experience. I felt intensely JoAnn Thatcher's struggle to hold on to her children, to survive. For me this was JoAnn's story.

Another writer might have focused on the story of how Colin Thatcher went from wealth and privilege to 25 years in prison with no possibility of parole. Or another writer might have found the twists and turns of the police investigation, how they nearly missed convicting Thatcher, to be the story.

But what moved me was the story of how marriages break down, how love turns to hate. This point of view informed all my choices. It also gave me an ending. An ending which had eluded me for months. Rather than end with the usual press scrum on the courthouse steps, I ended the four hours with the Thatcher children.

As directed by the brilliant Francis Mankiewicz, we see them out on the Thatcher land, and see in their eyes that they are the victims of their father's rage. They have been orphaned. They have been given a legacy of violence and loss. There is no dialogue in this scene. It is all in what we know of their story. They get back in their pick-up and drive off. Only the land remains as it was.

What Gives You The Right To Tell This Story?

Love and Hate was my first miniseries. I didn't tell Bernie Zukerman that I didn't have a clue how to write a drama based on a true story. I didn't want to worry him.

Back then, some eight years ago, there were no weekend seminars by "experts," no how-to books. If there were I didn't know about them. So I figured I'd try common sense.

For instance. Do I have the right to do this? To answer this, one would have to find a lawyer, one who knows, who can tell you if it's possible to portray real people in a television dramatization with or without their life rights. At a recent seminar at Osgoode Law School in Toronto, entertainment lawyers were adamant that producers must obtain life rights from the people involved. The project would be uninsurable without them.

At the same time, in the U.S., and I speak from personal knowledge, networks have been looking at ways to avoid paying for life rights. This helps cut costs, certainly, but it can severely restrict the drama in the docudrama. When the writer is restricted to public domain material it's a field day for lawyers. They will dictate what the writer can and cannot do and it will have nothing to do with turning out a good script.

What I mean is that there will be less drama and more "docu." Docudrama is a tightrope act at the best of times. A writer must balance the facts with the requirements of good drama. You only have two commercial hours to tell a story that may have taken years to live. Often your structure will dictate that whole chunks of the real story must be dropped or reshaped. This thing needs momentum, after all, pace. Sometimes there are too many people for audiences to keep track of. You might need to combine them into what is called a composite character, a character that combines the actions and motivations of several people. Sometimes there are too many lawyers. Just like in life. You might need to combine trials and appeals into one. You will want to do all of this but if you don't have life rights and you are confined to public domain material, articles, taped interviews, you may not be able to do any of that because the project might be deemed to be uninsurable.

Even more important is the private, emotional life of the people you are dramatizing. If you are unable to bring insight into what led people to act the way they did because you are prohibited from exploring moments in their lives, you may wind up with a story that does not resonate, that has no themes, no compelling moments. All of this begs the question, is this better as a documentary?

I've outlined some of the problems you might encounter without life rights. There are other kinds of problems when you *do* have life rights. Think about it. Someone wants to tell your story. Already you're nervous. Aren't you? — "What are they going to do, make me sound like, an idiot?" "Will the actress playing me weigh less than me because by the time the movie comes on the air I plan to have lost twenty pounds?" "I never said that back in 1982. I don't remember what I said but I couldn't have said that. Not with that accent."

It's impossible to predict how people will react to their portrayal. I gave the above examples because people often get litigious when their vanity is wounded.

An ideal situation would be where the writer and the people who will be portrayed trust each other. It can't be easy baring your soul and seeing yourself through someone else's eyes. Nor, on the writer's side, is it easy to deal with people who often can't see themselves objectively and don't know how to understand what is intended in a script.

I remember working from a book that a journalist had written. She was extremely upset by the finished script and sent twenty pages of notes denouncing what I'd done. I realized that she simply didn't know how the scenes would play. What she thought of as extreme and unrealistic were some of the strongest moments in the script.

So, let's say you have navigated all those shoals. Your agent or lawyer has made sure you are protected from personal liability in your contract. You've questioned yourself whether, ethically speaking, the story should be told. You now have a script that a network has approved for production. You are about to celebrate. Hold on.

Once a script gets the green light to go into production, writers are often required to submit an annotated copy of their script. This is a nightmare. Long after a writer has gone from the facts of the story to the dramatization, which might have involved combining two or more real people into one character and which always requires inventing dialogue even when the dialogue relates real-life events, the writer must now go back to the facts, find the incidents that inspired scenes and characters and sometimes provide two or more references to prove the incidents actually occurred.

Try this for fun. Imagine a script you've written or are thinking of writing. Think of each page and try to justify, to a lawyer, everything you've written. The characters. Their motivation. Actions. Dialogue. Line by line. Word by word.

Recently I started worrying about the final annotation and I hadn't even written the script. I was still at the treatment stage. This is not good. Concentrate on writing a great story first. Read further if you want advice on how your research can help or hinder this process.

And just when you think the nightmare is over, a new one begins. In one of my last MOWs the network lawyer would review the scenes and dialogue for the following day's shooting schedule and impose last-minute changes and deletions. This is why I am now writing fiction.

A bigger question, for me, is what right do I have to invade the privacy of the people who've lived through a tragedy? How will they feel seeing themselves portrayed on screen?

I have wrestled with this question many times. It has everything to do with responsibility, the writer's responsibility to respect the rights of others. Sometimes the answer I have found is that their right to privacy is transcended by the need to learn from their tragedy, by the insight it gives us into our actions, insight that might lessen the cruelties of this world.

What Do You Do With All That Research?

Let's hope you have some. If you don't, go out there with a tape recorder and get the story. From as many sources as possible. Meet the people whose story this is, if they'll talk to you. Go and see where the story happened. The feeling of the place can inspire you more than any description.

In some of the dramatizations I've done I've been fortunate to have books written by investigative reporters to rely on. Even then it's not a bad idea to question what you are reading, to do more research of your own.

Once I have what seems to be as much information as I'll ever need, I draft a chronology of events. I break down information into categories, where it refers to people, to incidents, to comments, whatever I think will be used in the dramatization. I create, in essence, my own research library.

This is invaluable. When I'm in the middle of a scene and I'm trying to remember what this person said to that person at that moment, I can find the information in seconds. And I'm certain to need it when it comes to annotating the script.

Finally the research is a touchstone. It represents what you know of the truth. Or what you think you know of the truth. Because truth is supposedly what this is about.

Often audiences will see, at the top of the program, a cautionary note.

What they are about to see is *based* on a true story, or *inspired* by a true story. Some of the characters have been fictionalized. Some events have been dramatized. Some language has been invented though it represents, in essence, what was actually said....

The writer, the producer, the network, sometimes the actors, can spend a lot of time questioning whether or not the dramatization truthfully represents the story.

One final reminder. Go there. Wherever the story took place. Where the people you are depicting lived. I'll never forget going to Saskatchewan on a research trip for *Love and Hate*. It was my first time on the Prairies. So much land, as far as the eye can see, with as much sky above. I understood then in a way I never could have before how someone could love this land so much that he'd do anything to save it. And going to The Pas, Manitoba. To a lake where Helen Betty Osborne's body was found. I made a connection with her there that stayed with me through countless drafts of her story. So go there. Breathe the air they breathed.

What's In It For You?

So other than gratifying your writer's ego, writing it, seeing it done, watching the director get the praise, what's in it for you?

One thing that's rarely talked about is how you live with a true life story. It's not something your fertile mind cooked up one day when you stood in the shower too long. It's not just entertainment. It happened. It happened to somebody.

There are times when you forget that. When the events are scenes and the people are characters. When you write a description of the murder and your mind in elsewhere as you type in details from an autopsy report. So many wounds. So much blood.

Then it hits you. It happened. It happened to somebody. And living with that for a year or more is part of what's in it for you.

For me it was Helen Betty Osborne. She was aboriginal. A young woman taking her first steps into adulthood. She'd left her reserve in Northern Manitoba for the big city of The Pas. One cold night she was dragged into a car by four white boys. Later she was found dead in the snow.

It's strange for me now to think how I turned this story down. Repeatedly. Bernie Zukerman kept calling me. Bugging me. He can get away with that. But I had to keep telling him, I can't do this. The story is so depressing, so bleak.

Then one day, perhaps the last day Bernie would call, I happened to read a quote from the late African-American writer James Baldwin. He said that to understand racism he needed to see it from the point of view of the white guy inside the Ku Klux Klan.

This is what I needed in order to understand how to tell this story. Helen Betty Osborne died and it took sixteen years to find the killers. Sixteen years because Betty's killers were white and protected by family and friends. Sixteen years because Betty was Native.

So I told a story of racism from the point of view of the killers. I structured it so Betty would be just another statistic. Just another Native girl people chose to forget. Then slowly, through the first and subsequent investigations we begin to discover her. Her life unfolds through an autopsy report, through interviews with her friends, through the music that was left on her portable player. Until, at the end of the four hours, the final scene is hers. She is leaving for The Pas to attend school. She hugs her mother goodbye. Her face is in the window of the little plane that is carrying her to her new life. In her eyes we see her hopes and dreams.

And it gets me every time.

When, a year later I was given an award for the screenplay of *Conspiracy of Silence* I said that some people had thought Helen Betty Osborne would be forgotten. But she wasn't.

Ultimately, this is why I write these movies.

Adapting Lost in the Barrens for Television

By Keith Ross Leckie

*K*eith Ross Leckie is a writer of television movies including The Bruce Curtis Story, Where the Spirit Lives, *the Emmy Award winning* Lost in the Barrens, Trial at Fortitude Bay, *and* The Avro Arrow Story, *among others. He lives in Toronto's West End with his wife, producer Mary Young Leckie and their three children, Toban, Kate and Sean.*

I was approached by Atlantis Films to adapt the Farley Mowat novel *Lost in the Barrens* into a television movie. The exciting part of this was that they apparently had production financing in place and wanted to shoot the film in about three months time. I had worked on projects through months and years' worth of drafts hoping and praying that financing would eventually be found. But on this, with the money and crew ready and waiting, all I had to do was turn in a decent script and it would be shot. It was a wonderful gift to a writer. The other element was pressure. I find, as do many writers, that I work at my best and most focused when I'm under pressure.

A script did exist but it required a major rewrite and the writer had taken on other commitments and was unavailable. I was given the option and would receive the same fee to either rewrite the existing script or start from scratch. I decided not to read the old script and to start from scratch. I would always take this option if possible. It can often take less time and is always more satisfying.

Farley's book was written early in his career and *Lost in the Barrens* is not his strongest work. It's a simple action tale of two boys, a white (who has come up to northern Manitoba to live with his uncle) and a Native, who becomes separated from a hunting party and must use his wits and skill to survive several months against weather, starvation and predatory animals in the subarctic.

In trying to make this story better and more contemporary, my first consideration was the old three levels of conflict: (1) person against the environment; (2) person against person; (3) person against himself. Farley had lots of number one. The whole tale was man against the environment. So I started to work on ideas about the "person against person" conflict. In Farley's book, Jamie and his Uncle Angus are immediately great friends. I introduced some effective conflict between them, but most important was to introduce conflict between the boys. The boys represent the central relationship in the story. In the book, the boys are great friends at the beginning, middle and end. There is no arc to their relationship. So I started working on the boys' backgrounds. I used my experience with *Where the Spirit Lives* and had the Indian boy Awasin just returning to his people after four brutal years in an Indian residential school. He hates white people. As for Jamie, he has just been removed from an elite eastern boarding school where he was top dog and dropped into this primitive northern environment which he despises. This set-up provided lots of opportunities for "person against person" conflict between them.

Before I considered number three, "person against himself," the inner conflict, I thought some research was necessary into where they were going and what they were doing in the story. With an assistant from Atlantis I gathered a body of material on the Cree and Dene (Awasin's people), specifically on their hunting methods on the edge of the tree line and in the Barrens beyond. I found out some fascinating things about these people. They are among the most skilled and successful hunters in the world. As with the Inuit, hunting for them is a spiritual undertaking. They must purify themselves and achieve a "state of grace" and in this state on the eve of the hunt, they connect with the animals, their prey, and "will" them to come to them. Through prayer they express the hunger of their families and themselves and ask the animal to sacrifice itself. This was rich ground for me to embellish Farley's story.

I went a little further with research and was pleased to find some scientific studies done in the early seventies that contributed to the primary research. The study revealed that when a band of Cree hunters stalk a heard of caribou or elk, several of the old, sick, lame or young animals will turn from the herd and walk towards the hunters! They sacrifice themselves for the good of the herd. There is documentary helicopter footage available showing this very phenomenon. So, beginning as a sceptic, I found there is truth to the spiritual connection between the Cree hunters and the animals; "need" and "sacrifice." All wonderful stuff, and I used it not only in *Lost in the Barrens*, but in a later movie, *Trial at Fortitude Bay*.

Having found this strong hunting milieu, I went on to explore three, conflict level "person against himself," the inner conflict. The contrasting backgrounds of the boys, so effective for conflict level two, also gave strong opportunities for conflict level three. Awasin has been forced to live in a white-run residential school away from his band for four hunting seasons. He has lost touch with the skills of survival. He is not sure if he can survive in the wilderness any more, so his inner conflict is fear of failure. If he cannot remember the old lessons and regain his spirituality, the boys will die. As for Jamie, he believes he knows everything and can be taught nothing. He firmly believes that Awasin's spirituality is all silly mumbo-jumbo, so when it works and they are successful in the hunt — a caribou sacrifices itself to them and saves them from starvation — Jamie is forced to re-evaluate Awasin and to re-evaluate himself and his biases.

Whether I write original stories or adaptations, I am very much structure-oriented and work hard to create a structured framework before ever writing any actual scenes. I usually begin by sketching out a general three-act structure that accommodates the story: the "beginning, middle and end." Within this I then write each scene in paragraph form. This document (an extended treatment) can be as much as 50 pages on an MOW. This is perhaps more than many writers do but it is where the bulk of my work is done and usually it takes longer than actually writing the first draft. The benefits are great because at this stage you can rework the structure with great objectivity. You can ruthlessly slash and burn if you need to. It's in a form that allows producers and editors to see exactly what you're doing and give meaningful input. When this process has been thoroughly done and the scene-by-scene treatment is in great shape, then and only then do I attempt dialogue and a first draft. Dialogue is where I begin to make my emotional investment in the writing. Dialogue is where my characters come alive and I quickly lose my objectivity. If the structure is working, then I have the freedom to play around with the characters and I know I'll be all right.

There are some writers who start at Act One, Scene One and just write, not knowing where they will go. I know Paul Quarrington, a fine writer, writes this way. But for me it's important to know just where I'm going. I find it enhances the scenes as I write them. And to write dialogue right off the top can be a dangerous trap for a writer who hasn't got the structure working yet. They fall in love with a scene or even a strong sequence of dialogue and they will fight to keep it, compromising an objective analysis of the overall story.

Working and reworking a scene-by-scene treatment until it's as good as it can be before attempting a first draft can save many days and weeks rewriting at a draft level. And when the hard work is done, and you know the outline is solid and the story works, the act of writing the draft — giving life and voice to the characters — becomes the greatest freedom and pleasure for me as a writer. I believe this method saved a lot of time on *Barrens*. My second draft was the production draft and this was only possible with a very strong, structured scene-by-scene treatment.

I went to Manitoba before writing *Barrens* because I believe more and more that writers have to go and experience the place they are writing about. I was once contracted to write a drama set in Africa though there was no money to send me there. The resulting script was very flat, lacking authenticity and probably the weakest thing I've written. Whether it be a wilderness environment or a murder site, the experience of being there is a tremendous inspiration to the writer, and producers must be made to realize this.

Probably the most important relationship for a writer is the one with the director. When you've rewritten the script five or eight or twelve times working with producers, network people, funding people and all their editors and the script has finally been green-lighted — just when you think, "Enough! It's perfect" — they bring on a director. There are some writers who will take their production fees and go home, but I believe this is the last and most critical stage of work for the writer to maintain control of his or her work.

When a director comes on board, emotions can be high because the director naturally wants to impose his vision on the script, the writer is feeling naturally defensive about his "baby" and this is the draft that will be shot and seen for all eternity. There are some directors who are "traffic cops" and they'll just shoot the script without really understanding the subtleties of the material. It's all just "blah-blah" to them. Then there are others who are "control freaks" and want to rewrite the whole script themselves. (This shows the ultimate disrespect for the script and the writer.) An ideal director is one who respects the script, wants to understand the writer's vision so he or she can make a better film.

On my first television movie in the mid-seventies, I had a producer who went to great lengths to keep me and the director apart. We actually had to have secret meetings! I think it is crucial for the writer to walk through the script with the director over the course of at least a couple of full, uninterrupted days, and it is the role of the producer to facilitate this process, bearing in mind that it was the scriptwriter whose work got him the green light. Some directors will resist this "mind-melding," but the good directors will ask for it. I talk the director through all the emotional beats, the character arcs and the narrative twists, and I'll answer all questions. We as writers live with those script elements every day and assume everyone must see them clearly on the written page, but a director's mind is full of visuals, locations, casting, schedules and budget. I remember once arriving on set to talk to the director just after a crucial scene was shot. We had not been through the script together. I'll never forget that chilling feeling when he said to me, "Oh, that's what you meant in that scene."

When I go through a script with a director, I accept that it is a give-and-take situation. I am obligated to keep open-minded to their new ideas and suggested changes. It must be a partnership. This "mind-melding" can be a long, hard process but invariably, it produces a better product. Ideally, the writer should be present for a "read through" by the cast. This is a wonderful opportunity for fine-tuning the script and staying in control of the material. It can make the difference between a good film and a great one.

Though time was tight, I had the opportunity of meeting and working with *Barrens* director Michael Scott in Toronto and Manitoba and wrote a production draft that incorporated many of his ideas. Mike is a warm, friendly guy, but he has strong opinions. After some give and take between us I left him to direct my script, satisfied we were seeing the same movie.

To be honest, I believe *Lost in the Barrens* might have needed just one more draft. There are some rough edges that still make me wince, but that's the case in every movie that I've had produced. *Barrens* did win an Emmy Award, and still has great circulation years later. And Farley says he likes it, which from Farley is high praise indeed.

Screaming in Patagonia

by Robert Geoffrion

A *baby boomer, Robert Geoffrion received his degree in psychology, then studied communication arts in Montreal and Los Angeles. He began his career writing and directing documentaries and industrials in Ottawa, then moved to Los Angeles in the late seventies. One memorable afternoon, while working in the art department of the quite forgettable* Deathsport *starring David Carradine and the late, lamented Claudia Jennings, he managed to commandeer no less than Roger Corman as his assistant. Since returning to Canada, he has written several movies for television and the big screen in North America, South America and Europe, in both English and French. He currently resides in Montreal.*

This is not a travel essay although I flew by the seat of my pants and hit brick walls on both sides of the Atlantic and the equator. It is not about cuisine, haute or otherwise, although eating and drinking remain one of the more enjoyable memories of the misadventures to which I am about to confess. And ironically, it is not an essay on screenwriting. Rather, it is about the frustration of not writing, or more precisely of not being allowed to write.

Wait a second — frustration? Isn't *not writing* one of the most rewarding, time-consuming occupations of writers? Of course it is. Writers are notorious procrastinators and every excuse to *not write* is a godsend. After all, what would a writer's life be without the blissful salvation of everyday responsibilities? Washing dishes, chauffeuring the kids and taking down walls are my personal favourites. Naturally, I will swear on the head of my first-born that while I am busy *not writing*, I am *thinking* about writing. Thinking about the movie that is, the movie that was, the movie that will be and, alas, the movie that might have been.

Writers are chronic thinkers. Make that chronic schemers, forever pondering new ways to love, hate, deceive, empathize, betray, confess, humiliate, cry, cheat, fight, rob, maim and kill. That's the fun part. And if all goes well, we hear voices. Voices of wisdom and insanity, of innocence and morbidity, of serenity and paranoia, of hope and despair — characters so memorable they will soar on their own to the big screen. Unfortunately, writing down our nurtured, inspired brainwaves is another story altogether.

Writing is a slow death. It is climbing Everest in a bathing suit. You are ten inches tall, your fingers feel like sledgehammers battering the keyboard, and page one is the quicksand that will suck you down where you belong: oblivion. *Having written* however is sheer exhilaration, if only because you can now return to your real purpose in life, like washing the neighbour's cat. But if not writing is a full-time job, not being allowed to write is a call to arms.

My draft notice came in the form of an unexpected phone call on a quiet day in the summer of 1990 while I was repainting the back porch and thinking about a script that has yet to see the light of day ...

Richard Sadler, an intelligent, congenial producer who has never quite forgotten he was once a philosopher, was at the other end of the line. "Do you know who Werner Herzog is?" he asked. I replied I did. "What do you think of him?" Images suddenly flashed through my mind. I remembered his exquisite *Nosferatu*, only to see myself dragging a boat over a mountain à la *Fitzcaraldo* with Herzog screaming, "Faster, faster! More emotion! Suffer!" I flashed on Klaus Kinski's hypnotic face in *Aguirre the Wrath of God*, then blinked to see Herzog point a gun at my face and say, "Write it, Robert. Write it now or I am going to pull this trigger!" I was excited.

The project, a Germany-France-Canada co-production, was called *Scream of Stone*. It was the story of two climbers. One older, one young. One the epitome of classic mountain climbing, the other the new wave of free-form rock climbing. Both men fighting for the love of the same woman and the glory of being the first to conquer the Cerro Torre, a three-thousand-metre needle of ice in Patagonia. Simple enough? After reading the existing screenplay, I was completely lost.

There was a movie in there somewhere, but it was buried under a structure that wandered all over the place, characters who floated aimlessly and dialogue that smelled of literal translation. It was perfect. I'm not being facetious. A famous sculptor, when asked how he achieved such exquisite human figures, replied, "It is simple" I take a block of granite and remove everything that is not my sculpture." I felt the same way about this screenplay — it was screaming to get out.

Also, with a strong cast already in place, the characters had a face. Vittorio Mezzogiorno, the brilliant Italian actor, was to play the older mountain climber. Stefan Glowacz, intelligent, extremely handsome and one of the top free-form climbers around, was to play his young, rock climbing rival. Anne Parillaud, fresh from *La femme Nikita* was the woman in the middle. And Donald Sutherland, as great an actor as there is in the world today, was the pivotal, Iago-type journalist who played both climbers like a violin for his own advancement

Still, there was something missing. And with the start of principal photography only one month away, this elusive element was now seriously gnawing at me. I was about to confess to Richard Sadler that I had no idea where I was going with this script when he miraculously interrupted me. "By the way," he said, "Donald Sutherland is rewriting his dialogue." I thought this was hilarious, considering the fact that I hadn't written, or rewritten, anything yet. I put on my best poker-face, raised my eyebrows, smiled and left the office.

On my way home, I wrestled once again with the elusive element that had stumped me so far. It always amazes me how one simple, inevitable question can lead to such anxiety and confusion. The question: what is this movie about? People who should know better often reply by telling you the story. As in: it's the story of a woman who falls in love with a man, then decides to kill her husband for the insurance policy instead of divorcing him, only to realize that he has also put out a contract on her, except that the hit man makes a mistake and kills her best friend so the policy now start an investigation and the woman falls in love with the lead detective who discovers her sinister secret and must now decide if he will turn her in or divorce his own wife and kill the woman's husband himself so he and the object of his passion can run away to Rio. By the way, did I mention that the detective murders the husband, only to learn that the woman has a terminal illness that will kill her within the week? Hello?

During my first class in writing way back when, the professor stood in front of us and asked pointedly: what do you want to say? Predictably, we all fell into the same trap, rambling on about the story we wanted to write. He listened patiently, then told us to condense our story into one sentence for the next class. Many of us proceeded to do just that: one sentence, the more clever ones in 300 words or less. We didn't get it. And even in this age of high concept where the one-line pitch rules the day, people still miss the boat. "Jaws" in outer space may sound clever but it tells you nothing about what the movie is trying to say. Mind you, very few producers are interested in what the movie has to say; they just want to see the poster. "Jaws" in Outer Space — "Alien!" Great, but make it a crab this time.

Be that as it may, the one-liner should not be the dazzle-them-with-fancy-footwork high concept it has become today, but rather the message, moral, premise if you will, upon which stories have been based since the golden age of Greek drama. Love conquers all. Crime doesn't pay. Money is the root of all evil. Ironically, the simpler — or perhaps the more simplistic — it is, the better. A good premise inspires character, conflict and resolution. And the fact that any premise can be interpreted ten million different ways explains why we still have the odd, original movie, even today.

Another of my profs, Milt Gelman, a man who was as funny and smart as he was generous with his time and his mind, based his whole professional career on the following: one man's hero is another man's traitor. I thought it was brilliant. I still do. Come to think of it, "one man's hero is another man's traitor" might have served *Scream of Stone* rather well, except that I didn't think about it at the time. My mind drifted instead to people who become so obsessed with their thirst for glory that it drives them to insanity, and even death. At length I formulated my own premise: the quest for immortality will kill you. Granted it was not bumper sticker quality but at least I had something to hand this movie on. I was on my way to Munich.

At their best, co-productions allow international stories to be financed by producers lacking the extraordinary resources of the Hollywood majors, and enable talent from around the world to come together in a spirit of cooperation and respect for their social and cultural distinctiveness. In this age of global markets, this is often the only way to go. At their worst, coproductions are two- three- and sometimes four-headed monsters fed strictly by monetary considerations and constrained by national quotas for crews and actors, to the detriment of the story, its characters and even its location. In these worst-case scenarios, French actors play American cops, an American actress portrays a German mother, a German becomes an Italian priest and an Italian a Native Canadian farmer. Let your imagination run wild — it's a free-for-all. Half a dozen languages are spoken on the set. Actors have no idea what they're saying and crews have no idea what they're doing. Invariably, those movies collapse under the weight of their own confusion.

In terms of a co-production between Germany, France and Canada, *Scream of Stone* seemed like a natural. Mountain and rock climbing were experiencing a resurgence worldwide. The film was to be shot in English, in Munich, Frankfurt and Argentina. The international cast was allowed to preserve, if not their native language for the most part, at least their nationality. As the jumbo started its descent into Munich, my spirits were high and I was filled with a sense of adventure and excitement. I was looking forward to working with the enigmatic Werner Herzog and becoming involved in the shoot, something I rarely do, as a dialogue director. This added responsibility allowed me to rewrite on a daily basis, even on the set if need be. As for meeting Herzog, it happened a lot sooner than I thought.

I was walking through the gate looking for the driver who would take me into town when suddenly, I saw my name on a white piece of cardboard. My jet-lagged eyes tilted up wearily to the face of the man holding the sign, then widened in amazement when I realized it was Herzog himself. He saw the flash of recognition in my eyes and smiled. I felt I was being reunited with an old friend. With Herzog was Walter Saxer, the film's German producer and co-author of the screenplay with Hans-Ulrich Klenner from an original story by Reinhold Messner, arguably the greatest mountain climber of them all. We hopped into the van and headed into town.

Munich is a mixture of Ludwigian splendour and post-war banality. Amidst the spectacular monuments and residences, whole neighbourhoods were rebuilt as five-story boxes totally devoid of character or originality. On the bright side, a wild, gigantic park splits the city from one end to the other and filters the noise and chaos that otherwise infect other urban centres. People here will tell you they are Bavarian, not German, and the massive beer gardens which dot the landscape are symbolic of their sociability and down-to-earth appeal. It felt good to be here.

The production offices were located in Walter Saxer's own sprawling apartment in one of the better neighbourhoods. This is where I would eat, sleep and work in no particular order. Lunch was ready fifteen minutes after we arrived and it was something to behold: an incredible penne arrabiatta served with a salad of tomatoes and buffalo milk mozzarella, washed down with Pinot Griggio. This was the work of Saxer's wife, a beautiful Peruvian woman he had met while working on Herzog's *Fitzcaraldo*. Through the ups and downs of shooting the monster *Scream of Stone,* the one element never to falter would be the food. I still miss it.

Prior to my arrival in Munich, the first draft of my rewrite had been sent to Walter Saxer and Werner Herzog. During lunch, trying to read Saxer's constant shifts from small talk to joviality to evasiveness had proved impossible — the man was a block of stainless steel. Now with the food off the table, the script magically appeared, no doubt from up his sleeve. He slammed it on the table and two machine guns suddenly burst from his eyes, spewing such vitriol that was no doubt as to what he thought of my modest contribution to *his* masterpiece. I coughed and burped my buffalo milk mozzarella.

Herzog turned to him and both men started speaking in German. I couldn't understand a single word they were saying but did notice that Herzog's cool was in direct proportion to Saxer's anger. I sensed an ally and managed to steer the conversation back into English. It turned out that Saxer didn't so much hate my rewrite as wonder why I had bothered in the first place. I replied the script had problems and that I hadn't been hired to correct the grammar. He took this as an insult, screamed that *he* was shooting in two weeks and switched back into German for what I construed to be a threat on either my life or my testicles. He paused for effect, then stormed off, slamming a distant door I couldn't really see. Werner shrugged and motioned for me to follow him. We drove to his offices at the Arriflex Studios and turned our attention to the rewrite.

Werner Herzog is an amazing man. He owns every single movie he has ever made and injects them with so much of his essence and personality that I asked him why he hadn't written this script himself. He admitted he had taken a stab at a rewrite, only to run into the same brick wall I had crashed into today. *Scream* was Walter's first project as a producer after a number of years as Herzog's production manager. Now that he was in the driver's seat, Saxer was determined to flex his muscles and assert his authority to make this *his* movie, not Herzog's. Walter's outburst suddenly made sense. While on the subject of flexing muscles, I asked Herzog if he had really pulled a gun on Klaus Kinski several years ago in an effort to have him do a scene. Herzog laughed and replied it had never happened. I felt somewhat relieved.

Herzog liked a number of things I had done with *Scream*. As we talked about the characters and their motivation, more scenes started popping out of the blue and the script magically took on a life of its own. Conflict was another crucial element that had been sorely lacking in the original script. "There is no harmony without conflict" is as old as drama itself and it is still true today. Simply, conflict is the engine that drives the story.

The climax of the movie where the young and the older mountain climber race to the summit of the Cerro Torre was a given. However, Herzog and I agreed that the long journey to the mountain top should not be a stroll in the park for anyone. One evident source of conflict was the sub-plot of the two climbers vying for the heart of a woman but we couldn't stop there. Indeed, it was imperative for the two climbers to struggle, not only with themselves in the form of doubt, fear and self-deception, but with each other as rivals, and also with the mountain, which transformed itself into the altar of their immortality. As we stripped away their protective layers, they became more interesting, seemingly larger than life and, ironically, more human. Moreover, they injected into the screenplay a behavioural tension and suspense that trickled down to the secondary characters and revealed their own vulnerabilities and idiosyncrasies.

Looking back now on those four days of intense rewriting, it is easy to see how it wouldn't get better than this. One of Herzog's most endearing qualities is his willingness to expose himself warts and all while maintaining a strength of character and purpose that is all too rare in the movie business. Also, he possesses an irresistible, charismatic ability to draw everyone he meets into his own world, on his own level and his own terms, and to make them all believers. I saw this with my own eyes when Anne Parillaud had to bow out of the film and Werner took it upon himself to call Mathilda May in Paris and convince her to come aboard on very short notice. It was over in ten minutes. Mathilda, a terrific actress still in search of a role that matches her talent, had turned to butter on the phone. Earlier, Donald Sutherland might not have been particularly impressed with the script but he was dying to work with Herzog. "I don't want to make this film, I want to work with you," he said. As for Herzog, he thought he was the only one who could direct this movie. Fateful words.

My own memories of our daily meetings were of a deep sense of collaboration and accomplishment. Meanwhile, Walter Saxer had calmed down considerably and there was still a chair for me at the dinner table — always a good sign. I had the distinct feeling that not only had he turned a blind eye to what we might have been plotting, but that he had forgotten we even existed. Seriously, I began to wonder if a producer could really look upon script and direction as two necessary evils that could be dealt with in the same manner as production vehicles or equipment rental. I was about to find out. As I wrote "The End" on the new draft, I had a strange feeling the fun was over. It was.

The screenplay began with the older climber witnessing an indoor competition on an artificial wall. He expresses such contempt for the new wave that the young climber accepts his challenge to scale the Cerro Torre, then compounds the arrogance by having an affair with his mistress. As if emulating the older climber, Walter Saxer read only ten pages and flew into such a rage that he turned beet red and veins bulged all over his face and neck. I thought he was going to have a heart attack. I remained calm and tried to explain that we needed a strong emotional punch right from the start to stoke the rivalry between the two climbers. Walter wouldn't hear of it and threw the script across the room. Now I became angry but Werner jumped in. He and Walter reverted to German and embarked on what would be a four-hour fight interrupted only by Werner's brief translations of a few choice words for my benefit. By the end they were physically spent and emotionally drained. I was discouraged.

Werner and I had agreed to meet the next morning. By the time I showed up at his office, something was wrong: he was making coffee silently, refusing to indulge in the idle chit-chat that had always characterized the start of our meetings. I was turning on my computer and reflecting on Walter's latest outburst when I noticed that Werner seemed to be wrestling with himself. If I feared the worst, I was not about to be disappointed.

Perhaps Walter was right, he said. Perhaps we didn't need an affair between the character of Stephan and Mathilda. I was stunned: this a complete reversal of everything we had been working towards since day one. I argued for the scene but it was obvious I was getting nowhere. Finally, I compromised and said that it wasn't so much the scene of the liaison itself that was crucial. Rather, it was the one where Mathilda returns to Vittorio's apartment late that night and *he knows* that something has happened between her and Stephan. Werner told me that we should also omit that scene. My jaw dropped.

He produced two pages he had written overnight. Stephan drives Mathilda to his apartment and, while still in the car, he takes her hand but she turns him down so he drives her to her own apartment. End of sequence. It was so stale and lifeless that I thought he was kidding. But he wasn't. We argued for another hour but he kept sidestepping the issue. I sighed, went to the scenes in question and pressed the delete key until they were gone. Doing so, I felt I'd been hit with a baseball bat.

Werner might have prevailed on a particular sequence but I was damned if I was going to cave in every time. Ironically, his rewrite brought him no closer to Walter Saxer who still held to his own agenda. In effect we now had three people from the top down heading in different directions, each with his own interpretation of what this movie should be. *Scream of Stone* had lost its voice and point of view, and from where I was sitting it was only going to get worse.

One place where I was no longer sitting was at the Saxer table. Also, I had been sloughed off to the garret room of some hotel a couple of kilometres away. I didn't particularly miss Walter's endearing personality but the thought of his wife's carbonara, gnocchi, penne, tortellini and other culinary delights, not to mention the wine closet, did leave quite an emptiness, so much so that one night I considered crawling back and begging forgiveness. I still kick myself sometimes but I resisted. And then the actors flew into town.

We were hustled to a French restaurant for a get-acquainted dinner. It was very nice actually and the bistro food was to die for. As for the get-acquainted part, well, Donald Sutherland returned to his hotel afterwards thinking I was a member of the cast. In all fairness, much of the confusion probably had to do with the non-smoking regulations which forced Mathilda May, the Columbian assistant director and I to spend much of our time between courses sipping wine and puffing away by the door close to our table while Donald entertained everyone with magic card tricks. As for the script, none of the actors had even seen one for a couple of months and the plan was for them to read it in the comfort of their hotel room after dinner. During dessert, I could picture them all fast asleep with the script open on their lap. Not a bad idea considering we were shooting bright and early the next day.

One of the first scenes involved a discussion concerning why climbers will go for a certain mountain. The obvious answer, and the one in the script, is that the mountain is there. Not necessarily. I was headed for the coffee table when Donald Sutherland intercepted me, wondering why I wasn't in make-up. When I revealed my true identity, always a dangerous move for writers, a look of astonishment crossed his face and he said, "Oh!" With that he led me to a table, whipped out his script and told me he had a couple of questions regarding his scene. An uneasy feeling began to overwhelm me and I said, "Oh?"

Donald had his own insight into why climbers will challenge a particular peak and "because it's there" did not enter into his equation. His theory was that mountains breathe, move, grow and attract the climber by becoming one with it. In no time flat we were talking symbiotic relationship between man and rock, osmosis, even transcendentality. Part of me wanted to run for the hills and part of me was fascinated. Deep down, I knew that so much of the script made so little sense now that it was completely open to these kinds of interpretations.

I placed my computer on the table and we proceeded to rewrite. The more Donald talked, the more he made sense. For one thing I knew that if he was comfortable with his lines, he would deliver them with great conviction and sell his character to the audience. Also, coming as I was from the creative wasteland of the last month or so, it was refreshing to sit down with someone to talk openly and honestly about what was on the page without flying off the deep end or slinking out the back door to appease sensibilities, however misguided they were.

The scene was rewritten and printed within the half-hour, then placed in front of Werner for approval. He had nothing to add. His mind was so preoccupied with how he was going to get through the day that he had little time now for what his actors were going to say. The scene was quite long and it involved six characters in a heated television discussion. Donald

Sutherland was spectacular, towering above everyone as the voice of enlightenment and delivering his lines like butter. It mattered little since most of the scene was eventually left on the cutting room floor, as was Donald's speech. Three weeks later I chanced to ask Stephen Glowacz, the only climber in the group, why he took on a mountain. "Because it's there, of course," he answered.

The precedent had been set and from that first day most of the rewrites, sometimes extensive sometimes not, were done with Donald Sutherland. Being the first to admit that he only looked at his own character, he was always careful not to tinker with any of the other roles; I would adjust them as we went along. It was the kind of close collaboration I had sought with Herzog, only to be ultimately denied.

Two nights later we were shooting in a vegetarian-cum-New Age restaurant. The scene involved Donald, in his Iago mode, convincing the young climber to appear before the television cameras and tell the world he had conquered the Cerro Torre although there was no proof because the summit photo had been lost in a tragic accident on the way down. I had rewritten the scene to make it more punchy and confrontational, but a huge problem remained with one particular line, a hold-over from the original script that I had wrestled with unsuccessfully a number of times before. During the course of dinner, another bottle is brought to the table. Donald's character grimaces and asks if this is the same wine as before, to which the snotty waiter replies, "Yes sir, it's organic!" We tackled the line once again but try as we may we couldn't come up with an alternative. He sighed and started strolling up the quaint street. Feeling rather diminished, I took off the other way. We were shooting in ten minutes.

As I walked, an old dictum came back to me: the funniest lines are always the obvious truth. I applied this to wine and it suddenly hit me. I raced back to Donald. When the waiter said the wine was organic, he would reply, "Ah! That would explain the undertaste of manure." We shortened it to simply, "Ah, that would explain the undertaste!" I felt so good I ordered a glass of wine.

The scene was a pleasure to watch. There was attitude, conflict, vulnerability, manipulation and various planes of emotion. Moreover, Mathilda May and Stephen Glowacz more than held their own and the three actors were working as one. It was then that I started to concentrate on how Werner was shooting all this.

Something didn't click. He was using only one master shot and cranking out take after take without going in for close-ups of the actual conversation to grab the little gems that were popping up here and there. I have always believed that movies sink or swim on the emotions they generate. Certainly those emotions must be in the script to begin with and the actors must deliver them. But more importantly perhaps, it is up to the director to capture them. Here, Herzog wasn't playing it safe, he was being downright timid for no reason at all. The actors were willing and the crew was ready to give him anything he wanted, yet he seemed to be watching the whole process from behind a plate-glass window.

A few days earlier André Gaumond, the Canadian assistant director who was working here as the script supervisor, had approached me with the same concerns. I had replied that Herzog was doing fine but André had been right of course: Werner seemed afraid of his movie. Looking at him more closely now, he reminded me of someone who has become so insecure he forgets which sock goes on what foot in the morning. The restaurant scene, which should have taken six or seven hours to shoot in the best of conditions, was over in three and everyone went home early. I never saw the finished product: it too ended up on the cutting room floor.

The final scenes to be shot in Germany, those that actually open the movie, involved an indoor wall climbing competition in an arena in Frankfurt. We spent three days shooting the sequence and here again, Herzog distanced himself so much from the intimacy of the action that one could find better coverage of such a competition on any televised sports show. Meanwhile, someone else was wrestling with devils of his own.

All of us had the greatest admiration for Vittorio Mezzogiorno, the Italian actor playing the aging mountain climber. But while the other actors were very loose and willing to enjoy a good laugh, Vittorio was extremely intense and the effort his role required was written all over his face. Although he had nailed down the essence of his character and spiced it up with nuance and subtlety, English was not his first language of course and he had great difficulty twisting his tongue around certain sounds. In my second incarnation as a dialogue director, it was my job to rehearse him and make him comfortable with the lines. I never did quite succeed.

Vittorio was a hard man to know. I kept wondering if his anxiety were not due to the fact that he was projecting forward to a future scene where he would have to stand by himself on the summit of the Cerro Torre, with no protection whatsoever except divine intervention. Not only would he be at the mercy of the hellish winds, but there was also the possibility that the unpredictable mushroom of ice under him might suddenly break off and send him toppling 3,000 metres down. A few weeks later when the time came, he did it of course. That is Vittorio Mezzogiorno standing on the Cerro Torre at the end of the movie, simultaneously triumphant and beaten while the aerial camera circles majestically around him to capture the incredible moment. Sadly, he would die three years later of a heart attack.

With Germany done, our ragtag circus moved to Argentina — sixteen hours from Frankfurt to Buenos Aires via Madrid. The next day, another four hours by plane landed us in Rio Gallegos, close to the southern tip of Argentina. From there it was nine bumpy hours by bus into the heart of Patagonia, a desert of whistling winds, snow-capped peaks and turquoise lakes of such awesome beauty they could have only been conceived in heaven. I cradled my computer the whole way to preserve it from the constant shocks.

We were to spend the rest of the movie in a valley offering a view of Mount Fitzgerald, the very same peak which appears on the Patagonia clothing line. The Argentinian government had built an outpost here to establish its national presence in an effort to circumvent Chile's territorial designs on the region. In a Herzogian twist, one of many, there were rumours of armed skirmishes between guerrilla units from both countries, but that's the last thing any of us wanted to think about. Further on, beyond a glacier 1,000 metres deep, was the dreaded Cerro Torre. We could not see it from where we were, but many of us could hear it calling.

After being assigned to the cabins the production had built, we repaired to the osteria, the main production house, for more delectable Italian food by Walter Saxer's wife and gallons of hearty cabernet sauvignon. It was a festive mood. The crossing of the Atlantic and the long journey into Patagonia had somehow dissipated much of the negativity built up over the last few weeks. Also there was a general feeling that Herzog, now out of the city and into the mystic wilds he feels so comfortable with, would finally come into his own and elevate this movie with his brilliance and sheer strength of character. His positive energy was infectious: we were geared up for our assault on the mountain. The script was still going through changes but even that would somehow take care of itself. Notwithstanding the lack of heat in the cabin, I managed to get a few hours sleep. And then morning came.

I will pass on the shower that wheezed dangerously and spat cold water since a torrential downpour soaked me top to bottom on my way to breakfast, and then again when I returned to the cabin. Refreshed, I placed my computer on the desk in my cabin and turned it on to see "Hard Drive Breakdown" flash across the screen. The machine was out of commission.

When I informed Walter Saxer of this tragic turn of events, a look of delight flashed across his face. I knew exactly what he was thinking: no computer, no rewrites. There was only one production computer and he would defend it with his life.

Grabbing a ream of paper and a couple of pens, I settled down by the wood stove in the dining room with a cup of coffee only to find the blank page staring at me, daring me to write something. I stared back. Nothing. My mind was a swamp. The white page began to look like a blizzard. It dawned on me that over the years, I had become manually illiterate — I could not think without my fingers on a keyboard. Walter Saxer sauntered by, smirked and asked me how it was going. A large kitchen knife flashed through my mind.

Plan B: borrow Donald Sutherland's computer. But Saxer was already waiting for me around the bend. Since he controlled the only printer and the copier, there was always a time sheet or other paperwork to monopolize the electronics whenever I walked into the office with new pages. When I pointed out that we were shooting a script (such as it was) and not a time sheet, his answer was always the same: time sheet first, script whenever, if ever. More often than not we ended up with only three or four copies of the script to be shared in the bush by Werner, the actors and the crew.

Screenwriters live and breathe their black and white page — a tidy and controlled, perfect little world where, simplistically speaking, nothing that can go wrong can't be fixed with a few more words or a hit of the "delete" key. Once the screenplay leaves our protective hands for the battlefield however, all bets are off. On any production, one learns to expect problems and minor irritants, obviously. On *Scream of Stone*, these escalated to hardships and near-tragedies on an almost daily basis. Some were beyond anyone's control; most weren't. Here is a partial list:

- Our clothing was totally inadequate. It might have been spring, albeit a chilly one, down in the valley but it was still very much winter up in the mountains and we were freezing our buns off in several feet of snow. Predictably, everyone got sick. Our ranks were decimated by colds, the flu, bronchitis, laryngitis and even pneumonia. Compounding the problem was the fact that our doctor, believing the weather would be balmy, had brought only one bottle of aspirin.

- The production office was equipped with Walter Saxer's pride and joy: a state-of-the-art satellite telephone. It conked out three days after we arrived and remained thus for at least the three weeks I was in

Patagonia, cutting off our only link to the outside world unless you considered the ham radio operator in the outpost.

- The cabin of actor Al Waxman burned to the ground four days after his arrival and everything he had brought with him went up in flames. One thing you must know about Al Waxman is that he does not travel light. Fortunately, he was not in the cabin at the time of the fire.
- Mathilda May took a bad fall on a horse and had to be airlifted to Rio Gallegos where she spent five days in and out of a coma. She recovered completely but the temporary loss of both the person and the actress cast a pall over the entire crew.

And then there was the shooting itself.

A number of scenes took place in and around a base camp offering a view of the Cerro Torre — a small, primitive hut up in the snowy mountains overlooking the glacier and accessible only by helicopter. This required a number of commuter trips in three small helicopters piloted by Argentinian veterans of the Falklands War. Gale-force winds could, and would, erupt at any time to ground the helicopters. We then had to scrounge for something else to shoot. Since the shooting schedule had been drawn up with no consideration for weather, we were playing it by ear more often than not. Sometimes we did shoot; often we didn't.

A case in point was the interior of the base camp hut. We could have saved enormous amounts of travel time by building it next to the osteria, adding removable walls to facilitate the shooting in cramped quarters. Werner would not even consider it — he did not want to deter in any way from the "magic" of the location. That was just plain dumb. In a small way, he was repeating his experience on *Fitzcaraldo* where he refused to shoot the river 100 metres from the civilized village where he was stationed, opting instead for a remote location 1,500 kilometres north in the jungle which proved to be a complete disaster.

Werner Herzog prides himself on the physicality of his movies, an admirable quality when it can be pulled off, a severe handicap when pushed too far. For reasons unknown, he was incapable of making that distinction. It could be that he is too stubborn for his own good, or else he only knows how to shoot movies one way. The way things were going, we were beginning to wonder if he would even finish this one.

One of the pivotal scenes involved Stephan Glowacz, fed up with the constant delays, convincing another climber in the team to ascend the Cerro Torre while Donald and Vittorio are away for two days buying more supplies. I was particularly proud of the job I had done on that scene since

I had managed a clever twist on Stephan's character. In less than one page, I had taken a vulnerable young man awed by his physical surroundings and the stature of the older climber, and transformed him into a manipulator fuelled by ambition and the scent of glory at being the first to reach the summit of the dreaded needle of ice.

The scene took place inside a tent. On the eve of the shoot, with inclement weather once again stalling the production, Werner surprised me by saying he had decided to fake the scene and erect the tent next to the osteria. This was an incredible reversal and for a split second, I actually thought he had seen the light. Then I noticed the piece of paper in his hand. He told me he had given the scene a great deal of thought and had decided he did not want to disgrace Stephan's character by turning him into a manipulator. I was stunned and asked to see what he had written. My heart sank. Once again this was a scene so flat and devoid of conflict, character and even reason that it added nothing to the movie and I couldn't even see the point of shooting it. I argued and argued but Werner would not budge and insisted on shooting it exactly the way he had rewritten it. "So shoot it, what can I say?" I replied. For all intents and purposes, this movie was over for me.

In the sequence that follows, we find the two climbers on the face of the mountain after what may or may not have been a successful climb. Suddenly the second climber slips and falls. The safety rope then tenses around Stephan's neck, effectively choking him. Fighting for his own life and unable to free himself from the noose, he finally cuts the rope to save himself and lets the other climber fall to his death.

This was as cinematic as we were going to get and I went to great lengths to write the scene shot by shot in the form of a storyboard, down to the finest details and every dramatic close-up. It was simple really: a suspenseful action scene specifically designed to make the director and actors shine, and put the audience on the edge of their seats as the tension mounted. Also, the resulting intrigue as to whether Stephan had actually succeeded in climbing the Cerro Torre would carry us into the rest of the film where, because he has lost the camera containing the alleged summit photo in the accident, he is cornered into climbing the Cerro Torre again, this time before television cameras.

There was no way Werner would leave this sequence on the cutting room floor this time because he did not shoot it. Look for it in the movie: it lasts less than one second and is so confusing even I cannot tell what is going on.

If Werner was timid about shooting the script as written, he certainly wasn't shy about putting his crew and actors through such physical hardship that I'm still amazed no lives were lost. At 2:00 one afternoon, we received word that the helicopters would be unable to fetch us because of severe winds in the valley. This meant a four-hour march back to our outpost. No one was particularly worried because we still had two hours to shoot, leave by four and make it back before the sun went down at 8:00. Mathilda May, quite a sight in a fur coat tied at the waist with a piece of rope, was released at three with one of the climbers. She later told me of being terrified for her life while negotiating a narrow path along the face of a cliff. As for the twenty or so of us left on the set, the shooting slowed down to a crawl.

Clouds were moving in and we had to stop until the sun came through again for the medium and close shots of Stephan. At certain point a half-hour went by before we rolled again. I began to wonder why Werner was suddenly so intent on coverage but the only answer that came to me was so sinister I had to wipe it from my mind. At any rate, my watch clicked on past four o'clock and I became more preoccupied with the mathematics of our situation. Never was I so uninterested in what was going on in front of the camera as each shot gave way to more delays. By the time Werner called an end to the day, it was 6:00. Two hours to complete a four-hour walk before the sun went down on us in the wild.

We started off at a brisk but comfortable pace, up and down rocky hills, through petrified forests and across dales of tall grass, then up and down ridges and hills again. Then the group began to stretch out as the ones up front moved faster and those behind started to lag. I was holding steady in the top five, perhaps out of a paranoid fear of being left behind, but the terrain was such that even now I was momentarily losing sight of those ahead and behind me.

I picked up the pace and moved into third place. We were maintaining a pretty good clip and felt confident we would make it back to the outpost in about three hours, before the dwindling light of sunset faded altogether. Fifteen minutes or so later along a forest trail, I came face-to-face with a herd of ten horses led by two gauchos sent from below to rescue us. Since there weren't enough animals to go around and I had psyched myself into thinking that I was going to beat everything Werner threw at me, I accelerated to join Stephan Glowacz and the grip who were about 100 metres ahead. Bad move.

After ten minutes I realized I would never catch the two leaders. Moreover I was now crossing interconnecting trails and couldn't even be sure the group I had left behind would find me if I waited. I was alone in the fading light. For a while the sight of fresh horse droppings confirmed that I was still headed due south on the meandering trail. Then I reached a swamp and hesitated before stepping onto the two rickety planks that spanned it, knowing full well they would never support a horse. Still there was no other way because this is where my trail had led me. I had been alone for half an hour by then and there was still no sign of the distant lights of the outpost. Not very reassuring.

Crossing another dale, I looked up to see an eagle circling 50 metres above me. I shuddered for a brief moment, then convinced myself there was no way it could mistake me for a sheep. I glanced back at it intermittently just to be on the safe side as I hurried along. At one point the eagle vanished, only to be replaced by a condor hovering approximately 100 metres up. I knew it was watching me but I had other things on my mind. Like the fact that I was lost. That the light had faded further to one-quarter of what it was. That I was deathly afraid of being attacked by a mountain lion. That I was soaked head to toe in sweat. That I knew I wouldn't survive if I spent the night out here. Good thoughts. Later I read that condors attack their victims from behind and take their eyes out before doing their nasty business. Still later I read that they are vegetarians. I still don't know which one is true but I'm relieved I didn't have to ponder those options on the trail.

I kept going at what can best be described as a nervous pace. I could feel the big toe of my right foot throbbing but there was no way I could stop. I started to think back on my life and realized it had been pretty good. Was this the beginning of the end? I looked up again and the condor was gone. I looked down and could barely see my feet. Every ten steps or so I went off the narrow trail.

I was on yet another mountain when suddenly, I saw the lights of the outpost two or three kilometres down below. I couldn't believe my eyes. A cold sweat went up my back. I almost cried. After an hour of increasing despair alone on the trail I knew I would make it. The mountain sloped down into a valley and I ran the whole way. I reached a field of tall grass and recognized a gaucho homestead where we had once rented horses. Then I saw the most incredible sight: an old Citroen 2 C.V. coming across the field with no one at the wheel. I raced for it and it stopped. I opened the door to see a twelve-year-old boy barely tall enough to see above the dashboard driving it. He offered me a lift. I couldn't stop laughing to myself as he drove to the outpost.

I went to my cabin and took a shower. My clothes were so wet they were dripping sweat. The nail of my right toe had almost been completely torn off from the constant pressure of the walk and was now dangling. Having nothing else, I wrapped my toe in a piece of toilet paper. I hobbled to the osteria in a euphoric state. Everyone else was there laughing and talking more loudly than I had ever heard them. I was so happy I was on the verge of breaking down completely and crying a river. I began to guzzle great amounts of wine. Werner came around. "Wasn't it exciting?" he asked. I didn't know if I should hug him or punch him. Either way it wouldn't have changed anything. It was the strangest feeling; it took me about an hour to realize I was still a living, breathing, social entity and not a ghost floating aimlessly in the room.

Three weeks after I had arrived in Patagonia, all the dialogue scenes had been shot and it was time for me to leave. Part of me was delighted at the thought of reuniting with my family after so many weeks; part of me was depressed to leave a ship in trouble on the open sea. Even the trip back turned into an expedition. It involved a helicopter, a single-engine plane, a Boeing 727 and a jumbo. It took me 29 hours to make it back home.

Months later, while he was post-synching in Montreal, Herzog told me of another incident while shooting second unit after the film had wrapped. He, Stephan Glowacz and another climber had just been dropped by the helicopter and were climbing the icy wall of the Cerro Torre when suddenly, Werner looked off and saw clouds surging in like a tidal wave. He knew exactly what that meant.

Reacting quickly, they dug a hole into the ice with their picks and bundled in seconds before winds of 200 kilometres an hour swept in and ravaged everything in sight. They would have literally been blown off the mountain. There was barely enough room for them in the hole but they were safe, at least for now. From experience, they knew that the unpredictable storms around the Cerro Torre could last anywhere from ten minutes to days. They knew this was a particularly vicious one but they remained hopeful. All they had was a walkie-talkie with which they could remain in contact with the outpost, and a piece of chocolate. They were radioed the storm was raging across the whole region. They waited. If anything, the storm only got worse.

The hours passed. They had to move constantly for fear of freezing, and began a ritual of climbing over each other to change positions every fifteen minutes. To fall asleep meant certain death. The light was beginning to fall. They were radioed that a rescue team could not be sent since the storm showed no signs of abating; they would have to spend the night in their hole. They ate a piece of chocolate the size of a fingernail, continued to switch positions and told each other stories to stay awake. By dawn they were in terrible shape but holding up.

The storm had calmed down considerably in the valley but not in the mountains. Another climber took it upon himself to reach them. He got bogged down in snow up to his neck and had to turn back. The clock ticked and ticked and ticked. There was a real fear of hypothermia. They could not even put their faces out of the hole the winds were so bad. They kept hoping, shifting positions, singing songs and hanging in there. Another day passed.

That night was the worse. The climber could feel himself fading fast. He told Werner and Stephan that if they weren't rescued by the next morning, he would die. They struggled to keep his spirits up and had to literally manhandle him so he would not fall asleep. They weren't in much better shape themselves but they had to fight on. The situation was deteriorating. Their strength was fading fast. Death was creeping into the hole. Morning came and there was still no break in the weather. They moved less and less now. Their voices could barely be heard as they radioed the outpost. Fate was the master.

The climber's eyes were closed more often than they were open. He was beginning to plead with them to just let him go. They knew they would have to give in at some point; they felt exactly the same way. More hours passed. The climber was ready to die. Werner and Stephan knew that if he went they would follow — they had run out of arguments.

Then miraculously, the wind died down and the clouds cleared. A rescue team finally reached them and they were taken down, suffering from exhaustion, hypothermia and frostbite. They had spent 50 hours in the hole.

"Was it exciting?" I asked Werner, remembering my own minor brush with death. He thought about it for a moment and answered, but I couldn't hear. I didn't ask him to repeat.

Scream of Stone turned out to be a nowhere movie — neither here nor there, never gripping and never knowing what it wanted to be. No one was making the same movie. Not I. Not Werner. Not Walter. Like so many others, it is only a movie that could have been. Take away the opening and final shots and everything between them could have been better written, better directed and better produced. But it was not to be. I have often asked myself if I would do it again. You bet.

I lost contact with Werner Herzog. Four years later I saw a one-hour documentary he had written, directed and produced on Kuwait after the Gulf War. It is brilliant.

Dialogue with Paul Quarrington
Interviewed by Anne Frank

Paul Quarrington *is a novelist, screenwriter and playwright. His screenplay for* Perfectly Normal, *which he co-wrote with Eugene Lipinski, won the Genie Award in 1992. He wrote the novel and the screenplay for* Whale Music, *and the screenplay for* Camilla, *starring the late Jessica Tandy and Bridget Fonda. He has been nominated three times for the prestigious Stephen Leacock Medal for Humour which he won in 1987 for his novel* King Leary. *In 1986 Quarrington was included on the Canadian Book Information Centre's list of ten best writers under the age of 45. In 1990 he received the highest honour for a Canadian novelist, the Governor General's Award for* Whale Music. *Other novels include* Home Game, The Life of Hope, Logan in Overtime *and* Civilization.

Can you talk about process, how you approach your writing?
If you want to talk about process, then I have to tell you the reason I write. I say this quite often and let people assume I'm being facetious, but I'm not, actually. The reason I write is because it gives me something to think about when I'm falling asleep at night. If I'm writing a novel, I think about the characters, and I think about what they're likely to do. Screenplays are the same thing, because what I actually do, and this sounds a little suspect, over a series of nights of falling asleep, I'll roll the movie.

I sit in some strange kind of imaginative movie theatre and each night the movie gets progressively longer. I ruminate about characters until they kind of gel in some hard-to-define way. I have to have a pretty clear idea of the whole thing and what the characters are like. I don't have to wait till I know the entire movie before I start writing, but I certainly have to know twenty minutes of it. I don't structure it at this point because really what I'm doing is rolling the movie. I can structure afterwards.

Sometimes, because of deadlines, you have to start writing before the characters are fully formed. It's largely a waste of time. The producers may call you up and say, "This character is not really fully formed," and I'll say "I knew that." Quite often when they ask about rewrites they'll ask, "How long will it take?" Your most honest answer is, "Well, it will take about 40 minutes, but I might not be prepared to do it for seven years."

It's the same thing with books. Books are like running the movie. You're not *reading* the book. Writing is just a way of communicating pictures.

Or a way of telling stories?
This emphasis on storytelling is kind of irritating. I think in terms of *creating fiction*. A strong traditional narrative is a tool. If you can find other ways to accomplish the same thing, that should be OK. I sometimes think in terms of "symphonic structure." Something like a long, complicated opening section, a slow middle, a furious ending. You could use a sonata form, introducing one character, then the other, then the variations of their intercourse, so to speak. I never think in terms of telling stories; I always think of it in terms of creating fiction and creating worlds. A story may or may not be a part of that.

There's no movie without character. This is my basic attitude. I heard someone say at one of these writing workshops, "Look, you know what the story of Hamlet is all about? It's all about this guy that sees his father's ghost and ..." They run through the narrative pointing out what sort of strength there is in the pure unadulterated storytelling of something like that. But you notice when they do that, they do it very quickly, and they think they're showing how pat and uncomplicated it is. But really, I think they're doing it quickly because that's about how much patience someone has listening to just pure narrative. Any pure story, any series of events, no matter how complicated and interwoven, are simply not interesting if you don't know the characters involved. People tend to speed through them when they relate them to you. Contrast that to someone who has gossip to tell, and think about how they go! "I know something you don't know," then you say, "Come on, tell me," "No I don't want to tell you." They'll take forever because this is where someone's interest is. I certainly think that the characters are the prime driving force.

Once you decide to move forward with your writing, how do you proceed? Do you structure your idea in some way? Do you write an outline?
I would just write, but with a fairly strong template or plan for myself in place. Like a lot of writers, I find that the actual writing of the outline is a dissipation of creative energy. It's not that I don't think they are a good idea; quite often you have to do it just because of the way things are set up. People like to see outlines. But where possible, I like to write them after I've written the draft.

When you're in the process of writing, what do you keep in mind as a reference point, a place you have to move towards?

I look back at what I've done and sort of project it from there. I try to see truly what I've done, and that will dictate what I must do. In terms of themes, you look and you see what it's about, not what you *think* it's about, or what you set out to write, necessarily. You have to look and see really what it's about. And that can give you a pleasant surprise or a shock. Whatever you find, I think you have to then go with it. Once you see what it's about, you continue that. The same with structure. I think I have developed, despite all my railing about being perverse about story and stuff, I think I'm good with structure. I conceive of it as — and I like to use the overblown word, of architectonics — I just look and see what I've done, and if there are valleys and hills, I see that there has to be a corresponding set of valleys and hills.

The kind of thing that too often goes wrong with a story is that it is in uneven blocks. A new storytelling impetus, a radical turn. You find this in some really quite well-respected screenplays. *Rain Man,* for example. It's got big lumps where new sorts of ideas and storytelling impulses rear their heads. There's that big, long Vegas interlude. It was brilliant, maybe, but it was a different movie. And I think this sort of thing comes with simply trying to invent action to drive towards the end of the movie. But if you were a painter you wouldn't keep staring at the empty parts of the canvas wondering how to fill them. You'd look at what you'd done, and then you'd move forward from there.

In a screenplay there isn't room for the kind of creative exploration that makes novel writing so exciting. When you write a novel you tend to have your characters and the situation, and maybe some broad ideas about plot, and then you let the characters go. It's as much of an adventure for you as for them, to wake up on the morning and see what's going to happen. But I don't find any of that in screenplay writing. You tend to know exactly when and where the characters have to be, and the process is simply one of solving the problems of how to get them there. So it doesn't really have the same degree of artistic satisfaction.

Do you find it more restrictive?

Oh, absolutely! I think people just overestimate the size of a movie. I think that basically movies are not much bigger than a short story. And that's about what they can hold. So they're about that restrictive, which I think, is very restrictive. You are very confined to what you can do and what you can't do. In a short story, you've got a paragraph to not only hook the readers' interest, but you have to set the whole tone for the short story. You have to more or less contain it all in the first paragraph. In movies, you've got five minutes off the top and then there's only a certain amount of complications that can go on. I don't conceive of movies as other people do, as a kind of huge sprawling canvas on which we can pour out all sorts of creative stuff.

When you adapt one of your books to film, does it then become a process of confining the story?
Not actually. It's a process of turfing out a lot of stuff. It's just that there's no room for it. You try not to confine what you do have. If you can come up with a kind of healthy, vibrant through-line, then you go with it. In *East of Eden*, the movie with James Dean, you have the story of Cal, his brother and their father. This story is not even a third of the book. But that's all that the movie could hold. So you just leave things out. And there's any number of examples like that.

Is it painful for you to leave things out when adapting from your own material?
When Alliance first asked if I'd be interested in writing the screenplay for my novel *Whale Music*, I was reminded of the old guy in *Of Mice and Men* who said, "Well you know it's my dog. I ought to shoot it." So to a certain extent I was better at getting rid of things from the novel than was the director, Richard Lewis, who co-wrote *Whale Music* with me. He'd often say, Well this was in the novel," and I'd say "So what?" The fact that it is in the novel means I don't have to worry about it any more.

And the good thing too about adapting your own stuff is that you are the writer most familiar with the material. And, you get another crack at things. Not that you've made mistakes necessarily in the novel. We wrote a script based on my book called *King Leary*. In the book there is one scene involving two characters. The director, Richard Lewis, who co-wrote the screenplay with me, said, "Why isn't the other character there? Why not?" and of course I didn't have a good answer. So you do get a second crack at things.

How do you start? Where do you begin when doing an adaptation?
You usually have to find a new way in — come at it from somewhere else.

And that's not always such a big problem as it seems. *Whale Music*, the movie, is much more about a kind of odd love relationship than the book, which is more about the relationship between the two brothers, I think. It wasn't my inclination to make it a love story. That is something you sort of decide on with the director or whoever you're working with. But it's a new approach, so you go from there.

Atom Egoyan was actually quite interested in directing *Whale Music* at one time. I wrote a screenplay with Atom once, and just thinking about his movies you could tell what would interest him. The dysfunctional family aspect is in the book, so his idea had a lot to do with Desmond's brother, and his parents. Desmond's parents were very much in that script. So you get that as true a representation of the book as anything else. But Richard, when he became the director, just decided, "Well, I am not really that interested in the parents who aren't there at all. I'm more interested in the love story." So you can see that to a certain extent, it's decisions made on that kind of a bloodless level. It's kind of an intellectual exercise. But when you're talking about process, you go through any number of them. And then you make other decisions, like, "Are we going to have voice-over?" Now you change your mind on that, and "What kind of conventions can we use?" It's rather arbitrary, and you might find that they don't work and so you change things. But basically you go in with your orders. It's best to make those decisions, and then you know what you're supposed to do and you try to accomplish it.

So you decide what the central idea of your screenplay will be and then you start writing? And if it shifts from the book?
It might shift because it was a bad idea. It will certainly shift from the book. I don't know that there's any way to avoid that. I would advocate respect for the book, respect for the book's fans, respect for what they saw in it, and try to replicate that. You kind of have an obligation to do that. In *Marine Life,* written by Linda Svendsen, for example, what that book's fans responded to was probably the last story as much as anything else, so I think there's kind of an obligation to deal with that. But I'm sure you'll find movie producers who will say," Well, you know, actually, the book only sold so many copies, so we don't really care whether they like it or not." As a writer, I wouldn't say it's my weakness, but certainly it's perceived as a fault by some of the people I work with, that I tend to be a little too respectful of the original writer and the creation — their book.

To the detriment of what?
To the detriment of commercial film-making. Which isn't a bad thing, commercial film-making.

Is the process different for you when you rewrite someone else's screenplay?
I came in as a second writer on *Perfectly Normal*. It was an original screenplay written by Eugene Lipinski. He wrote the first draft and I wrote the second draft. What you have to do if you are the second writer is think about the material long enough so you can find something that interests you — something that generates a first writer kind of excitement. Eugene's story had an angle on it that I thought had quite a bit of legitimacy and was something worth exploring, but it didn't have any particular resonance for me. The Turner character, played by Robbie Coltrane, basically wanted the hockey player to dress up in women's clothing because he got off on it. So it had to do with sexuality. For various reasons, not all from my point of view, the producers were reluctant to pursue this angle. It finally occurred to me that, for me, what the story was about was not so much sexuality, as just *difference* — that you can't really accept what's different in other people until you accept what's' different in yourself. And that approach has a linkage with matters of gender and sexuality. I found my own take on it, and then was able to tell the story from there.

Another movie I wrote — this one called *Giant Steps* — was the same sort of thing. There was a first draft written by another writer, Greg Dummett, and they wanted me to write a second draft. It was a coming-of-age story. One of the scenes in the first draft was about a young kid getting drunk for the first time. When the producers first talked to me I said, "Well you know, it would be hard for me to … I can't really remember getting drunk for the first time. I can barely remember when I got drunk last night." I forget how old I was at the time, in my late thirties maybe, well you know, a coming-of-age story wasn't really sitting too well with me. But because there was a middle-aged character in the script, and themes involving isolation and difference, both subjects that interested me, I was able to find a new way into the script. And sometimes you do that with your own material too.

What are some of your thoughts on the relationship between the writer and producers and directors?
My first — and best — experience was on *Perfectly Normal*. I was con-

tacted by Michael Burns, a producer who knew that I had written a novel about hockey. Because it was kind of a quirky hockey story, he thought that there might be some combination or connection. He was my first contact in this business, and we rapidly became friends. On that first movie he took me with him through the whole process. He would relate to me how he was trying to get the money, he would take me to see directors, and we'd talk about actors. So that's where I began to receive my education. And because he is kind of an old-school producer, by the time a director was hired I was very much of the mindset that this was Michael's movie.

When a movie is given the Oscar for best picture, it always struck me as odd that it would be the producer going up to receive the award. I'd have said that he was just riding on someone's coat-tails. But my experience really made it clear to me that this is the producer's creation and it was a revelation to me. Since then I am kind of put off to a certain degree with the — not the power that directors assume, because why shouldn't you assume all the power you can — but the power that is *bestowed* upon them for whatever reason. You hear all sorts of theories, like the French intellectuals coming up with their *auteur* theory. The director should really be a member of the creative team and answerable to other forces. We're discussing something that is written by one person, produced by another person and directed by another person.

We're going to see this change anyway because I can see in 30 years, it could be changed so radically that a director is simply someone who is sent out to gather information. A director would simply be a gun-for-hire. Any kind of visual information he comes back with is going to be manipulated. The editor is going to assume much more importance, which he should have now.

A director should adhere more closely to the model of a theatrical director whose attitude is to explore the script and discover what the writer is trying to say and then do his best, as a kind of midwife, to make sure that it gets expressed. But that's sadly uncommon. And you hear people say, I overheard one of Canada's hottest young directors at a party say, "Well they sent me the script. I liked it very much. I started rewriting immediately. I rewrote the whole thing." Well, what did he like about it?

I've had good and bad experiences. I teach a little course, "Self-Defence for the Screenwriter" and I go through everyone involved and put them into one of two camps, "Friend" or "Foe." I always put the producer as a "friend."

Editors are friends. They're kind of like the writers on the other end. They fix things that might have gone wrong. And they're usually working from the script. And actors? Friends. Actors are fabulous, especially if you don't expect them to say any of the dialogue the way it's written.

A director could be friend or foe. In a good situation, the director is there to make sure that everyone is making the same movie. I think this is where the experience and training comes in. You have to know how to speak to a camera operator so he or she will understand. How to speak to an actor so he or she will understand. To a costume person, a set designer. A director needs great powers of communication, and if he's got them, I respect that.

But why he or she can make *all* the aesthetic decisions is beyond me. I have this theory that writers are not, by and large, well people. You know? Writing is an odd behaviour and indicative of a large collection of obsessions. Writing is also its own therapy, so we end up being very healthy, but my point is that we're driven to create, we are carving something out from deep down, and the director is not part of that first order of creation. So if you want to know if the carpet should be red or green, why ask the director?

Mind you, most good directors are writers. And when it's working, then both the writer and the director are coming from almost the same place. It can never be the same place, though. Isn't possible. But it's close enough that the final product is satisfying for both the writer and the director.

3

SERIES WRITING

by David Barlow

D avid Barlow was senior producer on the 1995 season of the CBC series "Side
Effects," co-producer of the fifth season of the Alliance/CTV series "E.N.G.,"
executive story editor on the first season of "North of 60" (Alliance/CBC) and the
second season of the half-hour comedy series "Max Glick" (Fosterfilms/CBC). In
addition to episodes of these series, Barlow co-wrote (with Maureen McKeon) the
TV movie finale for Street Legal — Last Rights. During the eighties, he co-
created, produced and story-edited CBC's successful comedy/mystery series
"Seeing Things" with Louis Del Grande.

In The Beginning

Charles Lazer and I are currently writing the pilot episode of a proposed
series for Alliance Communications and the CBC. It is based on a series of
books, true-life adventures of a pair of wilderness ranchers in British
Columbia. Out of curiosity, and because I was writing this chapter, I looked
back in my files to check out when I first made enquiries to see if the television rights to these books were available. 6 July, 1987. It will be 1996 in
a few days. This seems like a good place to make the first point about series
development. Sometimes, developing a series takes time.

Nothing much happened with this idea for the first half-decade or so.
The few times I broached it with a broadcaster or production company, the
response was either, "Period series are a hard sell" or "The western is a dead
genre" or "The networks want half-hours not hours." There are a million
ways to say "No" but they all come out "No." Then one day in 1994, I happened to be talking to Christine Shipton, who is vice-president, Creative
Affairs for Alliance Television. And she happened to mention that she
might be able to sell a general-audience, period, hour series. Did I have

anything like that? Why yes, said I, blowing the dust off my notes. I sent a few pages to Christine, we talked some more, she set up an appointment to pitch it to Debby Bernstein at the CBC, Debby agreed to come in on development funding, and presto, a few months after my first conversation with Christine and only seven years after I had the original notion, we were in active development. Point number two — a good premise is not enough to get a series into development. Timing is essential, not to mention luck.

Not everything takes as long as this one did, but there are fads and fashions to series, just as there are in every other line of television and film writing. And, of course, the winner series are often the ones that break with the trends, offer something new and different. But they might be the hardest to launch. Frustrating, right?

"All in the Family," the ground-breaking sitcom of the seventies, was developed by ABC. After they rejected two versions of the pilot, the creators took the show to CBS where it ran for twelve years. "Barney Miller" went through three pilots. The seminal "Hill Street Blues" was almost cancelled in its first season or two until it reaped a raft of Emmy nominations and awards and audiences came around. Speaking of "Hill Street," developing television series is kind of like the police work on that show. The risks are enormous, failure is always a very real possibility, virtue is not always rewarded and the bad guys don't always get their just desserts. Oh, and one more parallel — a lot depends on who you know.

The sad reality is that track record means a great deal to the people who finance series development. Sad for new writers looking to sell a great premise, not so sad for those of us who have had the good fortune to have gained some experience on series. The caution of broadcasters and production companies is understandable; series production is a complex manufacturing process in which a given number of episodes have to be churned out on time and on budget. Figure $750,000 to a $1,000,000 or more per hour of drama multiplied by sixteen to 22 episodes and you can see that there is a great deal of money at stake. Take the low-end hour drama at $750,000 and multiply it by sixteen episodes over an eight-month production period and you'll be spending an average of $50,000 a day. It'll be less in pre-production and more when you are actually shooting, but any way you cut it, this is serious coin. And it all starts with the scripts. Write two people talking at the race track and we are outside with legions of extras, location fees and logistical problems galore. Change it to two people watching the race on TV and we are in the studio under controlled conditions saving piles of dough. But what if you can't decide what the two people should be saying? Well, then you've got a cast and crew of 40 to 100 people being paid to stand around and eat craft service while waiting for the script pages. So when broadcasters go to write that big cheque for a series, they look for names of people they can rely on. Reliable production companies and reliable producers, usually producer-writers, to act as showrunners — the people who will be ultimately responsible for delivering the series. Look at the most successful series in Canada and the United States and you will see that, almost without exception, the individuals who run the show are, or were, writers who created the concept or played a key role in its development.

But what about the new writers with the fresh new ideas? Are they frozen out? No, but they will most likely have to team with more experienced people their first time at bat or build up some credits in episodic writing and story editing until some broadcasters and production companies get to know them and develop a comfort factor with them.

The Premise

The two fundamental building blocks for a series are the creative personnel and the premise. I hope the previous few paragraphs explain, at least in part, why the creative personnel are so important. That leaves premise. There are two types of premises — high concept and ... not high concept. I don't know what to call the other kind, generically, but I know it when I see it and I will try to describe it to you.

High concept is just that, a situation or a set of characters where the continuing conflict is obvious from the moment the premise is described. Remember "The Fugitive?" Even if you don't, you probably know the movie. "Mission Impossible?" Same thing, stay tuned for the movie. Both were high-concept series. A bigoted, conservative blue-collar worker shares his home with his honest, loving wife, his independent, high-spirited daughter and his liberal, college student (unemployed) son-in-law. It's the politically turbulent seventies and the series is "All in the Family." No matter what person or issue came in the door of the Bunker house, you knew that Archie and Meathead, the son-in-law, would disagree, Gloria would side with one or the other or have her own particular take and Edith would be the peacemaker, while being written off by her husband as a "Dingbat." The rhythms were predictable and the audience revelled in the anticipation of "How will Archie react to this?"

"M*A*S*H" was high concept — anti-establishment doctors, anti-war and anti-army, isolated in a remote field hospital, forced to deal with the casualties of what was to them a senseless conflict. Set in the Korean War but telecast during the Vietnam War era, it managed to run longer than both. "M*A*S*H" also displays another high-concept characteristic: a disparate group of people are thrown together by circumstance and forced to live and work with one another because there is no prospect of escape. It shares this with a somewhat lower-brow but also successful series, "Gilligan's Island." Strange bedfellows.

Closer to home, there is the naive, Candide-like, Canadian Mountie thrust onto the mean streets of Chicago with the cynical, hard-bitten American police detective as his guide. To quote Paul Haggis, the creator of "Due South," his Mountie hero's objective is to clean up Chicago, one person at a time.

One example of high concept that backfired, if not commercially, then at least aesthetically, was "Miami Vice." The concept for that police drama was described as "MTV Cops." Catchy, conjures up the idea of a cop show done as music video clips, but it really describes style rather than substance. As I recall, this phrase came out of the mouth of a network executive rather than a writer, but I may be claiming that just to reveal my prejudice. Nevertheless, the series had great visual style and was a certified hit. But it struggled with scripts from very early on and I would suggest one of the reasons was that the basic premise, as encapsulated in those two words, does not give us a central and continuing conflict for the series. Maybe you need more than two words, no matter how catchy they might be.

Now, there is the other type of series premise and I am definitely going to need more than two words. To call it low concept would suggest it has inherently less energy or conflict, which it doesn't. And it would be wrong to say it is character driven, because all series are character driven. Even the most slam-bang action series has at its centre a character or characters whom the audience wants to go on the roller-coaster ride with week after week. But this other type of premise is softer; it does not lend itself to as brief and punchy a description of the central conflict. "Road to Avonlea" would be a good example. It takes us into the small-town world of Avonlea in the early 1900s, and provides us with the continuing joy of seeing a familiar and interesting collection of characters of all ages dealing with large crises and small. We realize in short order that certain characters can always be counted on to react to certain other characters, but there is no single, defining conflict the way there tends to be in high-concept shows. The CBC drama "Side Effects" is like this too, compared to the high-concept drama of an "E.R." which takes the medical show genre and treats it like an action series, with a life-and-death emergency coming through the door every twelve minutes.

While I would never describe "North of 60" as high concept, the creators did manage to sum up their premise in one succinct line. It works so well, they even put it on the show's T-shirts. "One town, two worlds, and the only bridge is trust." Whites and Native people living in the same community, trying to find a way to understand one another. Think of the possibilities for conflict that come out of that one word, "trust." Trying to earn trust, failing to trust, betraying trust — it is a tremendous one-liner.

Many children's and family drama series are also "not high concept" — I am thinking of "coming-of-age" shows like "Max Glick" and "My Life as a Dog" and "Jake and the Kid." But occasionally one will break the mould, like the underrated "The Odyssey" which dramatized the subconscious world of a boy in a coma.

I have gone on at length about this because it is important to know what you are selling. High concept is usually easier to pitch but you will have to be prepared to explain how the characters and situation will sustain interest over the long run. Shows with less overt situational dilemmas may be harder to pitch — you will need to find a way to quickly sell the appeal of your central characters. Which is not a bad thing to concentrate on because regardless of the type of premise, high concept or ... that other kind (I wish I could find a professional-sounding term), strong central characters, an interesting milieu and good opportunities for continuing conflict are what make a series run.

Characters

The central characters have to be people whom audiences will identify with, or empathize with, or people they can love to hate. The broadcasters want characters whom large numbers of viewers will want to invite into their living rooms for an hour each week. Characters whose unfolding story is endlessly fascinating to the audience. Viewers will get to know these characters as well as they know their friends and the viewer's anticipation of how their TV "friends" will react to their weekly dilemmas becomes part of the attraction of tuning in regularly.

One thing we have not been good at doing in this country is continuing to exploit actors who have established themselves as popular series personae. For example, why haven't people like Louis Del Grande, Al Waxman, Gordon Pinsent, Jeff Wincott, Sara Botsford, Art Hindle and

Mark Humphrey reappeared in new series? This can partially be explained by the limited volume of series development done in this country, and by the absence of any real star culture in English Canada but, excuses aside, it is simply a waste of valuable resources. Audiences respond to familiar characters; these actors, and many others, have already established a familiarity with Canadian viewers.

You can tell series' characters have been embraced when you encounter two people talking about a show the morning after it has been telecast. My favourite sample of this kind of conversation occurs when one regular viewer has missed an episode and the other is bringing them up to date. They describe the action by using the character names: "Green had to try and deliver a baby in the emerge …," or "Olivia caught Chuck in bed with …" When you hear those kinds of conversation, you know you've hooked an audience.

Unlikable characters can earn viewer loyalty too, but they're usually balanced by more sympathetic individuals. J. R. on "Dallas" and Arnie Becker on "L.A. Law" come to mind. A set of contrasting characters who can fuel conflict are ideal; think of the positioning of the idealistic Leon, the ambitious Chuck and the conniving Olivia on "Street Legal." Even a series like "X Files," which pits its heroes against a very formidable, often otherworldly antagonist each week, set up a continuing conflict between the two leads. One is sceptical, while the other is always willing to embrace phenomenal explanations.

An interesting milieu and the opportunity for continuing conflict are interrelated. There was an old question that used to be posed by network executives to test a series "legs." "Don't pitch me the pilot, pitch me the 43rd episode." Does your premise have sufficient depth to allow you to generate four or five years' worth of episodes? It is this question that drives series creators back to the so-called franchise" — cops, doctors, lawyers. These archetypes deal in life-and-death situations, encounter an endless stream of stories, and can touch any and all walks of life in the course of working at their profession. While the character conflict for any given episode may be a challenge, with these types of leading characters, there's no shortage of story conflicts.

I suppose the equivalent for family or young people's series would be the "coming-of-age" genre. Growing up is something we all did or are doing and so we can find somebody to identify with, or empathize with or fantasize about in series as diverse as "Beverly Hills 90210" and "Kids of Degrassi."

Another old trick to test the durability of characters in a series, especially in a sitcom, is to see how many stories can be generated among the regular characters without having to employ guest characters in a major way. The more stories that can be spun out of the interplay between the regulars, the more likely it is that you have created a constellation of characters that can endure.

Premises that have been tested in another form have appeal because this can be construed as an indicator that they've got what it takes to go the distance. So we have series based on books, "The Little House on the Prairie," series based on movies, "M*A*S*H" and "Max Glick" and series based on miniseries, "Road to Avonlea" and "Lonesome Dove." Remember we talked about the big bucks involved in series? Broadcasting executives and production companies want to know as much as they can about the potential appeal of series before they commit large sums of money to it. One way of hedging their bets is to say, "Well, this worked as a book or a series of books and/or as a movie or miniseries, it has already touched a chord with readers or audiences, that might suggest it has the fundamental qualities to appeal as a series."

Particularly in Canada, where the economics of development usually preclude making a pilot, being able to see the characters and the milieu in a movie, miniseries or book is a real help. And there can be an ancillary benefit. If the movie, miniseries or book was popular, then the concept has already been pre-sold to the public. There will be a recognition factor for the audience when a series of the same name appears.

If you don't have the advantage of existing background material to help paint the picture of your series, you may have to work harder, provide more detail, more visual aids. When selling "Traders," set in the world of Toronto stockbrokers, Atlantis executives took the broadcast executives by limo to an in-the-clouds boardroom of a Bay Street brokerage firm and used a high-powered trader as part of their pitch team. When Christine Shipton and I went to the CBC to pitch the western I mentioned earlier, I took a couple of paperback copies of the book and a map of the region. "Traders" is on the air and I am still in development. Maybe there is a lesson for me here.

Selling A Premise

I also had a couple of pages describing the premise. There is no standard form for this; it can be as few or as many pages as you feel is necessary. I always feel that the first document should be as succinct, as elemental as

possible, while still getting the idea across. Too much detail in the first document, like too much detail in the opening pitch, can overwhelm your
audience (in this case the network or production company executives) or
provide them with something they can hang a "No" on. Better to get them
interested in the central idea, then expand as they ask for additional details.
This gives them a sense of participation and allows you to make adjustments as you respond to their comments. You can't adapt every premise to
fit every audience, but many premises will be flexible enough to allow
changes in details or emphasis. As the creator, you have to decide what
improves your premise, what alters it without corrupting it and what suggestions are really incompatible with the fundamental things you want to
say with the series.

My feeling is that series are a collaborative effort, one person or team has
to hold onto the vision, but there isn't anyone who can't benefit from the
reactions of an audience. And your first pitches to a production company,
producing partners or broadcasters are your out-of-town try-outs. These
are your first forays into test marketing your idea. Listen to what's coming
back from these audiences of one or two or three people and don't be afraid
to use what's good.

If the feedback from a pitch has altered things so that your pitch document is no longer dead on, don't take it out of your briefcase. Tell the executives that if they like what you have had to say, you'll send them a couple
of pages on it that afternoon or first thing the next morning. Then scurry
back to your computer, incorporate the changes and fax it off to them. Free
editing and they have a sense of investment — what could be better?

I have included the first page of my first pitch document. I have never
felt particularly skilled at pitches or pitch documents, so do not use this as
a template, but rather as a sample of one way a series premise can be laid
out. These documents are also valuable for copyright reasons. They provide
the written record, the paper trail, of who wrote what and are essential
should there be any dispute in the future about who created the series.

NOTHING TOO GOOD FOR A COWBOY
A SERIES PROPOSAL BY DAVID BARLOW

RICH HOBSON and PANHANDLE PHILLIPS have a dream — to
carve a free-range cattle ranch out of four million acres of uninhabited wilderness in northern British Columbia.

A mismatched pair, one the Stanford-educated son of a Congressman, the other a hard-bitten Wyoming cowboy, these two men have the drive and the grit to make their dream a reality. They are part adventurers, part pioneers, part frontiersmen, part homesteaders. And they're about to add a city-born and -bred interior decorator to their partnership, GLORIA MCINTOSH, the woman Rich Hobson intends to marry.

As Rich and Pan struggle to tame the land, they also struggle with a conflict which is rooted in their very natures. If they are to survive and find happiness, they must reconcile the independent spirit of the explorer and cowboy with their desire for home and family. At the same time as they want to shake off the constraints and corruption of civilization they also want to build their own community of likeminded souls.

This is the classic dilemma that faced the men and women who opened the North American West from the 1860s to the 1880s. The difference with our story is that it takes place in 1939 at the beginning of the Second World War.

This makes the juxtaposition of the frontier and the modern world particularly acute. When Rich, Pan and Gloria make the four-day trip from the ranch to town they are riding from the nineteenth to the twentieth century. This provides the opportunity to tell everything from cowboy tales to small town, home-front-at-war stories.

NOTHING TOO GOOD FOR A COWBOY places the near mythic character of the cowboy, the rugged individual, in both his traditional setting and a near contemporary world at the same time. What's more, the story is true.

After the CBC indicated they were interested in developing "Nothing Too Good for a Cowboy" along with Alliance, there were a number of routes they could have taken. They could have commissioned a pilot script. As I mentioned earlier, it is rare to shoot a pilot in Canada; if the series doesn't go, both the broadcaster and the production company have sunk a lot of money into a single episodic hour or half-hour that will not really have much telecast or foreign sales potential. But the CBC could still have commissioned a single "pilot" script, or two scripts, or some combination of scripts and episode story lines, with the understanding that they would look at all this material before deciding on whether or not they would participate in production. As an example, Brenda Greenberg and

Guy Mullally wrote six episodes of "Side Effects" before the CBC ordered the series.

The Bible

Another alternative would be to write a bible for the series, with or without some scripts and/or stories. What's a bible? It's really an extended description of the series. The Independent Production Agreement between the Writers' Guild of Canada and Canadian Film and Television Producers Association has a pretty good, brief rundown on what a bible might contain.

> *Bible* means a written guide for a Series describing the central premise, story and characters, the setting, format, genre, style, themes and continuing elements. It may include detailed characterizations and describe the interplay among the principal and recurring characters. Character and story arcs, story line and dialogue examples and production requirements may also be included.

Character and story arcs are a description of what will happen to individual characters and continuing story lines over an entire season of episodes.

Once again, there is no standard form or format for a bible, and no prescribed length. A bible commissioned at this stage of development really has to serve two functions. It is, at this point, a sales document to help people picture the wonderful series you want them to finance. But should the series get ordered, it will become part of the package you give to writers and production people to help them picture the series before there are a lot of scripts or completed episodes to look at. When a series gets renewed for another year, the bible is often revised or added to at the beginning of each new season in order to lay out new directions, new characters and so on.

We did not get an order for a bible for "Nothing Too Good" so I can't include even a sample page. What we did get was an order for a TV movie script.

With hour dramas, a TV movie is a safer bet than a single episode pilot for the broadcaster and the producer. Even if a series doesn't result, a TV movie can have a life of its own. But writing a TV movie as a pilot for a series is tricky. TV movies are structured differently than a single episodic hour and you need to tell a bigger, longer story. And elements that you may have wanted to establish for the series could get swept aside if they don't feed that particular story. Two-hour pilots are done all the time, so obviously it is not that tricky, but it does have its pitfalls. Then again, I could be rationalizing — the CBC passed on the TV movie script for "Nothing Too Good."

If you have a series that has a fairly elaborate set-up, the two-hour format can work just fine. Of course, we are only talking about TV movies as a way of piloting one-hour series. I have never heard of piloting a half-hour with a TV movie, even though "M*A*S*H," "Max Glick" and "My Life as a Dog" all were based on feature films. Fortunately, because I need something to use for examples in the rest of this chapter, the CBC and Alliance decided to have another look at "Nothing Too Good." This time they suggested we do a one-hour script and several episode story lines. Remember I mentioned that series writing is a collaborative process? I asked Charles Lazer, who had story-edited the TV movie script of "Nothing Too Good" to co-write this material with me. That way, if I failed a second time, I'd have company.

We started with three story lines for three separate episodes. The first and second episodes of the series and a third one which could be, say, episode ten. Although it is not serialized, we do anticipate that "Nothing Too Good" will have an evolving series arc; time does pass in the series, so the episodes do have to be arranged in a certain order. With some series you can mix and match the episodes any way you want — each is independent and self-contained — but there is a current trend to seeing characters develop and change over time and so serial elements have crept in, be they recurring dilemmas in a character's personal or professional life or full-blown, continuing story lines à la "Murder One." As a creator, the degree of serialization is one of the things you will have to determine. The broadcaster and production company will certainly have an opinion about this, too — syndicators, for one, hate serialization; it means they actually have to telecast the shows in the order you intended. Apparently this cramps their ability to be creatively flexible.

The Story

What constitutes a story? Once again, there are no hard-and-fast rules. Let me tell you what I like to see as a story editor or a producer. For an hour drama, two to four pages laying out the beginning, middle and end of the main plot and the major sub-plots. If you want to call these the A story and the B and C stories, feel free. Actually, in an hour episode with four acts, it is more like the beginning, the middle, the second middle and the end. The A and B stories don't have to be interwoven in the story document; they can be, but they don't have to be. The story is really a general presentation of the main points of the important plots and character interaction for the episode. Just to confuse you, I'll say that it can be done in *beat sheet* form, but doesn't have to be. More on beat sheets later.

Here's a sample of a page from the first story Chuck and I wrote for "Nothing Too Good."

NOTHING TOO GOOD FOR A COWBOY
"A Woman's Place"
Story by David Barlow & Charles Lazer
November 30, 1995

FADE IN — ACT ONE
The SALOON in VANDERHOOF. RICH HOBSON'S stag is in full swing. A real Wild West bustup. PAN and the other RANCH HANDS are drunk and rowdy. So much so that Pan teases Rich: "When your big city bride sees these boys at the weddin', she's gonna leave you at the altar." Rich laughs, then stops, realizing Pan's got that right. He slips out of the saloon, where it could be 1885, onto the street where a cartage truck is parked. He hitches a ride with the driver to Vancouver — a journey of 300 miles and 55 years. It's 1940.

In VANCOUVER, at RICH and GLORIA'S WEDDING RECEPTION. In the middle of dozens of dancing couples, Rich trips the light fantastic with his new bride. She's gorgeous, he's elegant, they're both very much in love. She says it's too bad his "friends," the Ranch Hands and Pan, couldn't make it. He says they're way too busy. When EDGAR VAN DUSEN taps Rich on the shoulder, Rich thinks he wants to cut in. But Van Dusen has to talk business with Rich. Can't it wait, Rich asks, this is my wedding night. Rich's mother, ZELDA, appears to lead Van Dusen away, and GLORIA wants to know if they can sneak out yet. They do, as Gloria's BROTHER slips the ACCORDION PLAYER a ten spot.

In THEIR HOTEL ROOM, Rich and Gloria are in bed, trying to make love, but being diverted by the loud, incessant accordion playing next door. Finally Rich gets out of bed, takes his last ten dollars from his pants pocket and pays off the Accordion Player.

The next morning, Van Dusen knocks on their door, much too early. He's here to tell Rich that the ranch is a dead end. The investors think they should all pull out. They have better things to do with their money, and Rich can do better for himself back in New York. Gloria says no way. This ranch is Rich's dream. They're going to see it through. Van Dusen is persuaded to hold the investors together until Rich can bring a herd to market the next spring.

But when Rich and Gloria get back up to Vanderhoof, no one's there to meet them. BOB REED, the saloon/hotel keeper, says all the guys have signed up to fight the Nazis. They've gone off to war. What's Rich going to do? How's he going to run the ranch? Two kids volunteer to help him, TOMMY AITKEN and ED STREIGLER, both 16. Rich needs men not boys, but these are the best he can find. He reluctantly agrees to sign them on. How about me, asks KIT BRYANT, a smallish, skinny 14-year-old. No way, says Rich. You go back home. Kit stares at him, pleading silently, but Rich remains firm.

(FADE OUT — END OF ACT ONE)

The CBC and Alliance liked the story enough to have us proceed to outline, which we did. Let's leave Chuck and me working on the outline for the moment and talk about how you would proceed if you weren't writing a pilot but rather writing a single episode for an existing series. Along the way we will discuss that beat sheet format too.

You would pitch a story idea for an existing series in much the same way a proposal for a new series is pitched. Only instead of pitching to a production company or network executive, you would be pitching to people from the story department of the series. These could be any combination of executive producers, producers and story editors. You probably would have written out the story or stories in a few pages but you might use the same dodge that I suggested for series pitches, which is not to admit to having any presentable material that you can leave unless they seem to buy your pitch without modification.

The Beat Sheet

This is your lucky day, they buy one of your pitches. You're going to be commissioned to write an outline and a script, but before you do, you and the series story editors agree that a beat sheet would be a good idea. Notice I didn't say that the story editors ask you for a beat sheet. I am going to have to tiptoe though this section because I am a proud and active member of the Writers' Guild of Canada and if you go through the Independent Production Agreement you won't find any reference to a beat sheet. And WGC members aren't supposed to write things they aren't contracted and paid for. But, I am also a sometime story editor and producer and know how valuable this particular document can be for both the writer and the story editor.

OK, OK, enough of my angst. What is a beat sheet? It is a short, concise summary of the story, in which each major scene or plot point is described in one line or beat. An hour drama may have 24 to 35 beats. Double-spaced in courier twelve-point, it is going to come to a couple of pages. Well, maybe some of the beats take a line and a half or two lines to describe in all their subtlety and complexity, so we are up to four pages. Four pages, max. Which is, coincidentally, about the same length as a story. Which is why some people will do a story in beat sheet form. I prefer prose for a story because then I have a better chance of glossing the details I haven't worked out yet. But you are a better writer and don't need to stoop to this kind of deceit to get ahead.

So why beat sheets? The writer pitched the story, he or she is going to write an outline, why prolong the agony? Because when the writer pitched to the story department, they had suggestions and comments that the writer agreed would help the story (or that the writer is going to convince himself would help the story because he wants to make the sale). Then the story editors took the idea to the producers, who liked it but said, "What if we did this?" Then the producer took the revised story to the network executives in charge of this series who liked it but said, "Wouldn't it be better if we added this?" Now the story editor takes the story with all these improvements and suggestions back to the poor writer and discusses it. Just to make sure that everyone is clear, before the writer gets into a twelve- to twenty-page outline, everybody agrees that a beat sheet laying out the story as it is now constituted would be a good idea. And, believe me, it is. It saves writers from going off in the wrong direction and protects them from a story editor turning around after the outline and claiming they didn't include certain things they were asked to include. If you are a writer, think of it as an outline for the outline. If you are a producer, think of it as a way of double-checking your communication skills. And remember that you are getting a freebie.

The beat sheet for the first part of "A Woman's Place" might look something like this:

NOTHING TOO GOOD FOR A COWBOY
"A Woman's Place"
Beat Sheet — November 30, 1995
David Barlow & Charles Lazer

ACT ONE

1. Pan and the ranch hands throw a wild stag for Rich in the hotel in Vanderhoof. It looks like 1885.
2. Realizing he can't inflict this rowdy backwoods crew on Gloria and her family in Vancouver, Rich slips away and hitches a ride south. Reveal it is 1940.
3. Introduce Gloria and Rich, in formal wear, at their wedding reception. Gloria wonders about the absence of Rich's friends. Van Dusen tries to talk business but Rich and Gloria duck him.
4. Romantic wedding night is interrupted by persistent accordionist, Rich buys him off with the last of his cash.
5. Morning. Van Dusen brings bad news, investors want out. Gloria helps Rich persuade Van Dusen to hang in for a little while longer. He gives them 'til spring.
6. Rich and Gloria arrive back in Vanderhoof to find all Rich's cowhands have marched off to war.
7. Desperate, Rich has to sign on two sixteen-year-old boys. But he draws the line at a fourteen-year-old tagalong kid.

END OF ACT ONE

The Outline

Then we go to outline. For television scripts, it's called an outline, but some people call it a treatment, which is what the first stage is called when writing feature films. These terms can be as fuzzy as their formats, but if you lay out your outline something like the following sample, you won't go far wrong.

NOTHING TOO GOOD FOR A COWBOY
"A Woman's Place"
Barlow & Lazer

FADE IN — ACT ONE

1. EXT. HOME RANCH — DAY (1)
   RICH HOBSON and PAN PHILLIPS are leaving the Ranch to ride

to town. Establish beautiful, rustic setting, simple log cabin ranch house and barn. Cattle and horses grazing. It could be 1880. Rich is checking last-minute stuff with his foreman, JIMMY JOHN; Pan's anxious to get going. Rich has never known Pan to be in a hurry to get to town. The weekly train to the city doesn't go 'til Friday — three or four days hence — and it's only a two-day ride to town. Pan insists they have much to do before they can leave for Rich's wedding.

2. EXT. ON THE TRAIL TO TOWN — DAY (1)
The two cowboys ride through rugged, uninhabited country as background for credits. Pan reassures Rich about his impending wedding. Rich argues that he doesn't need to be reassured. Nothing will change on the ranch between him and Pan, even after he's married.

3. INT. REED'S HOTEL — DAY (1)
The old-fashioned western saloon in Vanderhoof. Rich's stag is in full swing. A real Wild West bustup, complete with someone riding their horse into the saloon. Pan and the other RANCH HANDS are drunk and rowdy. So much so that Pan teases Rich: "When your big city bride sees these boys at the weddin', she's gonna leave you at the altar." Rich laughs, then stops, realizing Pan's got that right. He slips out of the saloon. One of the partying cowhands doesn't want to let Rich leave. He tries to stop him, but Pan intercepts the cowboy and diverts him. Pan introduces him to one of the entrepreneurial local beauties. She's delighted to make the cowboy's acquaintance and "wants to get to know him better." Rich slips out the saloon door.

4. EXT. VANDERHOOF STREET — DAY (1)
Outside the saloon, Rich stops at the hitching rail to pat his horse, then turns to look down the broad main street. It's not 1880. It's 1940. But here in the Northern Interior, it's a blend of the two centuries. There are five street lights, some cars and trucks, but horses and wagons too. There are also banners and signs appealing for popular support of the war effort. As Rich looks down the street, he is startled by the sound of a large cartage truck starting up. He

hitches a ride with the driver to Vancouver — 300 miles down the road to another world, and what could be another time.

After you hand in the outline, it will probably travel up through the same chain of command that the story did. Story editors, producers, executive producers, production company executives and network executives will all have a read and give notes. Different productions have different procedures for who sees what stage of a script, but regardless of how short or long the distribution list is, the writer can always count on notes. The alternative is far less palatable — you are terminated at the outline stage and don't get to do a draft.

Chuck and I got notes, good notes I humbly confess, and proceeded to the first draft script. If you were a freelancer, writing an episode outline for an existing series, you might not be so lucky. The notes and changes on your outline might be so extensive that a beat sheet might be required. No way, say you, you already did a beat sheet at the story stage. Maybe, and you might not have to do a second one here, even if the revisions to your outline are major. The story department might do it for you. In fact, they might do an entire revised outline for you and hand it to you when they go over the changes. Or they might discuss the notes and then ask you to bang out a beat sheet before you proceed to script, just to make sure everybody's on the same page.

Know that all the need for changes might not be your fault. Series are constantly in flux; every episode that's written has the potential to affect every subsequent episode. And on any given day on a series, there may be a half-dozen or more episodes being developed, outlined, scripted, shot and edited. Change is the only constant in series and the writing (and rewriting) never ends. Lots of things could have happened in the week or two you took to do your outline that will require minor or major adjustments to your story. As well, truth to tell, we writers don't always get it right the first time and can usually benefit from a little guidance.

Some last words about outlines. They are a scene-by-scene, prose description of the episode. Write what we will see and hear when the show is telecast. Don't write what people are thinking; write what they say and do that reveals what they are thinking. If it is important to know what a character is feeling at a certain moment, describe how we experience what that character feels. And remember that this is a synopsis of the script. Each scene description should give the reader the essential action, the essential plot point, the essential emotional moment. Your framing up the episode here — save the decoration for the script.

The Script

This is the first page of the first draft of "A Woman's Place."

NTGC — "A Woman's Place" 1st Draft
FADE IN:

TEASER

EXT. FRONTIER CATTLE COMPANY RANCH — NEW DAY (1)
The big vista. Two cowboys, RICH HOBSON and PAN PHILLIPS, herd a string of cattle along a river. Lush green meadows, mountains covered with dark spruce trees, deep blue sky.
DISSOLVE TO:

INT. TEWKESBURY'S OFFICE — DAY (1)
A brightly-coloured map criss-crossed with rivers, long narrow lakes and mountain ranges. A MAN'S FINGER is drawing a wide circle in the middle of the map.

HAROLD (V.O.)
Hobson and Phillips are running cattle from the Batnuni Valley in the east to Tetachuck Lake in the west.

The map is spread on the office desk of a small town banker. Said banker, one ROLAND TEWKESBURY, mid-forties and prosperous, is listening to HAROLD, who looks like the kind of man you'd hire to snoop into other people's lives.

TEWKESBURY
But that's two hundred miles.

HAROLD
Yep. Four million acres. Lotta swamp and trees, but a lot of prime grazing land, too.

TEWKESBURY
How can they afford a ranch that big?

> HAROLD
> They bought up a couple old land claims, but mostly it's
> wilderness leased from the government. There's nobody out
> there but them and some Indians.
>
> TEWKESBURY
> (thinking)
> Still, an operation of that size needs capital…
>
> (CONTINUED)

I know, I know, this doesn't match the story or the outline or the beat sheet. Instead of starting with "Act One" there's a "Teaser" and who are these guys "Tewkesbury" and "Harold?" Like I told you, we got notes. Things change. Hopefully for the better.

Besides, you're really only looking at this for format. And speaking of format, make sure you get a copy of the format of the series you are writing for and follow it. Exactly. The bible and/or a sample script and a conversation with one of the story editors ought to give you everything you need to know. It's like that grade seven science project — presentation and neatness do count. From the producers' point of view, if you haven't got the smarts to imitate the technical layout of their scripts, how can they be confident you are going to be able to imitate their characters in your writing? And that's your assignment, to accurately recreate the voices of the series' characters while putting those characters through a new and interesting set of scenarios.

The second draft will probably be more of the same, notes from above and rewriting. Sometimes the story editors will not ask the writer for a second draft. Again, not necessarily because the writer blew it. The story department is almost certainly going to rewrite each script another couple of times at least; they may feel it's easier or would save time if they got their hands on it right after the first rather than the second draft. If you are serious about this work, get hold of the shooting script and note the changes. It may make you crazy to see what has been changed, it may seem that the improvements are not always improvements, in fact some may appear pretty damn arbitrary, but if you want to learn, you have to try to figure out the process. As much as it can be figured out. Depending upon your relationship with the story staff, you might be able to get one of them to tell you what motivated certain choices. Be warned that they may not be all that keen to review the script, particularly during the heat of production, and they may be working at such a pace that they simply may not remember why certain things were rewritten. "Why was the daughter's name changed to Julie?" "Julie? Oh yeah, the actress playing the mother thought that if she had had a girl, she would have named her Julie. And besides, she couldn't say 'Priscilla' without spitting on the other actors."

Who Writes For Series?

Now that Chuck and I are embarked on our second draft, let's end at the beginning. Who writes for series?

Mostly, the people who write for series are people that have written for series. It is the same as creating series; people tend to go with the devils they know. Thanks a lot, you're saying, I've read all this way and you're telling me it's a closed shop? Not quite — the market expands, the veterans get old and worn down (or promoted) and somebody decides that what a series needs is fresh blood. As a result, new talent does get a chance. I just want to make sure you realize it is a very difficult and very competitive market to crack. Conversely, the business embraces and rewards people who demonstrate proficiency in this quite specialized craft.

A majority of the episodes on many, if not most, series are written by the story departments. All the story editors and probably several of the producers on any series are writers wearing additional hats. This is not the place to argue the pros and cons of staff-written shows. I mention it only to make the point that for the freelancer, the real script market on a 22-episode series is not 22 but maybe eleven scripts. Or eight or none. To continue in this depressing vein, you can't walk into most series and pitch — you have to be invited. It's understandable, really, since there are probably limited script commissions available and the story department has a limited amount of time available.

Enough of the gloom and doom. How does somebody manage to get a gig? Aspiring episodic writers need to have samples of their work. Ideally, the samples should be generically related to the series you are pitching. You don't have to have a "Side Effects" script to be considered for "Side Effects," but it will be harder to judge your suitability for "Side Effects" if the only sample you have is a half-hour sitcom pilot about space aliens.

There is much debate about whether a writer should write speculative scripts of existing series or original material. One school of thought has it that an outside writer can never know a series well enough to write a spec script that will stand up to the scrutiny of the story editors and producers who are immersed in the characters of that show and their situations on a daily basis. So you will be judged too harshly and you are better off writing an original piece. On the other hand, people do sell spec scripts to series. Or sell themselves to series on the basis of spec scripts. To continue the pros and cons, in Canada a spec episodic script might have limited currency because we do not tend to do more than one or two series of a particular type, one medical show, one cop show, one western and so on. Also, a spec episodic script only works if the show is so familiar to most producers or story editors that they can judge whether or not you have captured the qualities of that particular series. Finally, if a spec episodic script isn't sold to the series it was written for, it is just a sample. An original script does double duty — it's a sample but some producer could also read it and say, let's produce this.

Speculative or original? What to do? I would recommend that you be guided by your feelings. Write what you want to write; write something you can get excited about. If that is an episode of "Due South" and you feel you know those two guys inside and out, go to it. If you'd rather write an original feature-length script about going to high school in Timmins and then use it to try and get work on "Madison," be my guest. And once you've written one speculative script, or rather rewritten it until it's great, then start writing another. After all, what's a writer? Someone who writes. You can never have too many samples of material.

The same advice, as obvious as it is, needs to be said about looking for work as a series writer. Do it because you like series television. Seek out shows that you want to write for, that you find entertaining, that you think will stimulate you to do your best writing. Don't try to write for series television if you think it's slumming. It won't do your own craft any good and you will waste a lot of other people's time and energy.

If you get a chance to pitch, study the show. Learn all you can about it and how it is constructed. Observe the rhythms of the principal characters and try to understand what motivates them. Remember that your stories should centre on the regular characters. Guest actors are only interesting to the extent that they create interesting dilemmas for one or more of the regular characters. Have two or three good "A" stories worked out in enough detail to pitch a beginning, crisis, complication and resolution. And most of all, keep in mind that despite the difficulties of breaking in and the competition for limited assignments, every story editor and producer worth his salt wants nothing more than to discover another good writer, someone who understands and can write their show.

If you succeed, you will be privileged to practise a wonderful craft. Writing for series television is like writing for an electronic repertory theatre. It is extremely demanding, the time pressures and production constraints can be overwhelming, the scripting-by-committee can be frustrating, but when you are in production, you can write a scene one day and have actors perform it the next, see it on tape the following day and cut together within the week. On the air a few weeks after that. If you are lucky, more than a million people will see it. It is immediate, exciting, a marvellous arena in which to practise the craft of screenwriting.

In *The New York Times Magazine* of October 22, 1995, the editor of *The Time Book Review*, Charles McGrath, articulated what the best of dramatic series television does:

> TV drama is also one of the few remaining art forms to continue the tradition of classic American realism, the realism of Dreiser and Hopper: the painstaking, almost literal examination of middle- and working-class lives in the conviction that truth resides less in ideas than in details closely observed. More than many novels, TV tells us how we live now.

There is a description that every television series would do well to aspire to. There is a reason to write for the medium.

4

pitchiNq

by Donald Martin

*D*onald Martin's *screenwriting credits include feature films, television movies and series. Feature films include* Never Too Late, *starring Olympia Dukakis, and* Pocahontas: The Legend. *Television movies include* Spenser: A Savage Place, No Blame, The Phone Call *and the Gemini Award winning* Coming of Age. *Television series include* "Side Effects," "My Life As a Dog," "Street Legal" *and* "Secret Service." *Producing credits include* Pocahontas: The Legend *and the series* "Women, Lifestyle & Money." *Donald resides in Toronto with his two dogs, Indiana and Dakota.*

Definition:

Pitch — the verbal presentation of a story or idea
(in the hopes of selling it or funding it)

It was a dark and stormy night…

I have an uncle who loves to tell stories. And each time he churns one out, it just seems to get better and better. He holds us captive with his vivid facial expressions, his whispered intensity … and his passion.

He only has about a dozen or so anecdotes in his repertoire and I've heard each of them at least a dozen times, but I never tire of them. He hones his story with each telling. He is my inspiration. When I prepare myself to pitch an idea for a movie, I simply picture my uncle in his chair by the fireplace, taking us all on a magical journey … with words.

The word *pitch* can instil such fear in old timer and neophyte alike in this business. It shouldn't. Pitching is merely storytelling. When you're chatting to a chum over espresso, weaving those story points together, you're pitching. When you're regaling your mother with that climactic chase scene through the park, you're pitching. When you're telling your child that brilliant moment at the story's outset, you're pitching.

There are, to be sure, several things to keep in mind when pitching, and we will touch upon them in this chapter, but the most important thing is this: just tell your story. Make them *see* the movie in your mind. Know it. Love it. And tell it. Dramatically. Briefly. Passionately. Pitch it.

There is the element of the salesman in every one of us, especially when we pitch. It is not to be dismissed. The word "salesman" need not be a negative term as not all salesmen are cut from the same cloth as Willy Loman. That *salesman* in you is essential to getting your wonderful story heard, *and* made into that award winning movie.

Says Jan Miller, executive director of The National Screen Institute and co-presenter (with Jim Burt) of the Pitching Workshop at the Banff Television Festival and the Canadian Film Centre: "Pitching is first and foremost a conversation. Just as everyone's style of conversation is different, so is everyone's style of pitching. My frustration with the word 'pitch' is that it sounds like you're throwing something at someone, which is a completely inaccurate representation of the art of pitching. Pitching is a circle of exchange. It's the process of inviting your listener into your idea."

The writer pitches the story to the producer; the producer pitches the story to the director; the director pitches the story to the actor; the producer pitches the story to the executive producer … who pitches the story to the distributor/broadcaster, who must pitch the story to his/her superiors in order to green-light the project. And so on.

That's a hell of a lot of pitching for one story. That is why it is so vital that the initial pitch, the one which comes from the original storyteller (i.e., the writer), must be so clear and distinct. It *has* to be. So don't overlook that salesman who lives within the writer. You need him. This is, after all, a business. You are creating a piece of work for a market place. Your goal is to sell that work.

Of course, you are brilliant and talented but, trust me, there are thousands of brilliant and talented writers out there creating terrific stories and scripts — how do you make sure that yours gets read? Gets financed? Gets made?

"I'm an *artist*," a screenwriter-friend sighs, "I have an agent. He can do all the 'selling' for me." Yeah. Right. My screenwriter-friend is still waiting tables in a trendy Toronto café. I'm not putting him down, mind you, but I am concerned about this *attitude*.

It does not serve his agent or his career. While my friend is indeed a talented screenwriter, the process of selling a story can sometimes be as challenging as writing it. It requires knowledge of the market place, positive attitudes and good communication skills. It requires that salesman lurking beneath the surface to be ready, willing and more than able.

When I have an idea for a film, I try to shape the notion into one or two sentences which capture the *heart* or *theme* of my story, and I work from there. My very first film for television was *No Blame*. The idea for writing that script was triggered by a dinner conversation with a friend. That same night I went home and wrote down these words: a woman overcomes the fear and ignorance of AIDS — by testing HIV-positive. That sentence became the lead-in to my pitch.

How do you pitch a movie? To whom? Where? When? Well, to anyone who matters (i.e., anyone who can be part of or a conduit to getting it made), anywhere (within reason, of course), and anytime (again, within reason).

What will a good pitch get you? Ideally, a deal ... but, more realistically and hopefully, it gets you another meeting. A pitch is one step in building a relationship. If the pitch gets you another meeting on the project, then you're taking one more positive step in the evolution of that relationship ... and, quite possibly, of the project.

I know a writer who pitched a producer in the sauna at the YMCA. True story. Did the script get read? Yes. Did he get another meeting? Yes, this time in the producer's office. Did the movie get made? Well, that's another story. Another screenwriter pitched a broadcaster at the funeral of a mutual friend. Did he get another meeting? No. Did the script get read? No. Hmmmm.

I have pitched people in elevators, in hallways, in cafés, on the street, in a Las Vegas casino and, yes, once in a while, in their offices. You don't get a lot of time in a pitch, especially in an elevator, so you must be able to get to the heart of the matter quickly and efficiently. Like any good storyteller, you need a beginning, a middle and an end. You need strong characters and conflict.

How long should the pitch be? One response would be to say three or four paragraphs, but that would be, in my opinion, far too general a reply. A pitch is as brief or as long as it needs to be, and you will know how long it needs to be when you are given permission, so to speak, by your listener to continue ... because you've got him hanging by a thread, wanting to know what happens next.

Let me play out a little scene for you — my first elevator pitch:

FADE IN
INT. HOTEL/ELEVATOR — DAY

MR. BROADCASTER, tall, early 40s, enters elevator, glad to be alone. The doors are about to close when, suddenly, MR. SCREENWRITER, short, early 30s, enters, glad to see he's not alone. Mr. Screenwriter presses button for the Lobby.

> MR. SCREENWRITER
> Oh, Mr. Broadcaster, uh, hi …

> MR. BROADCASTER
> Oh, Uh, Mr. Screenwriter, right?

> MR. SCREENWRITER
> Yes. Right, right.

> MR. BROADCASTER
> Good, good.

Awkward silence. Neither looks at the other. Mr. Screenwriter bites his lip.

> MR. BROADCASTER
> Look, uh, sorry I haven't returned your calls.

> MR. SCREENWRITER
> Oh, that's okay. I know you're busy …

Painful silence. Mr. Screenwriter takes a deep breath … *ah, what the hell!*

> MR. SCREENWRITER
> Listen, I've got this story …

Mr. Broadcaster looks at his watch, sighs … subtly. He puts on his professional smile, which Mr. Screenwriter takes to mean "go ahead."

> MR. SCREENWRITER
> It's the true story of a mother who helps her son become a woman — and, in doing so, discovers a whole new person: herself.

The elevator stops at the Lobby. The doors open. Other PEOPLE crowd in. The doors shut. Mr. Broadcaster and Mr. Screenwriter are now going back up to the rooftop patio.

MR. BROADCASTER
(*smiling for real this time*)
Do you have the rights?

The broadcaster gave me permission to go on telling the story, which I did, over a drink on the rooftop patio. A half-hour later, we had a development deal. Has the movie been made yet? No, but we're working on it.

Not every producer/broadcaster/distributor would have responded positively to that particular story, but this one did. I had figured he would. I had done my homework. It is essential in pitching to know your audience. You don't necessarily pitch action/car chase movies to a public broadcaster. Nor would your first choice necessarily be to pitch a local TV station for a historical costume epic, or an art house distribution company for a martial arts feature. Then again, like absolutely everything else in this industry, that could all change in five minutes with the public broadcaster suddenly *wanting* action/car chase movies! Moral of the story? It is important to be "in the know." Do your homework.

Know the company. Know its product. Know the person, or at least, know about the person you're pitching to. Know what they have given the green light to in the recent past. Know what they have tossed out as well. Knowing your audience at this early stage in a story's evolution is just like knowing your market once the film is made.

Is there a format or formula to a pitch? "No, absolutely not," asserts Jan Miller. "When you go in to pitch you must be clear in what you want out of that meeting but you can't go in there with a specific format or formula because then it's no longer a conversation — it's a monologue. What is so important in a pitch is that your listener has the opportunity to give input because that means they are buying into your concept, that they are participating in its evolution."

A pitch has to "hook" the listener and should answer such questions as: What is the dramatic/comedic paradox? Who's the protagonist? Who am I rooting for? Why do I want to spend two hours of my life watching this character on screen? What are his/her needs? What is his/her goal? what is standing in his/her way? How does she/he overcome such obstacles? Does she/he learn anything? How has she/he changed?

There is no by-the-rules format to pitching. The only rule is to tell a good story, and tell it well. Keep in mind that a good pitch deals with concepts, with the "big, picture." A pitch is baiting the hook, so to speak, with the *premise* of a story rather than the full plot. You provide your listeners with the story's broad strokes, essentially enabling them to fill in the rest with the way they hope the story will turn out.

Some producers and broadcasters I know actually don't like to be "pitched" in person. They *hate* it. They think it's as excruciating for the "pitchee" as it is for the "pitcher." They prefer to see the story on paper first. Which may be just one of the reasons why some writers are finding it useful to go beyond the verbal pitch and create a "pitch document." The document shouldn't be more than two pages maximum.

Such a document is viewed by some as an increasingly important element in getting one's movies to market. For example, if you're an untried writer and I'm a big producer or broadcaster, how are you going to get the opportunity to pitch me in person? It's unlikely. If you send me an unsolicited script, it's doubtful I'll read it. One of my professional readers may read it, or they may not. It may just sit on a shelf and collect dust, one of thousands doing the very same thing.

But if you should fax my director of development, or programming, or whomever, maybe even to me, a scintillating one-page document that whets my appetite, that triggers my curiosity, then I just might pick up that phone and request the script, or request a meeting to put the script into development. Whatever happens, the door has been opened — thanks to your pitch document. A pitch document can also be useful to leave with a person after you have made your verbal pitch.

This is, ironically, not a business in which people like to read. It is a business of emotions, images, issues, elements that trigger immediate and visceral responses. Your verbal pitch must do this, and your pitch document commits that magic to paper. Like the pitch calling upon the salesman within each of us, so does the pitch document. It is not a script. It may harbour pretensions of an outline, but it is not even that. It's a sales tool, and it should contain the essential elements of a good pitch: an opening hook that rivets one's attention, followed by the requisite building blocks of good storytelling: beginning, middle, end, strong characters and conflict.

Not to say that it is wrong to hand over an outline, or even a full script, following a successful pitch meeting. On the contrary. If the door is opened, thanks to your pitch, then anything can happen. Just be ready. Don't go in there and make a brilliant presentation, then have nothing on paper to leave them.

Having something on paper when you enter that pitch meeting is also important for clarifying that this is *your* story. Of course, in a pitch session, there are ideas being bandied back and forth across the table. It is, after all, a conversation … but it is your story, and one way to protect your ownership is through the script registration program at the Writers' Guild of Canada.

With movies, the person you'll end up pitching to can vary as much as stories do. You could be trying to interest an award winning director in your project, or a celebrated performer. And, as our industry evolves, attaching such individuals to a story becomes more and more integral to getting a picture made. It is not impossible that a good story can, on its own merit, get made but how many times have we writers heard the following refrain? "Terrific story! Come back once you've got it packaged."

Packaging. The long journey from script to screen can be made (a little) easier if there is an accredited producer attached — if the director is "hot" — or if the performer is a "name." Packaging. It's important, and it is often part of a pitch.

The writer does not necessarily become the packager of a project. A producer usually handles that. Or a manager. Even an agent. Yet the more elements a writer can bring to the table, the more he steps into that world of hyphenates — becoming, possibly, a writer-producer. Today's industry is filled with hyphenates. I'm a hyphenate (writer-producer), and I must confess that while it has its own set of headaches, it is a place that can sometimes be preferable to being a non-hyphenate.

A word of caution to the burgeoning hyphenate here: be careful that you package your project with the right people. What does one mean by the "right" people? Well, a producer whose last three films have flopped may not be the best partner for you. A director who can't green-light a picture on his/her own may not be your wisest choice. And an actress whose name elicits a reaction like "Who?" would not, frankly, serve your needs when it comes to packaging.

Packaging, like pitching, is a form of selling, so you want every element to be the best. And you want to do your homework to ensure that the individuals whom you are packaging into your project are suitable, marketable, and like-minded — that they see the same movie in their minds as you do in yours. Packaging is increasingly necessary in this era of dwindling licence fees, an age of financing movies with partners beyond our borders.

This is the new reality of the Canadian market place: it is more and more difficult to finance a film solely from Canadian sources. That is why having a "name" actor attached to a project can be so vital. A foreign rights distributor will require it. A European partner will need to add certain European elements to substantiate the financing in their respective domestic markets.

How does a screenwriter get to meet such potential producers? Distributors? Broadcasters? One way is by attending such events as the Toronto International Film Festival and its Trade Forum; the Banff Television Festival; and the annual convention of the National Association of Television and Production Executives (NATPE).

I attended NATPE in 1995 in Las Vegas. Can you imagine a more ironic (and vulgar) place in which to house thousands of television types, each hungry for a deal? Forget the casinos and the slot machines — the action was on the convention floor. People from around the world congregated for one reason and one reason alone: to hear/tell a story.

A pitcher's paradise (or nightmare). For three days, from mid-morning until sunset, I travelled from booth to booth, from one appointment (confirmed at least a month earlier) to another, carrying with me my briefcase and my list of stories, facing American, French, British, German and Italian executives, to name but a few.

Sometimes there were only fifteen minutes allotted — *fifteen* minutes to pitch seven stories?! Nerve wracking. An adrenaline rush. A veritable headache. Too much bad coffee and far too many doughnuts. At least, the French pavilion served cheese. But I did get to tell my stories. And one of those meetings, one, did manage to result in a deal. One.

As insane and repugnant as that entire experience was to the artist in me, it was also, on a whole other level, a revelation and a most positive journey. It amplified for me just how much every one of us in this industry, around the world, aches for a good story. In the chaotic frenzy of that convention floor in Las Vegas, everything stopped when someone heard a story that tugged at a heart string, that made one smile. That is why I love this business so much, why I love writing … and pitching. We are responding to something innate, to a need. Should every writer venture to a place like NATPE? I don't think so, frankly. It's more of a magnet for hyphenates.

Pitching for a television series has certain similarities to pitching for movies as well as numerous differences.

Similarities: Know your audience. Know your story. Make sure it has a solid beginning, middle and end. Know your characters. Identify the conflict. Keep it succinct and clear. And be sure to leave them something on paper if they like one or more of your pitches.

Differences: It is vital, before pitching ideas for a series, to get a hold of the series bible. This will enable you to get to know more intimately the characters, the through-lines and plot lines already mapped out, the locations and the tone. Of course, if it's a series that is already being broadcast, watch as many episodes as you can. Do your homework. Know these characters. Know what story lines have already been developed so that you do not appear redundant in your pitch.

And remember this: Every major story of a series is about its central characters and how that situation/crisis/whatever makes them grow. Your episodic pitches are not about the guest characters. They may supply the inciting incidents, but the stories are essentially about the central characters.

You should start your episodic pitch with one of the regular character's names, i.e., for a medical drama series you might begin your pitch by saying something like "Dr. So-and-So has a patient ..." or "Dr. Such-and-Such and Dr. So-and-So are at each other's throats when ..." The guest characters are important, yes, and they must be fully developed, but they are, in the end, merely catalysts for the central characters' evolution.

When you go in to pitch for a series, more often than not you will find yourself in a room facing various members of the story department and a producer or two. Unlike movies, where you can look that producer in the eye and tell your story in the quiet of his office — or in the elevator — or standing by a urinal (though I wouldn't recommend looking him quite in the eye at that point — you have a number of eyes here, several individuals with whom you must "connect." A majority of them, if not all, must "buy into" your story. So don't focus on just one individual, as so many of us can do when we are nervous. Try to be democratic with your attention.

Bring more than one story to tell. If you've got five or seven pitches, the arithmetic is that, probably, three or four of them have already been pitched/turned down or pitched/assigned before you enter that room. You don't want to walk in there, deliver one helluva great pitch (in your opinion), have them utter "uh, no, thanks" ... then have nothing else to offer them. No, you definitely do not want that. Go into that meeting *prepared*.

As with all storytelling, be sensitive to your audience. If they're not "buying into" it (i.e., when their eyes start to glaze over), do something to enhance the storytelling. If they're still not buying into it (i.e. when you hear snoring), then don't belabour it. Finish the story, and move on.

Or do something to wake them up. Who knows? They may feel so awful for falling asleep in your presence that you could well walk out of that office with a deal! It *has* happened, you know.

With series pitches you must be prepared to alter your story in the ensuring discussion. One writer I know went in to pitch eight stories to CBC's "Side Effects" — two of the stories piqued the interest of the story department, and one had been designed around the character of Dr. Knelman. The executive story editor, however, saw the two stories as one and as being more suitable to Dr. Barkin.

In the discussion, the writer (being flexible) combined the two stories and massaged the story points so that they started fitting comfortably into Dr. Barkin's idiosyncrasies. By the end of that meeting, the writer had the green light to go to treatment.

Storytelling is a process, and it is forever in a state of evolution. Don't permit rigidity, fear or insecurity to stand in the way of that process … especially in a pitch meeting.

The "Spec" Script

Many new writers ask about "spec" (speculative) scripts. Should they work on them? For movies? For series? My response is always this: if you are a writer, then *write*. As Canada's government development programs play less and less a reliable role in script development, the spec script becomes increasingly important. The spec script is a pitch all in itself. It's pitching your talents as a writer.

When it comes to movies, let me share a few stories with you. My first film would probably never have been made if I hadn't written it on spec. I was an unknown entity, in terms of screenwriting. Why could I expect any-one to hand over development funds to be based on a pitch or an outline? I had to write it, to show I could write. I had to prove myself. After that first film was made, the producer said: "What else have you got?" Well, I just so happened to have two other completed scripts in my filing cabinet which went on to be produced by the same team of producers and broad-casters. If I hadn't written those spec scripts … well, those stories may well have never made it to the screen.

Another anecdote: a friend of mine in New York wrote a spec script in 1978 for a wonderful film for television. He was an unknown quantity at that point, so he had no other option other than to write in on a speculative basis. He managed to get it read. People liked it, but they didn't want to produce it. Instead, they would hire him to work on another project. This went on for years, his brilliant spec script opening door after door yet never getting made. Nevertheless, it make him a career. It was his best pitch. He won an Emmy Award and did very well for himself. Almost twelve years after writing that initial script, he finally had the clout, or the contacts (one in the same), to get that script produced into a network movie of the week.

In series television, the spec script can also be an important way of pitching your talents if you're an unproduced writer, but be careful. Many story editors/producers say they do not want to receive scripts for "Side Effects" or "North of 60," let's say, when they are so focused on getting "Side Effects" or "North of 60" on the air.

If the speculative script you write for that particular series is so far removed from the current season's focus (i.e., the central character fighting cancer), as it most likely will be because how would you know that the story department is planning on having the central character battle cancer?, then the tendency is to disregard the spec script. The excuse may be that it plays on old themes, or that it's just too plain distracting to the task at hand (getting the series produced).

The advice one often hears from series producers and story editors is that they prefer to read a spec script which you've written for another series. This enables them to read it with enhanced objectivity and to examine more closely the writer's technique and talent. Again, use sound judgment. Don't send a spec script for a sex-and-violence show to the producer of a family drama. Or vice versa. Keep in mind your reader's frame of reference.

Here are some "dos" and "don'ts" on pitching from Jan Miller:
- Do know where your listener is and where she or he is coming from.
- Do know what you want out of the meeting.
- Do close the meeting knowing what it is you must do next to get what you want.
- Do acknowledge that you're talking to a human being and not a wallet.
- Do know and understand that every pitch is an opportunity to build a relationship, first and foremost, and — secondly — to sell a project.
- Don't ever pitch a project before it's ready — you can meet with people during its evolution and solicit their advice, but don't go to them with the big pitch until it's really ready.

And one more pearl of wisdom from Jan: "It is vital in pitching that you find the balance between specifics and economy in telling your story. I've found that writers, more often than not, provide far too many details in a pitch while most producers tend towards the generic. There is a fertile middle ground there. Find it."

Pitching is thinking on your feet. And, yes, there is a little bit of the b.s. factor thrown in for good measure — this is, after all, show business, right? But remember this: *a good story wins out in the end.*

5

How the Writer Deals with Story Editors, Story Teams and Story Conferences

OR

How to Survive All the Help You Didn't Know You Needed

by HART HANSON

Hart Hanson sold his first script to the CBC Anthology series "The Way We Are" in 1987. Since then he has written "Beachcombers," "The Black Stallion," "Ready Or Not," "Neon Rider," "Northwood," "Street Legal," "Road To Avonlea," and "Poltergeist." Hart has worked as story editor on "Fly By Night," and senior story editor, then executive story editor on "North of 60." He has written movies for television, "Trust in Me" (with Matt MacLeod) and "Broncos." Hart developed the series "Traders," for Global/Atlantis and is currently developing another series, "Cross Town," with Ark Films in Vancouver.

Congratulations! You have aroused "interest" in a project. It may be a spec MOW script; it may be an episodic television premise; it may be a glimmer of a feature film idea or a single character which suggests a television series. You may even have convinced someone that you are the right person to rewrite another writer.

Whether you used sex, charm, money, a brilliant pitch, intelligence, tenacity, charisma, talent or family connections, the next step is a constant of the universe.

Now you must face ... the story meeting.

A place and time will be specified. You will not sleep. You will drink too much coffee and smoke 'em if you got 'em. You will either get to the appointed crossroads too early and have to walk around the block, thus building up a sweat, or you will rush in late, sweating bullets.

You will be shown into a room with many more people in it than you expected, no matter how many you expected. There will be a plethora of introductions and hail-fellow-well-met skimble-skamble. People will say your script is delicious and piquant ... meaty, acerbic ... poignant yet zesty ... delectable. Although you may think these adjectives more applicable to a smorgasbord than to your script, bask in it, for it is praise and the first rule of the story meeting is *take your praise no matter how wrong-headed it may be.*

Preliminaries observed, someone will suggest that everyone in this room is here for the same reason: to take this wonderful work you've done and make it better. That sounds good to you, too. If that bright light is the perfect script, and the Voice calling you home is Calliope, chief of the Nine Muses, then why not fling yourself headlong, heart overflowing with joy? Because there are a thousand lights and a thousand false Calliopes, and the writer soon abandons the notion of flinging anything anywhere with a heart full of joy.

The Story Conference

My first few story meetings passed in a surreal blur. They subjected me to a trauma identical to that I experienced when I was whipped from the public school system into grade three at Sacred Heart Elementary: everyone in charge was dressed in black, they spoke a mysterious and intimidating ancient language, and there was a distinct atmosphere of Divine Judgement.

After my first few story meetings, I remembered nothing. I peered at my cheat sheet, upon which I'd scribbled notes. I couldn't understand them: " ... the chronology of the event should not be dictated by the exigencies of the event," and " ... contextualize the protagonist's franchise."

Huh?

What I did remember was "Make it shorter. Everybody talks too much," and, "The end of act one lacks punch." So I addressed what I understood and nobody seemed to notice that I hadn't dealt with exigencies or contextualizations.

What I didn't know then, that I know now, is that I'd been remfed, tyroed, and wonked. And I'd better get used to it.

Just as I learned the basics at Sacred Heart — don't sass nuns; nobody really understands Latin; the air of Divine Judgement is mostly incense — I learned the basics of story meetings. Patterns and rhythms began to emerge. A perceptible gestalt of measure and degree manifest itself through all the shadows and noise.

And because there's more wonk (see below ...) in me than I care to admit, what emerged like a *bas relief* from the lifeless grey stone of the story conference was ... archetypes.

I love archetypes. They're Jungian. They're reductionist. They're deep. Most importantly, they lend themselves to amusing and derogatory labels.

And though every project has its own structures, quirks and peculiarities, the archetypes prevail. You *will* face them.

So, a quick menagerie:

REMFS

If you write a script and that script is produced, a remf is involved. Without remfs, *rien*. Remfs are as constant and unchanging as the Manichean dichotomy, the love of a good woman, or television ice-dancing specials. Whether the script is a half-hour one-off, a feature film, an episodic drama, a sitcom or MOW, remfs will spray all over it like cats in heat.

R.E.M.F. is actually an acronym coined by American front-line grunts during the Vietnam War and it stands for "Rear Echelon Mother-F***ers. A finer acronym does not exist. It allows one to be extremely rude under cover of throat clearing.

Outside of ill-advised Asian police actions, remfs are particularly thick in the funding agencies, in the upper levels of the larger production companies, in the executive suites of the broadcasters and in screenwriting schools. They are marked by a fleeting — sometimes an utter lack of — *practical* experience in the actual making of film. Theory, yes; practice, no. Their positions are based on mucking around with other people's creative output and a flinty political cunning which allows them to found a sort of nebulous career on unsubstantive vapours and territorial challenge.

Remfs display a sort of grand detachment from the actual process of *making* something, like a film, often declining to read the script before commenting on it, though — and I'm not being facetious here — this fact seldom impacts in any meaningful way on the veracity or insight of their observations. This is the basis of their "whims of steel," whereby their comments take on the weight of Holy Script among the tyros, waybacks, poachers and wonks who work with them and may actually know better.

TYROS

"Tyro" is another word that originated on the battlefield. A "tyro" was a "recently levied soldier" back in the days when a season or two at "the war" was considered just the thing for a young man of a certain age in a certain strata of society. It always raises the image, in my mind, of a toothy, plucky chap in shiny new boots and haversack, rifle still sporting the price tag, ready to rush the barricades.

We all start out as tyros: no credits, no credibility, one of the mass of rookies trying to distinguish ourselves from all the other wannabes. Tyros often begin as readers for development officers. Others distinguish themselves by having a solid project which has simply evaded production through no fault of their own. Others are trying to make a jump from some other job: actor … grip … production assistant … progeny.

It's tough to be a tyro: you live waiting for someone to give you a chance to prove yourself.

Remfs hire tyros so as to pre-empt them from developing into writers. It's a way of retarding growth and ingeminating the remf species.

Take warning — if you forego the financial uncertainty of a scriptwriter's life to remain in a secure tyro-job until the rules of succession kick into gear, you become a remf.

WONKS

Wonk is an agreeable Anglo-Saxon word, which means " … a scholar who studies excessively, a grind…." Remember your English 101 papers on things like "sexual imagery in *The Rainbow* by D.H. Lawrence"? Wonks were Stockholmed into believing all that hooey we flung at the ivy-covered walls of the university and they are resolute in their determination to keep flinging it, usually at scriptwriters. They take refuge in rhetoric and semiotics and varsity terms like "objective correlative" and "affective fallacy" and "negative capability." If you say, "Isn't that ironic?" they are likely to reply, "Actually, no, it's a simple instance of ambiguity."

There are wonk sub-groupings, the most significant of which are Wonks Who Refer to Great Literature and Wonks Who Refer to Critics of Great Literature. Without belabouring the point, writers tend to prefer the first because, when it comes right down to it, the second are simply wonks who refer to bigger wonks.

Wonks tend to smell of armpits and old socks and sometimes won't admit to owning "television machines."

WAYBACKS

Waybacks are a bit like wonks in that they refer to a past canon of work, but instead of it being Shakespeare, Dostoyevsky or Ruskin, it's more likely to be "The Campbells," "The Littlest Hobo," or "Counterstrike."

Personally, I like waybacks. Their frames of reference are real shows that had real problems with scripts that had to somehow get up onto real screens for real people. Sure, there are waybacks who use their experiences as a kind of cudgel — "I'll have you know that 'Material World' was far ahead of its time!" And they sometimes have an odd, myopic indignance about whatever shows they worked on — "Don't you dare mention 'Danger Bay' in the same breath as 'Beachcombers'!" — and, unfortunately, most wayback opinions come freighted with a plethora of you-had-to-be-there anecdotes.

But waybacks have a great been-there-done-that weariness to them that is calming. Besides, when you're arguing passionately for a scene rivalling the death of Dr. Zhivago and a wayback says, "Yeah, we tried that on 'Adventures in Rainbow Country,' and it worked pretty well," you'd better listen.

Waybacks can also morph into remfs when their memories fade.

POACHERS

Poachers are bitter, drink too much coffee and comport themselves as a cross between Uriah Heep and General Patton. They are irritable dyspeptics who feel unappreciated. They are driven. So far, this general description fits most writers, but poachers are so driven that they will probably finish your next draft before *you* do. They know they can do it better than you can and their faces are tied in perpetual knots from the strain of this fact passing unnoticed. Often, poachers *can* write. But there is a world of difference between helping a writer realize his or her script through constructive criticism, and driving a writer *off* a project so it can get the treatment it "deserves" from the impatient poacher.

At first, a writer may feel that everyone in a story conference is a poacher who wants to wrest the script away, but the fact is, confronted with the real possibility of hands-on application, a remf or a wonk will back-pedal into the Age of Bronze, usually with platitudes about it being the writer's story and vision and so on. A poacher steps forward, sheds his or her camouflage, and cries: "Here I am! Use me!"

Sometimes poachers are tyros who are willing to trod across any number of bodies to get real experience. Sometimes they are waybacks who want one more kick at the can.

So What?

If you remember your Jung (I warned you I had wonk tendencies ...) you will recall the importance of personality types with regard to cognition. (If you don't remember, get really, really drunk and take a boo at the Collective Unconscious.)

And, as we all know from reading our Umberto Eco and listening to Lister Sinclair, cognition and language are inextricably intertwined.

Which brings us to the point of these archetypes. First, the writer must recognize them; then, the writer must learn to communicate with them; then — well, to be honest, it's unlikely but one can live in hope — the writer might win a few rounds from time to time.

The Platonic Story

Unfortunately, behind the archetypes and personalities, methods and mechanisms, is the simple, horrible truth of story meetings: the verity of the story must burn at a cellular level, deep inside somebody, and that somebody is you — the writer.

A story works on at least two levels. One is blatant and the other is secret. The blatant story has to do with plot and characters and drama. That's what most of the arguments are all about.

The *secret* story, what some call the "heart of the story" or the "subtext of the story," is much more mysterious and hard to articulate. Personally, I like to think of it as the "Platonic story," the perfect story, free of human dross and artifice, the version of the story which might be told by Shakespeare's more talented twin brother in Heaven.

The ideal story meeting is one in which all discussion revolves about the methods, machinations, and techniques the writer will use to reveal the Platonic story.

What are you trying to say in your story? What's it really about? To be sophomoric, what's the *theme*? What about it tugs at your heartstrings and made you think it was worth telling?

If you don't have at least an inkling of that, then you are as a lamb tossed unto the wolves. If you think it's a magic, miraculous and fragile thing that doesn't bear examination or argument, I heartily recommend you move into poetry. In the collaborative world of scriptwriting, your only worthwhile function is to defend that Platonic story to the death.

If you are strong in your Platonic story, you can be wonked, waybacked, tyroed, remfed, and poached without fear of losing the story — it might even benefit in that you can evaluate all that keen insight and scattergun suggestion against the Platonic story you alone understand.

If you don't know your Platonic story — the meaning inscribed beneath the surface — and you're a mature, centred, good writer, then all that battering and nit-picking will force you to clarify and understand, to rethink, reapproach, and re-evaluate.

If you're not a mature, centred, good writer, the project will either die on the vine, swerve into a wall, or be handed over to the next writer on the list.

So, Platonic story held closely to the heart, let us begin the story conference.

Identification

You enter the room for the story conference — sweating — your script or pitch or notebook in hand. Who are all these people? What do they want? Why don't their smiles reach their eyes?

The first thing to become apparent is the pecking order. Conceivably, you might meet with producers (executive, supervising, creative, co-) and a few story editors (executive, senior, junior, assistant). Then there are various consultants, interns etc. If the script is a one-off or long-form such as MOW or feature, you might also have to deal with a director or — in truly cruel circumstances — an actor.

Also in the room, sometimes in the flesh and sometimes only in spirit, is an executive in charge of production (the network's rep), various development executives (from the network, from the distributor, from Telefilm, from the provincial funding agency, from the production company) and, in some cases, the beancounter brigade (line-producer, unit manager, production manager etc.)

But someone is sitting behind the big desk or in the cushy chair. Even in the most collegiate and convivial of organizations, the boss will out. If you can't figure out who is the heaviest gorilla in the room, you probably shouldn't be a writer.

There will be a short period of small talk while people fetch coffee or discuss their various flights or recent meals. This lull is a gift from God to you, the writer.

Time to study up on your archetypes.

One of the first things that may happen — probably, but not necessarily at the behest of a remf — is that you will be asked what *you* think of your idea, treatment or script. Resist the natural impulse to say, "I think it's as perfect as an egg, don't any of you ham-fisted cretins crack it." Also resist the natural tendency to give a lecture on your intentions.

Let your writing do the talking — or all you'll achieve is to get the wonk all keyed up for debate and the poacher overeager to pounce on any sign of weakness. Don't walk into these traps.

Get *them* to talk by whatever means you can. I usually mutter something about being troubled by pacing or tone, both of which are so monstrously vague and unquantifiable that the conversation immediately turns towards something more concrete, like, "It's too long." (A poacher line.)

If you must talk, a valid strategy is to be (fairly) honest about your real concerns with the script. After all, if you're going to spend the next two hours dissecting your thoughts and ideas, you might as well steer the agenda as much as possible.

As Phase One of the meeting progresses, the archetypes should be increasingly recognizable:

The remf is the one who gets bored talking about specifics, preferring to discuss vague generalities of demographics, social significance or what the network/funding agency/Americans/broadcaster/etc. might think.

The poacher is the one who posits several "solutions" to problems which haven't even been discussed as problems yet, including several scenes, lines of dialogue, character names, painful details, often as not, well before their time.

The wayback is the one who has ensured that you know he or she is responsible for the real success of "E.N.G." and has indulged in a sort of *faux* cynicism that can be damned amusing.

The wonk is the one who wants to discuss your script in terms of *Middlemarch,* likes the words *paradigm, hubris,* and *hamartia,* and endeavours to discuss the image system and the allegory inherent in your piece with excruciating thoroughness to no immediately apparent, or applicable, end.

The tyro is the one who nods a lot in the corner scribbling notes and interjecting references to the various gurus like Field, Truby, McKee, Vogler or whoever is currently in vogue as though everyone has simply ceded to the frightfully obvious: these men are the Matthew-Mark-Luke-and-Johns of cinematic drama.

The Big Question

And as they talk and as you try to listen and make sense, one crucial, complicated, brutal question starts to clang in your skull like a blacksmith trapped in a dumpster:

How do I tread that fine line between being "easy to work with" and being a doormat? Between "having a strong artistic vision" and being an intractable snot?

How hard should I fight?

The Degree Of Accommodation

There are terrific writers who get less and less work as time goes on because they are hard to work with. On a series, with production realities chasing them down like an avalanche, very few producers or story editors want to deal with a writer — no matter *how* talented — who won't make their lives easier. Known in whispers behind their backs as "LTS writers" (Life's Too Short), they find themselves working only on long-form projects with more supple time-lines and — even in that more forgiving atmosphere — are soon poacher-fodder. You've heard it before: television and film are collaborative mediums and that means collaborating. That *doesn't* mean you should behave like a stenographer. (That's what tyros are for.)

A writer who responds to every whim and whoof of waybacks, wonks and remfs, in an effort to be nice soon finds themselves denigrated as writers who start out with promise, but never seems to be able to deliver the final goods. (The reason for this failure to deliver the final goods is that the early promise has been smothered by all the suggestions and demands of the archetypes.)

Forget the big bang, cold fusion or time travel. The central paradox for scriptwriters is The Degree of Accommodation.

Where lies the middle ground? It lies in the absurdity that *the archetypes are absolutely essential to the process.*

That's a hard pill for any writer to swallow — it's easier to think of these people as obstacles to creativity, to think of them as parasites on our creativity. Well, they are — but we need them.

Matter and antimatter make starships run. Debits and credits make economies run. Heaven and Hell make the world run. Archetypes and writers make stories run.

The degree of accommodation is contingent upon the answers to two questions: (1) Which story points should I argue about? (2) How do I best voice my displeasure and outrage?

Sure, the answer to question number one hangs on your own sense of the Platonic story, authorial authority and sense of self, but the cold heartless fact of the matter is that it's a direct function of the nature of the project.

The answer to question number two depends on your connection to the social contract, good manners, judgement and grasp on your temper, but the vital factor is which archetype you're facing down.

What Story Points Should I Argue About?

If you have a hearty-peasant constitution, you may be tempted to argue every point, as a matter of principle. This is exhausting and, in the main, fruitless, as the archetypes will simply regroup and tag-team you to death.

A better strategy is to evaluate whether or not the point in contention has anything at all to do with the Platonic story, that perfect story from Shakespeare's more talented brother. If the point *doesn't* impinge on the Platonic story, then the whole issue is small potatoes and should be treated as such.

If the point *does* affect the Platonic story, then you should dig in your heels, set your mouth appropriately and shake your head until they give up.

What's so important about the Platonic story? It is the core of the drama. Everything else, including the characters, plot, dialogue, settings, symbolism, tone, pace — all these things spring from the Platonic story.* If you allow it to be compromised or destroyed, then the centre will not hold, and no matter how well-executed the script is, it will be hollow and unsatisfying.

Story meeting arguments *should* centre around questions of execution, not of generation. Of Birth. Not Conception. Let us think of the Platonic story as something akin to the Olympic Torch — beautiful and fraught with meaning.

Say you've written a feature film script on spec between midnight and

---

*One of the best illustrations of the importance of the Platonic story to the writer can be found in William Goldman's book *Adventures In the Screen Trade* in which he outlines his reasons for *not* writing *The Right Stuff.* It comes down to a basic, fundamental, inarguable difference between his view of the astronaut program *versus* the producers' view. When he could not get them to adopt *his* Platonic story, he chose to turn down the job rather than compromise his own vision.

4:00 a.m. after your shift at the video store. In that case, you are not only the rightful bearer of the torch, you climbed Olympus and lit it yourself. Footnote

Say you're contracted to write an MOW based on a story by a producer, or on a real event or on a book. In that case you may be the best bearer of the torch but you didn't light it yourself. It was passed to you, and if it was passed to you, it can pass *from* you as well. If you can't agree on a Platonic story early on in the process — witness William Goldman — then *don't* agree to carry the torch.

Say the producers and story department of an existing television series give you the story idea for an episode. In that case you not only didn't light the torch, but you really only get to hold it on a small part of its journey. You may carry the torch higher, make it burn brighter, wave the torch in their faces but, in the end, you will have to give it back.

The ferocity with which you fight is directly proportional to how much of the torch is *yours*.

On that scale, the rule of thumb is: If you lit the torch, and the archetypes start trying to blow it out, fight off the poachers with all your might, debate with the wonks, evaluate how threatened you are by the waybacks, ignore the tyros and listen to the remfs if they're talking about how to get the torch to the next checkpoint.

In such an instance you know the *real* story behind these words and scenes and behind the structure. Anything they want you to change that weakens that real story is a *bad* change. If a requested change illuminates, strengthens or reveals the Platonic story, then it's a good change, even if it annoys you.

If someone else lit the torch and has hired you to carry it for a while (as on a television series), listen carefully to the poachers, debate with the wonks, let the tyros tell you what you need to know about format, see what the *others* think of the wayback ideas before you implement them and ignore the remfs.

In such an instance you can debate the Platonic story of your episode, but not the Platonic story of the series. (Your main job as an episodic writer is to provide an episodic story that resonates with the Platonic story of the series.)

To simplify: poachers rule on series, remfs rule on one-offs.

How Do I best Voice Displeasure and Outrage?
Speak the language of your archetype-opponent.

For example, poacher-talk tends to be quantifiable, pragmatic and oriented to what's on the page. Talk to the poacher in his or her own language. Argue the relative merits of two-handers versus three-handers at act bumps, story complexity, page count dialogue, act endings, story days, too many characters, too little action, actor limitations, cost considerations, *ad infinitum.*

These are not things that affect the Platonic story directly; they are craft considerations. Not only is the poacher usually right about such things but, in the case of a television series, the poacher will be rewriting you. It's a fact.

The more you argue, the more the poacher simply resolves to do it him- or herself. And since, in series, your main objective is to deserve having your name on the episode, it behooves the freelancer to give the series poachers what they want because the less it's rewritten, the more you get to write. *Ergo, ipso facto, Oreo,* Nabisco, *lodge only the slightest ego-preserving protests to legitimate poacher comments.* On series, poachers can be our friends.

On a one-off, they can ruin everything by considering themselves your co-writer and wielding inappropriate influence. (In fact, their ideas may be every bit as legitimate as yours, perhaps even more pragmatic, but until you get fired and they get hired, it's your Platonic story on the chopping block.)

I was recently assigned an episode of a new series that had production and broadcast commitments, but little else. There was a back-door pilot script — meaning that an MOW had been written in the express hope that it would turn out to be the pilot for a series — and a bible, but the actual series had yet to develop. I asked a bunch of pertinent questions of the fellow who was wrangling my script: What is the relationship between plot and sub-plot? Do you like acts to consistently end on the A line? Does every character's through-line come to fruition in the last act? These are poacher questions but, I thought, it's a series and poacher questions are the most important.

Unfortunately, I wasn't talking to a poacher, I was talking to a tyro-wonk — and he was at a complete loss. Floundering for non-existent common ground, the meeting turned to banal and obvious wonk-talk, "We're interested in round, fully-fleshed character developed stories," as I stupidly countered in the poacher dialect, "How many pages do you want?"

Now, we're enemies because we made each other insecure and, more importantly, because he's a cretinous fool. Fact is, as a tyro-wonk, he might have been invaluable during the conception of the series, even the writing of the pilot, but when it came to the nuts and bolts of my episode, he could really only discuss the wonk aspects of the series.

Wonk-talk, in a series, is mostly about the series, not about your particular episode. A series has themes and image systems and negative capabilities and all that hoo-ha that matters only in that it sheds light on the real story of the series — the series' Platonic story.

Wonk-talk on a more personal project might still be useful to you. If you are dead certain of your Platonic story, wonk-talk may expose you to facets you hadn't considered. If your Platonic story foundations are *not* solid, wonk-talk may lead you to understand it better.

Personally, I figure wonk-talk to be like late-night religious debate — diverting, trenchant, even edifying but slightly embarrassing in the light of day. And, if you're not vigilant, liable to force you to confront first principles — which is only good if you intend to rebuild the story from the ground up. If not, it's a waste of everybody's time.

I was once struggling with an MOW, agonizing over my two main characters, when a notoriously silly wonk said, "I think this story is about Order and Chaos." Instead of telling him what I thought, "Every goddam story is about order and chaos, snot-boy," I realized it was an element I'd assumed but had not injected into the script. It was part of the Platonic story I'd seriously underplayed.

In a series story meeting, the wonk can give you insights into the real story or core of the series you might not have picked up from watching it. Don't bother to argue that your episode is not "an analogue of the *Iliad*." If the series is an analogue of the *Iliad*, then so is your episode; and if your episode is *not*, then there's trouble in Troy. Even if the other archetypes roll their eyes, the wonk may know something they don't.

In a series meeting, the tyro is always the last one you talk to: "What word processing program do you use?" or "Will you be able to give us a draft by Christmas? How soon before Christmas?" If overly encouraged, the tyro might try to bring, say, Robert McKee into the meeting to back up his contention that the human value in question in your episode is not charity but hope. My advice is to nod — the tyro may have a point or, more likely, may eventually become immensely powerful.

Remember always, that in both a series and one-off context, the tyro has a power roughly equivalent to court reporter: when you have a pitched argument with the archetypes about who said what to whom and who agreed to what, it's the tyro who will have the official record. Think of your next story conference as a Court of Appeals in which the official record is vital to your escaping the death penalty. In such situations, the more noble of tyros may actually come down on your side, from time to time, if they're foolish or sleeping with someone of great influence.

The tyro, in a long-form project, can be heaven-sent. The tyro is a force which, like Yoko Ono, batters down the doors of artistic complacency and stultifying conformity. Tyros tend to talk about art and meaning with passion, and God knows we should encourage that if we can keep from yawning, snickering or snapping.

Tyros are good for counteracting the enervating influence of the wayback. The wayback can be negative and cynical and derisive in a way that is very convincing. They can argue their points backed up with years of experience and concrete examples of disasters and setbacks. The tyro is a grand force for your current day project, a constant reminder that just because something was true in the past on another project, it doesn't necessarily apply here.

Then again, it might. In any push-me-pull-you involving tyros and waybacks, my advice is to nod and promise to think about it later.

Waybacks can drive you insane. They always have an answer, they always tried this before, they always know how things are going to turn out.

Your best defence against a wayback is their own nagging suspicion that they might be over the hill, past it, non-hip and sclerotic.

Conversely, a wayback is a bit like a guardian angel. Always at your shoulder, playing the spoilsport, whispering the safe course of action, the conservative move — and this is a good thing. Waybacks can say, "We tried using an unsympathetic protagonist on "Bordertown" and people hated it."

Give their experience credence. Ask questions. Why didn't the unsympathetic protagonist work? How do you know people didn't like it? The typical wayback won't have a good answer, but your heretofore sleeping wonk will wade into the surf of debate like David Hasselhof, with a tyro Pamela Lee close behind. If nothing else, you've managed to split the wonk from the wayback and mystify the remf, who will suddenly have phone calls to make.

Dealing with remfs is the trickiest of all propositions. In series television, writers may be protected from direct contact with the remfs, but there is a definite supply-side, trickle-down remfonomic influence. In my experience, unmotivated soliloquies are often a result.

Writers are tempted to think of remfs as arrogant idiots, but that's suicidal. They may be woefully moony when it comes to story and scripts, but they know a hell of a lot about interpersonal relations, politics and self-preservation. If you allow a remf to pulverize your script or idea into seven-grain mush, it won't be the remf who suffers. It'll be *you*.

Still, there's a silver lining — if the remf is right in there in the room with you, ruining your life, it means that the organization — production house, funding agency, broadcaster, whatever — is taking the project seriously. Remfs can smell stillborn projects a thousand miles away and if yours has even a whiff of wet squib to it, well, they'll send in someone else, probably a wonk, with a fistful of inane notes.

Remfs are the bane of the writer's existence. They don't read the scripts and even if they read them, they don't *read* them. They don't care much about story; they are about selling the story and protecting their own butts. Remfs abhor personal risk and they are obsessed with reputation. They live in perpetual fear of people finding out they don't actually know how to *do* anything.

Except make the project happen.

Which is the most important thing of all.

When a remf realizes his or her function and pursues it, he or she is as vital an ingredient to a project as water is to rain. I remember doing a brilliant pitch to a remf and his entourage for a television series. The wonks and waybacks nodded and grinned. The tyro became enthusiastic. The poacher scowled and had an idea to begin the second season (we hadn't started the first yet).

But the remf was quivering like a whippet. Finally, he stopped pacing and smoking and said, "How the hell can I sell this to the Americans?"

My face suffused with nationalist indignation. My fists balled, my mouth gaped, all my facial features balkanized and declared independence from each other and from me.

Then, I *heard* him. Without the Americans, this project would not go. End of argument. The remf had spoken the single most important fact of this project: it had to sell in the States. All my perturbations and agitations dwindled to one annoying little nub: do I want to do this or not?

I suspect that a remf's eardrum is specially modified to pick up only the nuances and dynamics that matter to remfs. They're like foxbats who can hear gnats sighing but miss sirens.

That's why we need remfs.

God help us when a remf does take a sudden, ephemeral interest in the actual story you wish to tell. They pass on ill-considered suggestions that, as mentioned earlier, take on the authority of the Ark of the Covenent. In my first collision with a remf over a half-hour one-off, I got this actual story note: "It would be better if the script started out with the two characters sitting on a bus talking about what was going to happen in the script." This, apparently, was to make the plot clear.

My argument that this wasn't exactly a snappy or dramatic opening was a poacher defence. My affirmation that the entire story was an *homage* to the myth of Hippolytes' Girdle was a wonk rejoinder. My contention that Syd Field said never to begin with exposition was a tyro supplication. My declaration that I had never seen a two-hander, on a bus, under credits, clear up anything was pure wayback desperation. I was twisting and turning and feinting and bobbing and weaving, but I could feel this classic remf idea tightening around me like a boa constrictor.

Then, the stained glass window spoke.

The stained glass window, God bless her, simply said that an extremely important person, for whom we were all ostensibly working, had once reprimanded the stained glass window for a similar scene, on a train, in an MOW which, though an homage to Hitchcock, failed to transcend.

Wow! The stained glass window had effectively soothed all archetypes in one fell swoop. The remf back-pedalled smoothly, the wonk nodded, the tyro scribbled, the wayback twisted his mouth sardonically, and the poacher sighed in huge relief. The universe reeled back into alignment.

The Stained Glass Window

Stained glass windows are somehow both seamlessly beautiful and bluntly clunky. From outside, they aren't particularly impressive, but once inside, they illuminate and edify. Stained glass windows are made up of hundreds of facets but somehow they make sense.

When you walk into a story meeting, what you really want to see is a stained glass window sitting calmly among the archetypes because then you know you've got *help* in the room. A stained glass window has a knack for finding the heart of your story, the Platonic story, and helping you realize it.

Depending on the light, they morph and mutate, but the big picture doesn't change. There's both immutability and modulation. I love stained glass windows and so should you.

A stained glass window has the ability to channel the spirit of any of the other archetypes when necessary. If your story is in danger of being self-indulgent and self-absorbed, the stained glass window will speak in a remf voice.

If the project is losing it's heart in an avalanche of craft details, the stained glass window will adopt the voice of the wonk, taking you back to first principles and themes and subtext and human desire.

If you are drowning in philosophy and abstruse psychological arcana, the stained glass window will play poacher and bring you back face-to-face with the act, the page, the scene, the dialogue and what the hell the actor is going to do.

If you are too derivative or stretching the envelope, reinventing the wheel or trying to do without it altogether, the stained glass window will pull wayback rank, bringing experience to bear.

In short, the stained glass window is a morphling, something like Tony Randall in *The Seven Faces of Dr. Lao*.

The stained glass window is a godsend. It's as though the writer has back-up in defending and improving upon the *real* story he or she is trying to tell. While any number of people are capable of manifesting characteristics of any archetype, it is the stained glass window who adopts the right archetype at the right time.

I was once co-writing a science-fiction feature with a terrific writer. We were lumbered with a remf-poacher-producer (the worst of all possible combinations — someone who knows very little but wants everything done in a particular way).

The stained glass window was brought on to help me and my partner, who had taken to lying on the floor at story meetings cradling his head and moaning at a subsonic level. She sussed out the situation and, the first time we were alone with her, suggested we quit the project. She had good reasons for this on the wayback level: ("He wants a rip-off of *Starman* ... ") the wonk level (" ... and you guys want to investigate the themes prevalent in the story of Absalom."), the poacher level ("The story and the budget are nowhere near compatible ... "), the remf level (" ... and I don't see Telefilm putting this at the top of any lists.") And she even managed a tyro move, reading us back some of the producer's more outrageous comments from her copious notes. ("I know aliens and this is not how they behave.")

We quit the project and my partner was once again able to withstand gravity.

Unfortunately, stained glass windows are rare. You can't count on one popping up at every story conference.

Which leaves it up to the writer.

Sitting there, getting advice and prognostications and proclamations, you have to be able to keep a firm grip on the Platonic story with one hand, a firm grip on your temper with your teeth and a firm grip on the realities of production with your other hand.

That done, the story meeting is a pleasant meeting of the minds in which we're all aiming at the same goal — to make this project as excellent as we can.

So, that being said: what do *you* think of the script?

6

Writing For Children: A Child is a Child is a Child

by Nancy Trites Botkin and Dennis Foon

Nancy Trites Botkin has numerous credits as writer, story editor, producer and director in both television and film. She has received over 50 international awards for her work as well as many nominations. She is producer/executive story editor of "Fred Penner's Place," and has written for series such as "Madison," "Northwood," "Inside Stories." She was co-writer and originator of the MOW Race to Freedom: The Underground Railroad, wrote Red Shoes, Tramp at the Door and Heaven On Earth and was co-producer, director and story editor on For Angela which won the 1995 Gemini Canada Award. Ms. Trites Botkin teaches scriptwriting at the University of Winnipeg and is on the executive board of the National Screen Institute.

Dennis Foon is the recipient of the British Theatre Award, the International Arts for Young Audiences Award and two Chalmers Awards for his work. His script for the CBS After School Special, Maggie's Secret, won a Scott Newman Award, and his drama, Skin, received a Gold Medal in the New York International Film and TV Festival and was a Gemini nominee (the playscript was a Governor General's finalist). Little Criminals, an MOW broadcast on CBC, won the International Critics Prize in Monte Carlo, 1996. Episodic television credits include "African Skies," "The Odyssey," "Northwood," "Black Stallion," "Mom P.I.," "Friday the 13th," "Fred Penner" and "Nilus the Sandman." Current projects include the feature What You Need, for Acme Films, "The Short Tree," an animated series with Waterstreet/CBC and The Queen of Light, with Metaphor Films.

What Is A Child?

Someone who is short, not stupid. Someone who has the fullest range of human emotions possible and is fully capable of expressing them all — in five-minute cycles. Someone who, at the age of three, asks on average, 350 questions a day. Someone who laughs over 400 times a day and will grow up to laugh maybe four times a day. Someone who doesn't know they can't fly until they are told.

The actual *length* of the journey through childhood is very short. It is not simply a time of "waiting to become." Childhood is "being and doing" in the present. The eternal now. To a child, the process of living is learning.

What if someone told you that you could spend fifteen minutes or a half-hour every *day* with millions of children — one on one — in their most intimate setting, no barriers. And that during this time you could make them see their world differently, offer them a whole new range of feelings and thoughts to explore, make them laugh, and let them know how unique they are. This potential for making a difference keeps a lot of excellent writers plying their trade for an audience of children.

Kim Todd, producer of the series "My Life As a Dog" and "Ramona," said the first thing she would say to a writer who said they wanted to write for children is to ask what they had to say. "If you haven't got something important to say — write for another audience. Writing for children is not just a job — it has to come from a passion that you have something vital to say to children and you are willing to get down — eyeball to eyeball — to say it."

The goals of the best TV shows for children are to create safe and wonderful worlds where children visit each day to laugh, think and feel that they are welcomed. When healthy core values are modelled, individual dignity is affirmed. Creativity is celebrated. The capacity to love and be loved is expanded and self-respect is the constant by-product. All of this through story.

Writer/story-editor Jill Golick who has written for "Sesame Street," "Fred Penner's Place", "Groundling Marsh" and many other children's shows feels that some writers understand this responsibility. She says that, "Our craft — the art of storytelling — has always been among the most potent teaching tools that a community has. Stories have taught generations of children right from wrong, safety rules and strategies for solving problems. Every community and culture has told stories that help children learn religious ideas, values, skills, history. We use tales to help our children deal with their fears, to inspire them to greatness, to console them in the face of defeat and to encourage them to try again. Through the ages, stories have been a part of childhood and part of child-rearing. And today we are still using them in the same ways, only today our stories are told on TV."

There is perhaps no other vehicle with such potential and power for influencing and shaping children as the medium of television. Creating excellence in children's television is not solely about entertainment. It is to create entertaining and educational shows *rooted* in core values which can help children forge tools for the rest of their lives. This is one heavy-duty order.

What Does It Take To Write For Kids?

Determination. You'll get lots of satisfaction but little respect. Jill Golick laughs as she says, "Face it — writers who write for children are an easy mark even for other writers, 'I'm writing for Hammy the Hamster today — he meets a frog in my episode." Our society doesn't show respect towards children; even in government-funded projects we give the lowest amount to those involving children. Kids deserve at least equal resources. But they don't vote and pay taxes or buy. Writing for children conjures boring educational goals or fluff. And when we do tell a story with meaning and deep feelings, it gets bumped from early morning markets to family prime time slots."

Ask any writer who writes for children and they'll tell you the same thing. Pay scales are driven by the market. Kids don't have disposable income. Writing for children is often on a lower scale than writing for "other" kinds of television. And writing for animation isn't covered by any kinds of guild rates in Canada or the United States. So don't plan on getting rich fast.

But as vital as it is to gain pay equity in writing for children's TV, money isn't the only measure of reward. As writer/story editor Yan Moore who wrote for "Degrassi Junior High" and "Degrassi High" says, "it's fun to write for them because it forces you to connect back with your own childhood which is healthy, educational and sometimes startling." Jill Golick adds, "I never write for kids — I write for myself. I'm always entertained. I always have fun. You don't deal with the pessimism you have in writing drama or episodic television."

In Canada, most writers are capable writers for a wide range of shows and refuse to be pigeon-holed in one category. Writing for children's television should be an elite market, the requirement being that we hire only our best writers. That isn't always how it works. The best are there often because of their own commitment to children and our global community. Children deserve our best. They are a most discerning audience. Add to this the fact that in many cases parents have handed over the responsibility of morality and values to television. Add to that the element of political correctness. The box gets tighter and tighter.

Writing for kids is one tough gig. The following sections cover the list of "abilities" a writer for children must have.

Ability To Respect

Power for the child, not over the child. A child deserves the respect given to any audience. To know them, their needs, their dreams. To see them clearly. Writer/story editor Yan Moore says, "You have to respect your characters. Just because they're little people doesn't mean you have the right to look down on them. Kids pick up condescending adults in a snap."

It's interesting that "Mr. Roger's Neighborhood" has a very small age window during which children watch devotedly. It is round about ages two to four. By five, kids are usually "too big" for him. His slow, steady pacing often drives parents wild, but to watch a little one in front of his show is a study in perfect fit. Mr. Rogers not only knows his audience well, but he has tremendous respect for them. There is never a moment of tongue-in-cheek towards his audience.

Writing with respect means to tell good stories. "The Odyssey" writer/story editor/producer Charles Lazer who also wrote for "Max Glick" and "Road To Avonlea" says, "I don't write for kids, I write for an audience that I believe appreciates and understands good stories. And I tell them the best and the most powerful stories I can think of." Children need strong stories to make sense of their world.

Michael Mercer, writer/story editor, who has written for "Black Stallion," "African Skies" and "The Campbells" says much the same: "To me the key in writing for children is not to write for children. To do so is to perceive them as people other than self — younger and less experienced — and there are few things children can sense more quickly than someone speaking down to them. I can only write convincingly about those things that interest and excite me personally, so when writing for children, I choose rather to write for the child in myself. I can be sure of one thing. I have never, in living memory, spoken down to, or patronized myself."

Ability To See

Can you see the world through the eyes of a child? With wonder, whimsy and honesty? At no time in life is there as much passion, imagination and creativity in life as there is in early childhood. Kids know if you can see their world, and they also know if you are telling the truth about what you see. They have little mercy for shallow solutions or characters — kids know.

Talk to kids about the shows they watch. What do they see? Did they like it? What did they like about it? Is it how they know their world? How would they make it happen differently? What was funny? What was not? These questions will spark some fascinating observations about your audience and yourself.

Ability To "Get Inside"

Know who your audience is — what they know, feel, think, want, understand, love, hate. What makes a kid a kid? The more you know about children, the better. Age, context, viewpoint, place in family all inform your audience. Think kid. What is a child's reference point? If you were three what would you feel, see, hear? How would that be different if you were seven, ten? What is going on inside? Can you see it, feel it and capture it?

Jill Golick agrees, "You have to know kids, listen to them talking, hang around with them, know who you were when you were a kid, know what a good story is. I try to listen to the words they are using, phrases, language and expressions."

Whether you're writing for the whole family or for a specific age group, the more you know about child development the better off you are. Remember (or learn) the huge developmental difference between children. An average three-year old's attention span is quite short and they can't distinguish between fantasy and reality. A five-year-old has a longer attention span but still has trouble separating reality from fantasy. (If you dare ask parents with teenagers, they will tell you that by the time a kid reaches sixteen, they have zero attention span and have completely lost touch with all reality — but that is another topic.)

Don't take our word for it. Find out for yourself about the physical and mental changes kids go through year to year. That information itself is a gold mine of detail which will help you build character, situation and story. Remember you are the scout on the hill, the first to find the character and story, but it can be a long, hot ride.

When you're writing for families, the greatest catch-all is to include an age spread of characters in order to cast as wide an interest net for your audience as possible. And if you do that, the more knowledgeable you are about the specifics of each age, the better off you'll be.

As part of your research you will want to read all the theoretical overviews you can get your hands on. But most importantly you need to talk to children. After all, their world is significantly different than yours was as a child.

You will inevitably be drawing from your own experiences and feelings, but if you are writing about contemporary kids, you had better have a sense of their reality. What are the issues of families today? Some relate to basic human condition which makes us all crazy (and good writers), but some of the pressure points are specific to today's world.

Yan Moore goes farther when he suggests that: "It's critical when writing for kids that you run your work by kids because you're so far away from that age. Don't assume you know how to do it. Test your script with a bunch of kids you know, or in classrooms or workshops. And don't assume because you're a parent, you understand what's going on with kids."

Not only do you need to get inside the child's world, but as well you must be able to get inside the show you are writing for, know what the show is about. The show's bible is a good starting place — but ask questions. Read scripts. Watch the shows. What are the producers and/or story editor's *really* looking for and why? A few shows are aimed at specific age ranges: most expect you to write catch-all scripts that have interesting hooks for adults too.

One of the biggest problems facing writers for younger audiences is that the interests and cognitive levels of children vary widely and it's often a guessing game to try and write a script to fit a given age group. Adding to this confusion is that the popularity of a show is often measured by it's merchandising marketability, not its intrinsic worth.

Ability To Sing

Music is a key element especially in shows for younger children. Children don't have to be taught to sing — they do it naturally and unconsciously up to a certain age. Music captures their attention and brings them back time and time again. Music can be used in many ways: to feel, move, dance, as mood, to create, as pacing, even as story.

On "Fred Penner's Place," we feel that music works best when it is so integrated into the story line that it becomes a part of the character arc. Songs can inform the drama, move it forward, become a turning point or resolution. In one episode when Nikki, one of the puppet three-year-old characters has lost all sense of worth, Fred sings his "Nikky" song to her about how unique and wonderful she is and the song facilitates her turning point. By mid-point of the song, she takes back her self-confidence and is ready to take on the world again, singing by the end, at the top of her lungs.

The more the child is involved in music, the better, Make 'em move, dance, clap and wiggle. What makes a good song? Ask these questions:

1. How does it make you/a child feel?
2. Does it work for your target audience?
3. Does it draw attention?
4. Is it easy to understand?
5. Is it humourous?
6. Would it work to initiate participation?

Ability To Play

Play is how children learn their world and their roles in that world. The skills children learn for dealing with life are learned through role playing. Play is a child's work. It's important stuff. Creativity is far more important than knowledge and, in fact, it's the road to get there. The good writer for children looks for opportunities to "play" and in doing so, stimulates the child's own creativity.

When looking for writers for children, producer Kim Todd looks for those who can structure a good story, tell a yarn and capture an audience — writers with a sense of play. "They must have a sense of humour, imagination and whimsy combined, so when they hit those hard choices, they will take the road less travelled and make it work. Children work on gut reaction — they can't be bought cheaply. Cheap sentiment doesn't work. They are a tough audience because they are so honest. The writer's bag of tricks (or the producer's even bigger bag of tricks) doesn't wash for kids. They can see right through it."

Play is an effective way of creatively solving problems as adults too. The best writers know how to "play" well. We do it all the time with characters. It's one of the delights of being a writer — you get to make up all sorts of people and worlds in your head — and get paid for it. In fact no one thinks it's odd that writers for children buy strange little toys for their offices, even when they don't have children around. They assume it's in case a kid wanders by. Little do they know — we indulge. "I keep toys in my office," says Jill Golick. "Juggling bags, bubbles. Magnetic words. I constantly acquire toys for myself. There is something about the toys that generates creativity. Because on "Sesame Street" we're targeting that very young group of kids, I love getting action into the scene that is just playing — bringing playfulness for the sake of playing to the scene."

Ability To Laugh

Humour is an essential element to writing well for children. Laughter is an important key to reaching a child. They love to laugh. Young children can find humour in almost anything. It doesn't have to make sense to be funny for a child and what works in person may not work on TV. Verbal humour is lost on real young children, but the sound of a word, or repetition of a word may be fall-down funny. Physical humour works well. So does slapstick. Children appreciate the surprise, wit, whimsy and silliness of slapstick.

Ability To Take Risks

Write so that the characters take emotional, spiritual and physical risk. Every choice a child makes has a risk. As writers we can model the freedom to take those risks and be affirming for those choices the child makes, even if they don't work out the first time.

Charles Lazer talks about risk taking in his series: "In 'The Odyssey,' we valued loyalty, bravery, courage and let our characters make those choices, even at significant cost to themselves. They'd risk everything for their friends. The mistake many people make when writing for kids is to tell easy stories, not to force the characters to make difficult choices. An obvious choice isn't a choice at all. Kids today are a sophisticated audience. They get bored with stories that are lame."

Ability To Include, Not Exclude

On "Fred Penner's Place," we ask our writers to think of the camera as the point of view of the "child." Whatever the camera is seeing, is how the child is seeing this world. We always have Fred look directly at the camera, constantly engaging the child. "Mr. Dressup" does it so well. Only when this happens is the child (audience) always part of everything happening. The child is "in" on everything, either with the guest or host or both.

This creates what we've called the "Triangle." It is not an evenly weighted triangle. The host and the child (audience) hold down the bottom — the guest is in tangent to each of them, having his own relationship with the host *and* the child, but being the guest of *both* the host *and* the child.

This perspective is essential to our shows because we have found it's what makes the magic happen for the child. The child is not just included, but is a vital part of the shows. She or he is the consistently special friend. When the show's guest acknowledges the child's pre-eminent position, the mix works every time.

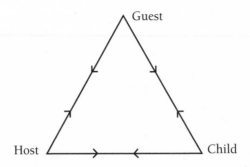

The same principle holds just as true for many adult shows. Take "The David Letterman Show." We, the TV audience, are on the "inside track" with him. He confides to us that the next guest is crazy — but hey — see what we think. So "Letterman and I" talk to the guest. We are not the butt of any of his jokes — we are his silent partner, often included even more than the live audience.

One could make a case that the failed CBC show "Friday Night Live" with Ralph Benmergui, was cancelled in part because the triangle with the audience was ignored. In fact, the audience often became the butt of the joke. The connection was not with the band or the guest (who was often on the outside of the triangle too), but with producers who were off-screen.

Each show has a different relationship to audience, but it's important as writers to figure out that connection.

Ability To Tell A Good Story

Who was it that said writing is easy? You just stare at a page until drops of blood form on your forehead. Writing for children is just as simple. Bottom line is that you just have to be a damn good writer. Be able to tell a story well. Make it come alive.

The magic of any children's show of quality starts with the writing. Children's Television Workshop who produce "Sesame Street" reminds us that, "the layperson will see a Muppet bit and marvel that the muppet was so brilliant and skilful in ad libbing, when all the time the ad lib is a word-for-word reading of a script. "Sesame Street" is a highly and carefully structured show which is the work of writers."

Structure, plot, character, dialogue, pacing — these are essential when writing for children. It's crucial to remember that all the best drama is about something. If it's not, you have no content, no conflict, no story.

Jill Golick talks about the need to write for children in such a way as to "engage the intellect to get the children at home thinking. To know a beat before the character does. Know what the right answer is — to build an opportunity to feel smart — to get it. Children should get the clue and figure it out and feel good about it. And get a pay-off for their intellectual work — and for the same price — get a good laugh."

Know Your Message

Think kid, talk kid. But as well you have to understand the complexity of message, meaning, context, educational goals and entertainment within a structure for children's show. There is a message *received* from every show (children's or otherwise) whether you intended to send it or not. Make sure it is the one you wanted to send.

Just because the messages are "care-filled" and aimed at the target audience of a younger child, does not mean these messages are insipid or weak. In fact, by addressing a child's moments of great joy and/or great trauma, we are encouraging tremendous strength and empowerment. This mirrors well a child's own personal potential and power.

Think of the strength and fury generated by a two-year-old in full-blown tantrum, or conversely, the unmitigated power of joy in seeing a rainbow for the first time. Writers for children must take their audience, and their life's moments, seriously.

Concept words such as *sharing* have little meaning until they are illustrated. Don't tell me — show me. (Of course, in order to share, you must first *own* something, something that belongs to only you. Many economically disadvantaged children have never owned anything. In fact, one out of five children in Canada now lives below the poverty line. This must factor in the overall consideration of meaning and scope in responsible programming for Canadian television. And this becomes a shared responsibility among writers, producers and broadcasters.)

Pre-school shows in particular have educational goals, but it's not uncommon to have shows that are aimed at say, twelve-year-olds make similar demands.

This can be a demoralizing task, because most of us believe story and education are like oil and water. It instantly puts you in the realm of boring, moralizing drivel. But it doesn't have to be that way. The first obstacle to overcome is your own allergy to "education," because most of us have at least a few negative memories of that time in our lives. In fact, we became dramatic writers just so we didn't have to ever do math again. Except at tax time.

So if you're writing for a show that has an educational objective, you've been given your content. Your job is to find the emotional stakes, because if you don't, it will be a very dry and deadly experience for both you and your audience. You have to take this environmental lesson, or counting review, or shadow explanation and bring it to life. Our tools are the palette of every writer: the conflict, story, characters, dialogue and humour.

Children's Television Workshop's rule of thumb for educational effectiveness is: "Get in quickly, do what you came to do and get out quickly. Try to keep all distractions at a minimum. All the lines of meaning (sound, symbol, visuals etc.) should intersect at one point … and only at one point … and this should be the concept you are teaching."

Don't do too much. Consider the length of the piece you're writing and the target audience. Figure out what the educational objective is and stick to it. Don't try to teach more than one thing. If you do, you'll lose both your dramatic and educational focus. If your producer is asking for too many goals in the script, try to get them to clarify what's really important so you can do your job successfully. And have fun. If you don't enjoy it, neither will the child.

So, you still interested in writing for kids? We hope so. There are some other areas which should be considered.

Animation

In the last few years, one of the fastest-growing markets for writers in Canada has been animation. There are a fair number of excellent animation houses across the country who are producing series that are distributed worldwide.

The two giants, Cinar and Nelvana, are now joined by many others such as Breakthrough who produce "Dudley the Dragon," Delaney and Friends who with Cambium produce "Nilus the Sandman," Ciné-Groupe, "Little Flying Bears," Alliance, BLT and Limelight who co-produce "Reboot", and "Beast Wars," co-produced by Alliance and Mainframe Entertainment. International co-productions in the animation field make a lot of sense because it's a simple matter to replace the dialogue and it's a logical way to share the costs in a form that is quite often more expensive to produce than live action.

One of the biggest ways most producers keep cost down is by having the bulk of the animation done overseas. The key creative work is done here — scripting, character creation, storyboards — but the rest is shipped out.

Another way most producers reduce costs is by not being signatories to the Writers' Guild of Canada (or America) contracts. This savings is tiny compared to shipping out the animation, but it's the one that affects writers most. Generally speaking, it means less money for the writer, no benefits and no protection if the producer turns out to be less than honourable.

Luckily, most of the established animation companies in Canada and the United States are reputable and pay rates that, while usually less than scale (and with no hope of royalties down the road), offer reasonable compensation and treat writers in a very professional way.

This situation may not make Guild member's day, but it is encouraging news for aspiring writers who may have an increased chance of breaking into this market. Though with the increase in animation production and the increasing competition worldwide, animation companies are beginning to pay more attention to script quality. Many are now hiring experienced story editors and a few are even signing Writers' Guild of Canada contracts, despite the fact they do not have to. At least for now.

Writing Animation

We all know that a great script has to have a strong theme, terrific story and brilliant characters. This is the bottom line whether you're writing live action drama or animation. However, there are some technical difficulties and opportunities in animation which are important to bear in mind.

Energy

Action, movement, whatever you call it, characters sitting and talking is death in animation. It's not so hot in live action either, but you can get away with slightly more static dialogue in live action because you have the complex activity of human facial expression and a wide emotional, physical palette. Cartoon characters are like sharks; if they don't move, they die.

Imagination

The most exciting aspect of animation is that anything is possible. You can turn a sea to a desert in a blink, have a character soar off into space, splatter into a talking pancake, and drill through the ground all the way to China. Live action can do all this stuff, but you're talking big budget special effects as opposed to what is the norm in cartoons. It's a blast to be able to stretch reality wherever you want to take it and that's the joy of this genre. But remember: (1) every animated series defines its own reality and you're expected to play within those ground rules; and (2) none of your great fantasies mean a thing if they're not helping push the story ahead.

Humour

It's interesting that one of the most successful film comedians of our day, Jim Carrey, plays live action cartoon characters. His superb gifts at physical comedy remind us of how rare and special that kind of humour is. Animation owns physical comedy. That's where it lives and breathes. Sight gags, double and triple takes, pratfalls, you name it — animation loves the stuff.

Pacing

Because everything can and must happen so quickly in animation, pacing is an important word. You're working in a form that's instant, so nobody should spend much time debating their next move. The story has to move fast and clearly. Set-up is essential — but the pay-off must come fast.

Violence

Ever since Road Runner dropped a ten-ton boulder on Wile E. Coyote, people have been talking about violence in cartoons. Today, Road Runner seems like Gandhi compared to what your basic super hero does to an evil robot. But robots don't bleed, so pulverizing them is open season. "Action" shows make for international hits because, unfortunately, violence is a language everybody understands.

But until the day Transformer means spiritual rebirth, we have some realities to face. One is that "action" in some form or another is still alive and kicking. The other is that there is a powerful lobby trying to change it. In animation, more than any other form, writers are straddling the fence. To survive in the realm of "action" shows — and to be somewhat socially responsible — we are obligated to find new and imaginative ways to have characters neutralize each other.

Thankfully, not all animated series are the blast 'em variety. But in many cases, these shows use physical comedy, and as we know, even Tweety Bird and Sylvester are synonymous with the Terminator in some circles. That's because many of the old classics rely on aggression for their humour. For some tips on non-aggressive physical comedy, look at Buster Keaton or Chaplin. There's an ancient and well-tested vocabulary in this genre that can provide a wealth of ideas and new directions that might help us escape this conundrum.

If you are going to write for children, the issue of violence will come up, in one form or another. We are including excerpts from the excellent paper

Jill Golick wrote on behalf of the Writers' Guild and presented to the Canadian Radio & Television Commission.

"Television violence does not:
- Make children into violent adults; real life does. Real experiences with violence, poverty, neglect and abuse breed violence. Television violence has a greater impact on children who have had first-hand experience with violence.

Television violence does:
- Make kids fearful; they think of the world as a scary and dangerous place.
- Desensitize children to violence; they think that violence is an acceptable way to solve problems.
- Interest children in violence as a form of entertainment.
- Affect the behaviour of pre-school children in the short term; young kinds imitate what they see and hear, but do not become violent in the long term.

The final point requires some elaboration. In the current debate in which Power Rangers has become an important issue, it is vital to recognize that children under the age of seven or eight tend to use imitation as a way of learning. They recite the alphabet with "Sesame Street," sign along with Fred Penner, and fight beside the Power Rangers. By the age of eight, most children are capable of at least some abstract thought and can watch the same programs without immediately jumping up and imitating what is on the screen.

Knowing what effects violent television will have on our children, we can begin to look for ways to mediate or minimize those effects.

We may wish to first consider the special needs of the small segment of the population whose real life experiences make them most sensitive to television violence. Because the source of these problems is real life — real violence, poverty, abuse, neglect — the best source of the solution is probably real life, primarily in the form of social services. Taking the "Power Rangers" off the air will have far less impact on young lives than providing these children with love, food, clothing, safe environment and education. It is simplistic to think that we can solve the very serious problems of these children by regulating television more closely.

Just as we teach our children to look both ways before they cross the street, we must equip them with the skills to navigate the television world safely. We must make them better and smarter TV consumers though media education.

It is with both the historical context and newer issues in mind that we as writers enter into the discussion. We are concerned about the harmful effects of television violence on children. We agree that education and media literacy are part of the solution. We are less convinced that classification systems, v-chip technology and control of cable carriage of foreign signals are either effective or practical.

However, we do believe that stories from other communities are a large part of the problem. Canadian programming produced in Canada is almost violence free. The fact is that the violent programming that concerns so many people is imported, largely from the United States.

Our final point is that an essential part of the solution has been overlooked: storytelling, including television storytelling, remains one of the most powerful child-rearing tools that we have as a society. It is our belief that the solution to the problems created by the effects of television violence on children lies not in the silencing of the voices of storytellers, but in assuring that our own stories are told. It is in our children's best interests to nurture the art of storytelling and the craft of writing in this country, so that our children are exposed to Canadian stories which are told from the heart and not created exclusively in a commercial context.

Merchandising

Animation more than any other form is dependant on merchandising. Many shows find their initial development dollars from toy manufacturers who want to tie in early. Of course they are more likely to buy into a show based on an already popular toy. And then everybody gets to worry about the big anxiety in the business: lack of shelf space in the department stores. If Toys 'R Us won't stock your action figure, your show spot on Saturday morning may go to somebody who is on the shelves. It is amazing to think that the key player in this industry is the big chain store.

So you can image how hard a sell completely original cartoon shows must be. A producer will inevitably be finding foreign investment and each investor will be making demands on the form and content of the show. Story editors get old very quickly on shows that have multinational producers who are inevitably making contradictory demands.

These days the biggest target group is eight- to twelve-year-old boys. It seems they have the biggest buying clout and their taste (say the marketing people) is for "action," in other words bashing and blasting. A quick look through the TV guide will confirm whether this is true or not. The main thing to remember, whether you're talking Cybercops or giant robot-cars, is that even Capital Chippy The Flying Lazer Gun needs a good story.

So, You *Still* Want To Write For Children!

One day when writer Janis Nastbakken and the two of us were deep into the design of a course to teach writing for children, we filled page after page of big sheets of paper — wrestling with the question of what we really wanted to teach these new writers.

Dennis wrote the following: "The simplest miracles — we breathe, we grow, we see, we smell, we taste. We touch the garden bursting with activity over the bee, stinging us in a magic act. Can we be open to the magic? Can we break through the cathode tube and make the cathode rays blossom, burst through the glass. Can we make real magic appear through this mechanical thing we stare at when the true magic is the child — the miracle of growth, eyes, hair and cells — staring, playing, talking in front of our odd manufactured illusion."

This is one reason we keep writing for television children. Jill Golick summed it up when she wrote, "We can tell our children Canadian stories that help them see that their country and the communities within it are safe, non-violent places to live, work and play. We can tell our children creative, imaginative stories in which problems are solved in a whole range of ways and not always by violence. We can tell them stories that are funny, moving, thrilling, inspiring. We can tell tales which will hold our children rapt. Let us teach them our history and values, give them skills and guidance, spark their imaginations and inspire them to greatness."

7

A View from the Network

by Peter Lower

C*urrently an independent producer and script consultant, Peter Lower is the former executive producer, Drama at the CTV Television Network where from 1990 to 1996 he oversaw the development and production of Canadian dramatic programming including "E.N.G.," "Neon Rider," "Lonesome Dove," "The Sound and the Silence" and "Due South." Prior to joining CTV, Peter was story editor, writer and producer for the CBC docudrama series "For The Record" and executive story editor for "Street Legal." He produced* Oakmount High, *winner of two Gemini awards and the Gemini nominated drama* My Brother Larry. *Writing credits include* The Unexpected, Reasonable Force *and* The Exile. *Peter has taught writing and production courses at the Summer Institute of Film and Ryerson University; is on the Board of Directors of the Academy of Canadian Cinema and Television and the National Screen Institute. He is also on the Academy's Rules and Regulations Committee and the TV Drama Programme Advisory Committee for the Canadian Film Centre.*

With the recent phenomenal success of films based on the works of Jane Austen, there's been a rush to book stores to buy and, presumably, read the original works. You can bet, however, that no one is lining up to buy the scripts. The film is what matters and the script it is based on is all but forgotten. You can buy published screenplays of course, but the market is small and specialized, consisting of film buffs, students or aspiring screenwriters curious to see what *Leaving Las Vegas* or *Pulp Fiction* look like on the page. And no matter how brilliant the episode, there are no line-ups at local bookstores for scripts of "Seinfeld," "NYPD Blue" or "Due South" the day after broadcast. Therein lies one of the paradoxes of writing for film and television. No form of popular writing undergoes such intense and lengthy scrutiny as do scripts written for television or film production. But once produced, these scripts are largely forgotten. Multi-draft (seventeen for *Four Weddings and a Funeral*) and multi-writer (seven for *Toy Story*) ordeals lasting years are not uncommon in a business where more scripts are written than produced and where the phrase "all writing is rewriting" is accepted as gospel. Some insight into the paradoxical nature of professional screenwriting can be gained by taking a closer look at the unique relationship that exists between writing and the hugely complex entertainment industry that spawns it.

Television is the producer's medium and feature film traditionally belongs to the director. The writer who neither produces nor directs is often relegated to the sidelines as the machinery of production takes over and the previous pages are all but forgotten as the lights kick on and the cameras roll.

In general, feature writing is simpler in its overall structure with fewer people involved in the ongoing torture of the writer. The feature writer will often enjoy a longer time frame than his television counterpart which, depending on age and personal wealth, may or may not be a good thing. Many feature screenplay writers work totally alone on their scripts until they are ready to be sent to their agents for strategic circulation among performers and/or producers. Others work on scripts under long-term development deals with directors, producers and, increasingly, performers whose success has allowed them to form their own development and production companies.

"Long-form" television programs — movies and miniseries — bridge the worlds of the large and small screens. Both the feature film and the television movie offer the writer a large canvas on which to work with respect to both narrative and character development. Aside from act (read "commercial") breaks and more rigid content considerations, the television movie can offer the writer a satisfying and financially rewarding alternative to the rarer feature film production. Moving from television movies to hour and half-hour episodic dramas and comedies takes the writer further into the heart of the commercial television industry. Here the producer takes over the driver's seat and writer/director consultation is brief if it happens at all.

The world of episodic television is the world of the television network which exerts as much or more power over the proceedings than the producers who actually make the shows. Not that the network is absent from the process that brings forth the endless spate of MOWs. Far from it. But it's the prime time dramas and sitcoms that truly define the battlefield where wonderful talents, massive egos and millions of dollars duke it out for the eyeballs of the nation. Here the networks reign supreme. They decide on the size of the field, they make up the rules, they hire the players and coaches. They buy the referees. They name the teams and pick the uniforms. The game starts when they say so and they get to blow the final whistle anytime they want.

How does the writer take his or her place in this overheated landscape where the script is both the indispensable "blueprint" and the eminently disposable and forgettable bundle of coloured pages? How do networks regard writers and their craft and what do the networks really want?

The relationship between the writer and the "business" of television writing is not unlike the relationship between Little Red Riding Hood, her basket of goodies for Grandma and the big, bad wolf. The writer gets to play the heroine, while the script is the basket of goodies being transported through the deep, dark woods to Grandma's house. The producers and network executives play the big bad wolf doing their utmost to prevent the writer from delivering his story to the audience. It's a perilous journey and few make it through unscathed. In fact, getting mugged along the way is very much a fact of life for many television writers. To survive, the writer must surround a core of distinctive writing talents with well-honed craftsmanship and a first-hand knowledge of the business.

In the beginning, however, the story is the first point of contact between the writer and the industry that transforms and transports the words from the page to the screen.

A story is a dynamic, living thing. A good story brings originality, vivid characterizations, strong structure and a high degree of empathy and recognition for our audience. A good story takes us on a journey — from the introduction of the setting and main characters, to the incident(s) that begin the story, to the conflicts that are progressively compounded and intensified by the twists and turns of plot, to major climactic moments and, finally, to the resolutions that restore some kind of order and equilibrium. The degree to which an audience becomes caught up in the lives of the characters and is swept along by the succession of events is the measure of the strength of the story.

The ability to recognize good writing, to know a good story and how to develop a movie premise, series proposal or pilot script that deftly combines originality, topicality and mass audience appeal is the hallmark of the creative executive at the network or production company. These are the people who decide which projects go forward and they are the ones the writer must know how to work with. Here's what they are looking for in a proposal for a new dramatic program or series:

1. There must be craft. The writer's ability to use language to convey his story must be highly evolved. The writer must demonstrate superior skills in the depiction of people in conflict through the use of spoken language and actions. Any writer with ambitions to write for the screen who does not have a talent for expressing the largely internal realms of thought and emotion solely through action and dialogue should quit before he or she begins. As the expression goes: "Show. Don't tell."

2. There must be originality and freshness. Avoid derivative characters and storylines at all costs. Consistent, predictable characters who are true to "type" and nothing more are the bane of television writing. Characters must surprise you with their freshness. There must be authenticity — the "ring of truth" that is immediately convincing and strikes a resonant chord deep within. The ultimate challenge faced by the writer is to present the familiar and the commonplace in ways that are totally unexpected yet real and affecting. My test is to look for a commonplace scene, preferably with high emotional content, and see what the writer has done with it. If I'm startled and moved by a writer's handling of these scenes, then I know I'm on to something.

3. There must be conviction. The writer alone bears the responsibility of convincing the harried, distracted or plainly disinterested development executive that this is a project they should pay attention to. As the writer of the script or creator of the series concept, it is your unshakable belief that will draw others in. It may sound corny but the power of positive thinking can work wonders. Remember that the network's fear of saying yes is as strong as your fear of rejection.

4. There must be industry and audience awareness. You should know which network is looking for what and which production companies are currently supplying their programming. The television industry is highly volatile and demands close attention by you if you hope to stay well informed. Doing your homework will pay big dividends.

5. There must be flexibility, not malleability. If you've got a good idea/story/script, then stick to it. Write it and propose it with all your

might, but don't create a *fait accompli* by adopting a "take it or leave it" attitude. On the other hand, don't become all accommodating by offering to do anything the network wants. The network responds to quiet confidence and panics if confronted with either overzealous cockiness or abject compliance. Both extremes betray an irrational component which in this most irrational of businesses, is anathema.

6. There must be a plan. When approaching a network or production company come prepared to discuss the next stage of development just in case someone says "yes." The idea, proposal or script is not enough on its own. Be prepared to discuss how you and your production partners would put the production together from a financial point of view. You may only be looking for script development and that may be well understood by everyone, but remember it's the long term that's important. If you don't have a solid business plan in place, then have an "ideal" one at the ready.

The business of writing for television is the business of relationships. These relationships take many forms and unlike other professional relationships, are never clear cut. Men and women sit around meeting tables trying to make something out of nothing to entertain millions of viewers, cause prospective advertisers to stampede, employ hundreds of talented artists and craftspeople and cost millions of dollars in the bargain. And all the while nobody knows exactly what it is they are talking about because it hasn't been made yet!

As projects gather momentum they also gather people. And once a show goes into production, a population explosion follows as the hundred plus artists and craftspeople are assembled to execute the well-laid plans that often began over lunch or a meeting at the production company, agency or network.

WHO DOES WHAT?
What follows is a brief description of the key personnel involved at the earliest stages of a project and their relationships to one another.

The Network Executive
The cost of an average episode of prime time drama comes in at around $1 million. A television movie routinely requires an investment of $2.5 to $3.5 million. The network frequently provides a significant amount of the development and production financing. The network executive is the guardian

of the network's interests and acts as a liaison between the network and the producer to ensure both the quality and the suitability of the programming being produced for the network. The network executive is also charged with overseeing the development of new programming.

The Production Company Executive

A development executive from a production company is a key player in the process that brings new programming into being. In most instances it is the production company which commissions the writer and secures the interest of a network in a particular project. It is the role of the development executive at the production company to put ideas and people together in creative relationships that will result in production orders from networks.

The Writer

The writer remains the primary driving force in new program development and script production for ongoing series. The majority of program ideas originate with a writer and if they don't, it usually isn't very long until a writer is brought on board.

Networks and producers often come up with bare bones ideas for movies derived from books they've acquired the rights to or stories they've read in the newspapers. Without a writer, however, these raw materials remain like so many inert chemicals without a catalyst. It is the writer who is charged with creating the magic. The writer is usually a free agent without specific ties to production or broadcast organizations. This unencumbered state is highly prized by many writers and, in fact, provides a necessary bubble of autonomy which acts like an invisible shield to cushion the buffeting that will come their way once a project is undertaken.

While a writer is free to create and sell materials on a purely speculative basis, the majority of writing for television is undertaken by commission. When writers are commissioned by production companies, they are paid for their writing services and in return grant the producer rights to exploit their material on an exclusive basis. The writer will be contracted under the Writers' Guild agreement and will be paid in stages as the work progresses. If the writer has an agent, then the agent will negotiate a contract specifying the kind of writing to be done and under what conditions.

Writer's Agent

The writer's agent will try to negotiate development deals with production companies and/or networks. These will usually be exclusive deals that guarantee a first look at anything the writer produces over a given period of time. These deals can be very lucrative for the writer. The writer's agent does not normally participate in the creative development of the property.

The Script Editor

Long-form projects like movies and miniseries often employ the services of a script editor to work with the writer and producer on the script. The script editor is consulted on matters of overall structure, character and story development. The script editor can be an invaluable asset to the development of any script providing a relatively objective pair of eyes and bringing a fresh sensibility to bear on a given project.

In the US and Canada the term "story editor" and its many variations is usually reserved for a staff writer on a continuing series. The UK industry has traditionally employed the services of non-writing script editors on all drama projects including series. The CBC adopted the UK model and although largely phased out, occasional use of non-writing script editors is made on movie and miniseries projects. Script consultants are routinely employed in the development of feature screenplays where they act on behalf of the producer in matters of script development.

The Director

On a major television project, like a miniseries, or on a feature project a director may be present at the development stage. The director may play a vital role in script development working closely with the writer. If the project is, for example, an adaptation of a well-known book, both director and writer may be brought on board early as part of an overall package that will be useful in raising financing for the project. In a similar way, a lead performer may be attached to a project early on and may play a part in the creative development of the project.

Director/writers are not uncommon in the feature world and occasionally play a significant role in television movies or series. (David Lynch on "Twin Peaks" comes to mind or George Bloomfield on "Due South".) This is more the exception than the rule in television, however, where the director is often the last person to come aboard and is handed a completed script, a principal cast, a predetermined look for the show and so on. Exceptions arise in the case of series pilots where the director can play a vital role in setting down some of the key parameters that will then be repeated in subsequent episodes.

The Producer (s)

If the writer is not a writer/producer or "showrunner," a creative producer will often be attached to a project from the outset by a production company. If no large production company is involved at the outset, an independent producer may establish a relationship with a writer to develop materials that will subsequently be presented to production companies and networks.

Agency Representative

A representative from a creative agency may also be present at early discussions to represent or broker the interests of a network or production company. More a US phenomenon, but increasingly important in the Canadian industry, an agency will represent a production company to one or more networks. The network may feed specific wants on the series or movie front through the agency representative who in turn passes them on to selected production companies. The production companies then develop and pitch their ideas back to the network directly or through the agency representative. An agency can be instrumental in putting together creative "packages" that might include particular writers, producers and performers.

Private And Public Funding Agency Representatives

No overview of the development process would be complete without noting the presence of both public and private funding agencies at the earliest stages of dramatic program development. Though by no means exclusive to Canada, we have cornered the market on development and production funding from non-commercial agencies. There are approximately 50 public and sixteen private funds available for program development and production financing. The primary funds like Telefilm, McLean Hunter, Rogers Telefund, the Cable Production Fund and the various provincial agencies require broadcaster commitment as a prerequisite to their participation.

By and large, following initial assessments of the business and creative aspects of a project, these agencies leave the creative development of the show up to the production company and networks. Their representatives do not, as a rule, sit down with the other players as a group.

The Process — And How To Survive It!

Now that we have some idea of the various people involved in the business of writing, let's take a brief look at the development process itself, keeping in mind that the development of the relationship is as important as the development of the actual idea. How do new programs get started? What role does the writer play and how does it all look from the point of view of the network?

The process begins with some form of written or verbal proposal for a program or series. It's amazing how few people have great ideas on what to do with a blank page and how many suddenly do when that page is filled. Unsolicited as well as solicited materials arrive at networks and production companies daily and in volume. The range of materials is awesome: from fully produced twenty-minute trailers or "minipilots," to comprehensive packaged series proposals featuring show concept, main character bios, key sets and sample story lines, to a napkin from lunch with the word "Friends" written on it.

These materials come to the attention of networks and production companies in a variety of ways. Among the most common:

1. Writer alone. Writes idea, treatment or script then sends it to a development person at a network or production company. Waits for response.
2. Writer's agent hears that network A or production company X is looking for an hour-long, contemporary urban drama with some kind of supernatural or paranormal component. Writer writes brief proposal, often on spec. Writer or agent sends in material. They look for a development deal of some kind.
3. Network calls writer or writer's agent directly. "Got anything cooking that might interest us?" A lunch or meeting ensues where ideas are discussed. If something catches then a development deal is set up.
4. Production company (or studio in the US) invites writer to write. Development deal is struck. A network is approached with fully developed proposal and one or more scripts.
5. The network puts out the word that they're looking for "X" kind of show. Production companies bring in selected writers and put together a proposal which is pitched to the network.

Exclusive development deals with writers and producers who have winning track records are the wave of the future in an increasingly competitive environment. With the emergence of major production companies such as Alliance Communications, Atlantis Films Ltd., Paragon Productions, Nelvana, Cinar and hundreds of smaller ones, development deals struck between these companies and particular writers have become the primary means of securing and developing new programming. These relationships are commonplace in the US and while they reduce the level of autonomy enjoyed by the writer, they provide a level of stability and security that is often hard to come by when working on a strictly project-by-project basis. The writer signs on for a negotiated fee and undertakes to develop series proposals, bibles and pilot scripts which can then be shopped around to prospective broadcast or cable network partners.

The relationship that exists between the writer and the production company can also exist between the writer and the network. The network may contract the writer on individual projects or on an overall development deal encompassing a number of different projects usually over a specified period of time. If the network has initiated the project, then the network development person has a very specific mandate which is to put into motion a creative process involving two or three other parties, including the writer, that will result in a program that the network can exploit to the maximum benefit of its advertisers and audience.

In these development deals, the buyer (whether network or production company) has exclusive rights to the material created and very specific options regarding the future use and development of such materials The reasons for gaining exclusive rights to the services of a particular writer or writers are twofold: In a business founded on relationships, the exclusive deal provides a means of bringing the needs of the production company or network and the talents of the writer together in a way that will intensify and focus the creative forces at work. Secondly, and on a more practical level, an exclusive deal effectively makes an individual writer unavailable for a period of time and nicely outflanks competitive producers and/or networks. In the US these deals are often brokered by agents associated with one of the large creative agencies such as William Morris. They will negotiate deals on behalf of their clients with the major producers and studios.

In some ways the writer has the easiest role at least in terms of the various agendas involved. The writer brings a willingness to exercise his talents under the auspices and direction of the representatives of the production company and network. Fees are agreed upon and deadlines set. Intensive discussions take place on exactly what the writer will undertake to write. When the talking is done the writer retires to the keyboard and beings writing. While most writing at the development stage takes place over weeks and months, it is not uncommon for writers or teams of writers to spend one or two years developing various properties for productions companies and/or networks without actually seeing any one of the projects go into production.

The "relationship" factor resides at the heart of the program development process. Decisions on what to develop or order or buy are rarely based solely on the specific elements of the project at hand. If it's a series that's being pitched, then it's important that the show fit with the general needs of the network, but equally important is the reputation and experience being brought to the table by the person who has created the show and who, presumably, will produce and run it. Vitally important is the relationship that may or may not exist between the two parties across the table.

For example, "Due South" came into being when Alliance Communications' head, Robert Lantos, and then CBS programming president, Jeff Sagansky, sat down to talk about developing a show "whose Canadianness would be an asset" in the fiercely competitive US prime time schedule. They began with the notion of a Crocodile Dundee-like character who would be totally out of his element in a city like Chicago. Of course, that basic concept was only the beginning. The series proper was created by Paul Haggis, the writer of the pilot and eventual executive producer of the series.

What's important to note is the fact that idea of a by-the-book Mountie teaming up with a seat-of-the-pants Chicago detective arose from a well-founded, multi-faceted business and creative relationship that was ideally positioned to put the idea into motion.

As I mentioned off the top, writing for film and television is writing for production. And while the script is much more than a mere "blueprint" for the final filmed product, there remains the fact that great writing for the screen exists for the sole purpose of being transformed into something else — the film itself.

And because of the multitudes of enormously talented and dedicated people who descend on any script prior to its production to create sets, costumes, props, hairstyles, car chases, gun fights or trips to the moon … nothing comes under such scrutiny and takes such a beating as does the script. And no one is more important and, at the same time more put upon, than the writer who, like Little Red Riding Hood, skips on her merry way through the deep, dark woods clutching the script tightly and dodging the multitudes of wolves that threaten her at every turn.

So the bad news is you may get eaten alive. The good news is that in both television and film production, writers currently enjoy a level of unprecedented prominence and power because the business of writing for film and television remains the business of telling great stories within the context of an often uneasy but frequently highly productive and creative alliance.

8

Writing Documentary Films

by Steve Lucas

Writer-producer Steve Lucas received an Academy Award nomination for his first documentary, After the Axe, in 1983, and both a Genie Award and a Hot Docs! Best Writing Award for his most recent one, The Champagne Safari, in 1996. Other documentary film credits include Soviet Space: The Secret Designer, Distress Signals, Who Gets In?, Transplant, The Breath of Life, and Pitchmen. Dramatic feature film credits include Diplomatic Immunity and (as story editor) April One. Lucas also writes episodic television, advises at the Canadian Film Centre, and, for the past five years, has taught screenwriting at Maruska Stankova's "Directing, Acting, and Writing for Camera" Workshop in Toronto. He is a National Writers Forum Delegate (Ontario) to the Writers' Guild of Canada.

You've got this idea. Would make a great documentary film, you figure. Friends, family members, people you buttonhole at industry functions all agree: your next logical step is a meeting with a bona fide producer, distributor, broadcaster, funding agency representative — someone, anyone, who can help provide you with the development money and guidance you need to get your film made. Only one problem: all those people need to see something on paper first.

At this juncture, there are two things you can do: you can hire a proven documentary film writer to help you pull your project together (the current Writers' Guild of Canada Members Directory features 165 such writers to choose from) or you can become a documentary film writer yourself.

At some point or other, the investors in your film may encourage you, may quite possibly force you, to team up with someone who has done this sort of thing before. For now, though, let's just assume you're the type of person who likes to go it alone. You're eager to learn. You can't really afford to hire anyone else right now, anyway. And, besides, this is your idea, right?

So you begin.

The Proposal

If your party pitch is ever to become a documentary film, now defined by the *Random House College Dictionary* as "a film or program portraying an actual event, life of a real person, period of history, or the like, in a factual way, especially one containing sections photographed of actual incidents as they occurred," you'll need money and lots of it. A compelling film proposal is your first step.

WHO ARE YOU TALKING TO?

Documentary film-making in Canada used to be a one-stop shopping proposition. As recently as a decade ago, you went to the NFB, or the CBC, or a few provincial TV networks, or a handful of independent production companies. You pitched your idea. The executives there like it (and you) well enough to fund your film all by themselves, or they didn't.

While such opportunities still exist today, unfortunately they are mostly limited to entry-level documentary films in the $50,000–75,000 range. For documentaries with larger budgets, it is now the norm to have a broadcaster and two or three different funding organizations involved in a film's development phase, with even more investors involved in the actual production. Money is tight. Every year, there is more competition for it. This puts added pressure on all phases of the documentary writing process, starting with the proposal: now that you have to please more people, your written submissions have to be that much more accomplished.

Before you can confidently commit any thoughts to paper, however, you need to know whom you are addressing. Where is the money for your film coming from? Who are the decision makers involved? What are their likes and dislikes?

Let's say you plan to go to the CBC: it's important to know that journalistic balance has long been a cornerstone of their broadcasting policy. Let's say TVO is your broadcaster of choice: it's good to know that Ontario's public television network has recently shown an interest in just the opposite sort of film — subjective, personal, film-maker-driven. And so on, all down the line: whatever broadcaster, distribution company or funding agency you have in mind, try to acquaint yourself with their tastes.

Finally, and most importantly, you need a strong sense of your show's intended audience. Clearly you can start writing your proposal any time you like: you can't really finish it until you know who your show is aimed at and what their interests really are. Finding out may take some doing but you really need to know.

WHAT MAKES A GOOD PROPOSAL?

Documentary film proposals are mysterious birds. They can be impressionistic, mythic, poetic — or hard-hitting and chock-full of facts. They can be a few pages long, ten pages long or even 25 (although, at this length, you are likely dealing with a documentary series proposal). In the end, there is no set formula, no standard way of doing things. All that matters is that your proposal be sufficiently fresh and intriguing to raise the development money you require.

There are two parts to the proposal. The first deals, explicitly, with your film: Who are its principal subjects? What are their relationships with one another? What is the film's central premise, that is, what significant dramatic questions get raised at the beginning and answered at the end? What story lines do you intend to follow? What are their possible outcomes? If, as often happens, you are writing about events which have not yet occurred, what surprises are you allowing for? What shifts might spontaneously arise? How do you plan on dealing with them? How do you intend to tell your story? How much weight will you be giving the pictures? How much weight will you be giving the words? What themes and issues do you want to explore? What will the tone of your film be? What visual approach will you employ? Will sound play a major role? What about music? What sort of film are we likely see in the end? And so on.

The second part of the proposal deals, often implicitly, with you, the filmmaker: What is your perspective on the material (and why)? Do you understand the logistics of what you're trying to do? Are you being realistic? Can you really make the film for the proposed budget? Do you fully appreciate the psychological and emotional terrain you are about to enter? (A film about circus clowns is one thing; a film about holocaust survivors is another — investors need to be assured that you can handle yourself accordingly.) How much film-making experience do you possess? Are you willing to work with other people who have more? Are you genuinely interested in a team approach? And so on.

As with résumé writing, the key to film proposals is always to be honest — and never to offer up anything negative about yourself or your film. Investors, having been burned before, are constantly on the lookout for film-makers who are greedy, flaky, dishonest or flat out insane. You do yourself a large favour by presenting your ideas in a clear, concise and sensible way.

In the end, a good film proposal, true to its phrasing, simply gives its readers a strong sense of the film being proposed. Granted, some guesswork is involved. Yes, the proposal will be more suggestive than conclusive. Still, the intention, feeling and quality of the final film should all somehow be alive within the proposal's pages.

HOW-TO?

As for format, a proposal works along with the same lines as a newspaper column, feature magazine article or movie review. The basic operating principle is this: lead with your strength.

What is your film's most appealing element? What drew you to the subject in the first place? A colourful, famous or infamous lead character or, better still, a group of them? A hypnotically fascinating story or process full of improbable twists and turns? A burning theme or social issue of the day? Stunning visuals? A mesmerizing soundscape? Whatever your film's greatest strength, my advice is that you lead with it and build the rest of your proposal from there, always trying to shape and pace the material as if it were a drama.

A word of caution: you do not have much time to hook your readers. The decision makers you are approaching, be they publicly or privately funded, deal with the printed word every working day of their lives. Most of what they are obliged to sift through is appalling: bad ideas, poorly executed. The sooner you can demonstrate that your idea is a cut above, the better.

If, having come up with a genuinely interesting idea, you go on to execute it well, your chances of going into development are considerably enhanced. To this end, I recommend that you hone your pitch repeatedly, even at risk of permanently alienating family members and friends (be sure to note those moments when their eyes glaze over: those are the parts you need to rework).

You might also try to get hold of some sample proposals for other documentary films, preferably ones you admire. You may want to seek advice from the people who made them. (Film-makers often turn out to be generous people; it does no harm to call around.)

To make a convincing documentary film, you generally need to become something of an authority on your subject. Often this means meeting some of the people involved, visiting a few locations, doing some interviews and going to the library — all in advance of writing the proposal.

One last cautionary note: crafting a good proposal can take weeks, even months. Several drafts are often needed. Plan for them. Give yourself the time you need to get the piece right. Be sure to get someone (quite possibly a few people) to read and, if necessary, to edit your material before you make your submission. A poorly written proposal invariably suggests a poorly made film — and no investor in his or her right mind wants to be party to that. Make sure your proposal is well written. It helps.

The Shooting Script Or Treatment

Depending on your film's subject matter (and, to a certain extent, depending on your track record as a film-maker), a shooting script or treatment, as it's also known, may not be necessary. If you plan on making as "occurring documentary" or "process film" in which you will be focusing on unfolding events, the outcome of which cannot possibly be known — a political convention, say, or a medical procedure — then a proposal may be all you require to get into production. Anything more may be either impossible or inappropriate.

If, however, you are making a "constructed documentary" or "essay film" which is based primarily on existing historical or biographical material, both your broadcaster and your investors will likely want to see a shooting script.

Everything that applies to the writing of a good proposal applies equally, if not more so, to the writing of a good shooting script. With your proposal, you were trying to raise tens of thousands of dollars in development financing; with your shooting script, you are likely trying to raise hundreds of thousands (and sometimes, though rarely, millions) of dollars in production financing. So the pressure on the writing increases.

RESEARCH AND DEVELOPMENT

The research you do prior to the scripting phase is absolutely critical: there is nothing worse than a documentary film script that makes bright promises the film it anticipates cannot possibly keep.

Often, during the research and development phase of a project, things fail to work out. Characters you assumed would be colourful turn out to be deadly dull. Stories become non-stories. Issues somehow get resolved. Films on the same subject open to stunning reviews. And so on.

If, during your R & D phase, any of this happens to you, my advice is, either come up with a fresh angle or call a halt. Sooner or later, your investors will forgive you; some may even thank you. It is exceedingly bad business practice to knowingly overhype a documentary film. If, desperate for fees and dreaming of future glory, you consciously elect to stretch the truth about your project, you are asking for trouble — of the you'll-never-work-in-this-town-again variety. Film ideas are still a dime a dozen, despite inflation. If yours turns out to be a dud, far better to admit it and move on than to bull your way through.

If your research serves only to reinforce your initial enthusiasm for the project, however, you'll want to proceed to a shooting script without delay.

GOALS

A good documentary shooting script explores, realizes and ultimately refines the ideas first set forward in your proposal.

A shooting script's primary goal is to give investors a strong, appealing sense of the movie they are going to see. In many ways, the script amounts to an insurance policy: if worse comes to worse, you are saying to your investors, "I'll have this plan to fall back on, this kind of footage from which to make my film."

A shooting script's secondary goal is to help you, the film-maker, define your intentions. The script is a warm-up exercise, a forced preparation that enables you — and everyone else involved in the project — to understand the direction in which you are headed. (Things can get fuzzy on a film set; it's easy to get lost on the day, to forget what you came here hoping to find.) Writing a shooting script obligates you to think your film through.

FORMAT

The old-style format for a documentary shooting script had the film's proposed video components listed on the left-hand side of the page, and its audio components listed on the right. Some scripts are still written this way and, as blueprints for the director, I suppose they're fine. For everyone else, however, a shooting script written in such a manner is virtually unreadable.

My advice is to go with a user-friendly format instead. To my mind, that means writing the script as an essay — again, a good one. Fade in on your proposed opening scene. Introduce your first few film subjects, say what it is they're likely doing, state the premise of your show, the principal dramatic questions that are to be raised and answered and so on. Then stitch your other anticipated sequences together, beginning to end, as best you can. Again: try to make your writing as vivid as possible. Give us a clear sense of the scenes you have in mind. Use the most colourful quotes you collected during your research and so on. To see how this can best be done, you might want to take a look at the film and television reviews in *Variety*: week in, week out, the American trade magazine's plot synopses are among the most accomplished written anywhere.

PROCESS

Outside reads remain important throughout the scripting phase. Are you making sense? Are you being clear? Have you left anything important out? What can you safely delete? You need a trusted outside reader to help you answer these questions.

Finally, as with the proposal, your shooting script should once again answer the questions customarily raised about a documentary film: What is it about? Who's in it? Where will it be shot? When? How? Why (to what end)? For how much?

The Narration Script

While a proposal can get you into development, and a shooting script may lead to production, a narration script is often what gets you home. When people talk about "writing a documentary film," voice-over narration, also known as "continuity" or "commentary writing," is normally what they're referring to. While compelling film footage and a solid overall structure remain the two basic ingredients of documentary film-making, a good narration script can often enhance and sometimes even save a documentary film; a bad narration script, of course, can ruin one. In terms of pressure, no other writing phase compares.

DO YOU REALLY NEED ONE?

Avoiding narration at all costs used to be quite the vogue and, for all I know, still is. One thing is certain: a documentary that needs no explanation should never be given one (Nicholas Broomfield and Joan Churchill's *Soldier Girls* and Bruce Weber's *Let's Get Lost* are excellent examples of films where narration was neither added nor required). If your picture can possibly do without a voice-over, by all means, do without.

If you are in any doubt, a test screening should settle things. Invite half a dozen friends over to see your film. Sit in the back of the room and watch them watch the screen: if they fidget, squirm, doze, get audibly impatient or stare at you in stunned disbelief once the lights come up, chances are your film is in need of some narrative assistance. Then again, maybe not.

First you might want to try restructuring your picture, using more sync sound from the principals, both on- and off-camera, even going to title cards, which worked in the silent era and can still be made to work today. Then screen the film a second time, for a different set of friends. If the audience again remains unmoved, voice-over narration may be your only option.

HOW MUCH? HOW LONG WILL IT TAKE?

The late, great Donald Brittain saw narration as a series of "golden hinges" used to link sequence to sequence, scene to scene and, sometimes, parts of the same scene together.

If you find that your picture needs only a few such hinges — if it has been well-structured, if its sync sound material is largely intelligible, if a handful of connectors between the sound bites is all you really need to sustain viewer interest from beginning to the end — then the writing of a satisfactory narration script can be accomplished, with a draft and a polish, in a matter of days.

If you have always known that your picture would need a great many hinges to sustain itself, that, too, should be no cause for alarm: you just keep refining your ideas through successive drafts until you're done.

However, if test audiences have suddenly informed you that you have a dog's breakfast on your hands, which only a substantial narration script can possibly sort out, be forewarned: a good deal of film doctoring, several drafts, a few more months and a big whack of extra cash may all be needed to get you through to picture lock.

"How did this happen?" you ask yourself. You wrote a nice proposal. Your shooting script was fine. The shoot went well. Everyone liked the rushes, or said they did. How could you possibly wind up here?

The sad truth about filmmaking in general, and documentary film-making in particular, is that nothing is ever for certain. No matter how well-prepared you try to be, you can never really know ahead of time how things are going to turn out. Dramas are somewhat (and only somewhat) more predictable: a drama you can write and rewrite, again and again, prior to the shoot. A documentary requiring a substantial amount of narration can only really be written (and, of course, rewritten) once a film has been shot.

IN FOR A NICKEL

Your film may have been in the cutting room for weeks, sometimes even months, before you finally realize that narration is desperately needed. By this time, the combined costs of the editor, the editing machine and the editing room itself (not to mention the bridge financing) have likely grown worrisome. Your next "drawdown," or scheduled payment from investors, is at the fine cut stage, whenever that is. Your delivery date to the broadcaster is imminent. So panic starts to set in.

The advent of Avid, Lightworks, and all the other non-linear editing systems has done little to alleviate matters: while a film can now be restructured in a heartbeat, no way has yet been found to similarly accelerate the narration-writing portion of the human brain. Whatever machine you happen to be using, the addition of a new and substantial narration component means that now, when people ask you for a completion date, you don't know what to tell them. So the panic escalates.

My advice is this: try to get a grip. Yes, you have spent hundreds of thousands of dollars of other people's money, invested what may be years of your life in this project only to wind up in creative difficulty — but, the truth is, you are probably closer to completion than you know. Besides which, you are duty (and quite possibly, legally) bound to carry on.

Broadcasters have the right not to accept delivery of a show, if it fails to meet their standards. Funding agencies can follow suit. Then, too, there's your career to think about, your reputation: a turkey of a documentary that took years and somewhere in the mid-six figures to make can hurt you every bit as much as a barker of a low-budget first feature. After all, if you can't pull a documentary film together, what exactly can you do?

What you can do, what you must do now, is, carry on. In this case, that means either hiring a narration writer or writing the narration yourself.

FINDING THE PREMISE

As a narration writer, your primary concern is to determine the real premise of your film. In law, a premise is defined as "a basis, stated or assumed, on which reasoning proceeds"; in documentaries (and dramas, too, for that matter), a premise is the basis on which the rest of a film proceeds. Normally suggested by a film's opening scene or sequence, the premise raises the most interesting and involving questions your film is capable of raising; the balance of the film then goes on to answer them. Once a film's premise has been fully explored, once its key questions have all been answered, the film is over and your work is done.

To give you a more concrete idea of what I mean by premise, here are a few examples from some of the films I've worked on:

• A middle-aged executive is seen being fired. Will he ever find another job? How? At what cost? What must he go through? (*After the Axe*)

• A would-be immigrant is seen being refused entry to Canada. He didn't get in. Who does? What does it take to become a Canadian? (*Who Gets In?*)

• A millionaire-industrialist-explorer is seen being wildly successful in the middle of the Great Depression. But World War II is fast approaching. Soon this man, too, will be forced to choose a side. It is the one task for which he is ill-suited. All his life, the only side he has ever really been on is his own. (*The Champagne Safari*)

It can take a succession of drafts to come up with both your film's premise and the right words to frame it. The process can be frustrating in the extreme — but it is absolutely critical to the successful completion of your film.

GETTING THROUGH TO PICTURE LOCK

As is true for every stage of the documentary film writing process, there turns out to be no set formula for completing a picture, either. That said, and for what it's worth, I will give you a short sketch of the process I normally go through when I'm brought in to do a film's narration. None of what follows is carved in stone. My advice is, use whatever works for you and disregard the rest.

Typically I come onto a picture late. Often I am the second, third, sometimes even the fourth writer in. Time is running out; the heat is on: it's a little like firefighting.

Initially I try to plough through all the pertinent research material as quickly as possible. If the film is in something of a confused state, I work with the other creative personnel (the director, the editor, the producer and, sometimes, the broadcaster) to get a new rough cut together. Please note: narration writing and structural changes go hand in hand; a documentary film that doesn't work is likely to be a documentary film that has been improperly structured. Sometimes a little tinkering will do the trick; sometimes a major overhaul is needed.

As soon as the rough cut comes available, I put it in the VCR, take out a hand-held tape recorder and attempt to free-associate my way through the footage, recording whatever thoughts come to mind. My goal at this stage is solely to generate a flow of film-related ideas. From this, I cobble together paragraphs, copy lines and, eventually, finished cues to time.

Returning to the cutting room, I go through my draft with the director, the editor and whomever else is handy, reading the script live to picture to save time. I then make whatever writing changes are needed, and the editor makes whatever picture changes are needed to pull together a narrated rough cut we think might work. We then record the narration and the editor lays it in.

Test Screenings

It was your investors' understanding going in that you would be making this film for an audience. Unless that has changed — and let's hope for your sake it hasn't — test screenings now become an essential part of the process. Depending on your picture's ultimate destination, the money left in contingency and the number of people attending, your choice of venue may vary. But whether your test screenings take place in a cutting room or a theatre, what's key is simply that there be test screenings — if at all possible, plenty of them.

Encourage those you invite to take notes, either during the screening or immediately after. In the old days, we used to have round-table discussions in the screening room. Now I prefer follow-up phone calls or one-on-one meetings. It's my experience that some people are too shy in a group setting, while others aren't shy enough. In any event, if you've cast your test audience correctly, you'll soon learn everything you need to know about where your newly narrated film is at.

Just seeing a picture with an audience can sometimes be enough. It's a little like stand-up comedy: you know when you're on a roll; you also know when you're dying. Granted, the process can be painful but better this than a festival screening, with upward of 400 people walking out of a theatre, all cursing your name and hating your film.

Drafts

I've done one or two and a polish. I've also done twenty. It all depends. My advice is: get ready for a worst-case scenario and hope to be pleasantly surprised. All the language customarily associated with this part of the documentary film-making process — cracking it, nailing it, locking it up — suggests something difficult, violent, as pleasant as dentistry. In my experience, none of this is too far off. As it turns out, some pictures are harder to make than others. When you're done, you'll know it and you'll feel it. In the meantime, as ever, try to hang in.

Voice

Whenever I do a narration, I try to appropriate the film-maker's voice as much as possible. He or she is the person who generated the picture and has slaved over it all these years. If you are writing your own narration, clearly you are looking to do more or less the same thing for yourself: accessing your deepest feelings and attitudes towards the material in the hope of finding your real voice.

A Few Narration Dos and Don'ts:

- The technical underpinnings of a good narration script are exactly what you'd expect: you set up your ideas, you develop them and you pay them off. (Where the images and sound are borderline unintelligible, you are also sometimes obliged to go so far as to tell your audience what they're going to see, what they're seeing and what they saw.)
- Narration is another way, often the final way, of achieving momentum in the viewer's mind. You achieve momentum by telling the viewer what he or she needs to know precisely when he or she needs to know it; you sustain momentum by cutting quickly to the next scene.
- If you are confused as to where to begin, take a look at your principal character. What is his or her goal? What obstacles stand in the way? Does your principal character overcome those obstacles and go on to achieve his or her goal, or not? Why? Why not?
- As a general rule, good narration tells you what you can't already see or hear on the screen. Again: where necessary, a script can also tell viewers what they should be looking and listening for.
- In terms of cue length, 45 seconds of narration, for whatever reason, is about all viewers can absorb at any one time.
- In the interests of economy, if you find you need to close off a scene with narration, try to do so in a way that kicks off the scene to come.
- Narration can always be shorter. Get in and out as quickly as possible. Never say more than you need to. Sentences of twelve words or less tend to be the way to go. As laid out in Strunk and White's *Elements of Style,* never use two words where one will do.
- Narration writing is a form of oratory. Try to write your copy lines the way you'd speak them. If you're uncertain, record the cue on tape and play it back. Did you hear the cue's central idea? Did it register? Or did it blow right past you? If it did, you need to rewrite the cue.
- By and large, you are looking at subject-verb-object sentence construc-

tion. Modifiers tend to be unnecessary. The film's footage should provide the colour customarily provided in print by adjectives and adverbs.

- Facts are better than fiction. Try to save the windy generalizations for another day.
- Tone matters. Do you like the narrator's attitude? Would you want to spend time with him or her at a party? If not, make the appropriate changes.

MODELS

For exemplary narration, you might want to look at the following documentary films: Donald Brittain's *Henry Ford's America* and *His Worship, Mr. Montreal*; Ken Burns' *The Civil War* and *Baseball*; Jon Else's *Day After Trinity*; and Stanley Jackson's *Enemy Alien*. For the most part, all these films achieve their effects not through visuals but through the interplay of visuals and words: see what you can apply to your own work.

Summary

For most of the people who make them, documentary films are less a straightforward commercial proposition than a labour of love.

Documentary film-makers, as a result, are seldom flush with funds. So you should know, going in, that becoming a documentary film writer is unlikely to make you rich.

Documentaries also tend to make more demands on their viewers than dramas do and, again as a result, are less watched. Glory, such as it exists in the documentary world, tends to go not to writers (or editors, for that matter), but to those producers and directors who generate the films, develop the films and ultimately complete them; in my opinion, this is as it should be. Unless you plan on carrying out one of the other functions, however, you should also know, going in, that as a documentary film writer, obscurity will likely be yours.

That said, documentaries have a long-standing tradition in Canada. We continue to make them rather well. For young film-makers and writers alike, documentaries remain an excellent way of getting into the business and learning about it, particularly about the mysteries of the cutting room. The form tends to be more elastic than drama and, as such, more forgiving.

There is some money to be made, truth be told. Documentary work can also be interesting, more often than not teaching you things you didn't know. Plus, the form is life on planet earth as opposed to "life" on a

Century City sound stage. As much as documentary cameras may alter the reality around them, the images they record are still likely to be more authentic and true-to-life than, say, your average episode of "Full House."

Finally, there is nothing quite so thrilling as a documentary film that works. There are still those among us who will take one *Hoop Dreams* over 100 Hollywood confections; I suppose I'm one. Whatever toll the last documentary may have exacted, however firmly I may have sworn that I'd never work on another one, there is always the dim possibility that this time, it's going to be different, that his one is going to be great. In the end, I guess that's what keeps me coming back for more.

9

Writing for Interactive Media

by Paul Hoffert

P aul Hoffert has spent his life seamlessly integrating culture and technology. In 1969, Mr. Hoffert joined a team at the National Research Council of Canada which designed a digital musical system. He has written software for computer music, animation applications, and has developed audio compression algorithms, microchips and consumer electronic products. Mr. Hoffert is also one of Canada's most recognized creative artists with nine gold and platinum recordings, four Juno Awards as well as Genie, Clio, Anik and San Francisco Film Festival awards to his credit in the music, film and television industries. He was inducted into the Rock and Roll Hall of Fame in 1995 for his work with the group he co-founded in 1969, Lighthouse. Mr. Hoffert has written and conducted original music for more than 30 feature films, composed orchestral music and conducted symphony orchestras in Canada, Europe and the United States. He is a director of the Academy of Canadian Cinema and Television, the SOCAN Foundation, and president of the Guild of Canadian Film and Television Composers. He has been executive producer of the Gemini Awards and director of PROCAN. He is chair of the Ontario Arts Council, professor at York University and director of the CulTech Research Centre at York University.

What Are Interactive Media?

Interactive media are technologies that allow a user to change the course of events in a story, game, reference or other work. Although there have been interesting experiments in interactive theatre and cinema, the great majority of interactive media works being produced use computer disks, videodiscs, CD-ROMs or Internet-like technologies to deliver the interactive works.

Multimedia Is Not New

Multimedia is usually defined as works that include sound, visual images, and (optionally) text. The sounds may be speech, music or sound effects. The visual images may be graphics, animations, photography or moving pictures, and the text may be descriptive or titles. Film, television and theatre are multimedia formats. They are also linear, moving inexorably from beginning to end with an order set in stone — Scene 1 is always followed by Scene 2, followed by Scene 3 and so on. The term "new media" has come to represent formats which are multimedia and also interactive, like computer software, CD-ROMs and the World Wide Web. From the perspective of a writer, interactivity is a greater challenge than multimedia.

Interactive Is Not New

The most natural form of storytelling is interactive. Anyone who's had a young sibling or child knows that children have an insatiable appetite for stories. And their imagination prompts them to interrupt the course of storytelling to demand that the name of a character be changed (perhaps to that of a family member), to add dwarfs to the Cinderella story or to perhaps change the ending of *Red Riding Hood* so that the wolf has a change of heart and instead of trying to eat the young girl, befriends her.

Storytelling is, after all, an oral tradition in which even adult storytellers react to their audience and context by elaborating on certain story elements and eliminating others. For example, you would naturally modify the story of World War II if your audience were primary school students, university students, war veterans or peace activists. You would also modify the story if you knew your audience was keenly interested in, or opposed to, violence. The linear dictatorship of film and TV have, in this sense, conspired to deprive us of our natural storytelling instincts. These media have encouraged writers to create essentially passive experiences, while audiences are prevented from having input to the story path.

Sometimes it's difficult to explain what interactive storytelling is all about. I like the example given by Ira Nyman, a non-linear author who led a discussion at *Interactive '96*, a conference for artists and creators. He began with "Mary had a little lamb. Its fleece was white as snow. And everywhere that Mary went … *Pick one of the following choices.*"

Interactive Media Is New

The key to interactive works is the concept of branching, allowing the user to change the flow of events by making a choice. There are historic examples that allow users to take part in the creation of a work, but they are few and generally have not flourished. A notable example — Mozart wrote a piano piece constructed of entirely interchangeable four-bar modules that may be rearranged in any order by a performer.

The rise of interactive media is directly related to the use of computers in interactive media appliances which enable branching. The first commercially acceptable works that incorporated user interactions were computer programs. Because computer chips have branching built into their silicon, it's easy to construct computer languages which also feature branching. In addition to the "if ... then go to" type of instructions, software languages also allow for random branching so that each experience of the work is different.

Branching

Branching allows the user to change the flow of events by making a choice. The first large-scale implementations of user interactions were computer programs which had branching built into their underlying languages. These also allowed for random branching so that a creator could guarantee that each experience of the work was different.

In storytelling, as in other interactive processes, there are three basic types of branches. *Cul-de-sacs* leave an audience hanging without the ability to continue. These dead ends are frequently used as diversions, leading the audience down a calculated story path of disinformation. They have to backtrack to re-enter a main story branch. *Loops* take the audience on side trips that add information or entertainment, but ultimately return to the main branch at the point you left it. They generally allow the audience to gain extra context and depth, or provide entertainment. The third type of branching stays within one of the possible story spines — generally a classic three-part structure with a beginning, a middle and an end.

Branching at the end of a story spine is relatively painless and doesn't involve a lot of additional work. It has its parallel in the film industry — shooting alternate endings for a movie. In the case of interactive works, the audience, not the producer, makes the decision to change the ending. Branching at the beginning of a story, on the other hand, can involve generating complete multiples of scripts and productions because changing the premise can affect the entire story path. The successful interactive writer understands the implications of controlling the framework of interaction, and chooses carefully where the audience is allowed to branch out of a story spine so that dramatically unrewarding story paths are minimized.

Hyperlinks

The most recent technology for interactivity is the *hyperlink*, a basic technology that has enabled the wildly popular World Wide Web portion of the Internet. Hyperlinks allow multimedia objects to contain information about actions that should be taken if a user selects them. For example, a hyperlink might be attached to a picture or book which, if selected, would display a table of contents of that book. When the multimedia objects are words, the technology is called *hypertext*. Clicking on a hypertext word normally performs the action of branching to another part of the document, or to another document altogether. An example might be hypertext links in a book's table of contents. Clicking on a chapter heading would display the text in that chapter.

Branching and hyperlinking have enabled authors of CD-ROMs, computer programs and World Wide Web pages to create interactive media works.

Now's The Time

When it comes to holding an audience, timing is everything, and one of the problems with creating effective interactive works is that the writer can't model the time flow of the work. In a traditional medium like film, we expect that a screenplay might be 120 pages in length and that the running time might be 100 minutes. The length of the script has a direct relationship to the running time. For interactive scripts, there is no longer a linkage between length of the script and the running time.

Running time for an interactive script is dependent on which story paths the user chooses. The length of an interactive script, on the other hand, depends on the number of branching options and where the branching takes place — early branching requires more scripting than late branching. The following illustrates the difference between running length and script length for an interactive work:

> Two writers are each asked to create a simple interactive story for a kiosk in a mall. Each story is to have three parts, a set beginning, a choice of middle parts and a set ending. Each part will run one minute and will occupy a single page of script. One writer constructs a beginning Scene 1, an ending Scene 3 and two options for the middle, Scene 2a and Scene 2b. The second writer also constructs a single beginning Scene 1 and ending Scene 3, but allows for ten choices in the middle. Scenes 2a, 2b, 2c, 2d, 2e, 2f, 2g, 2h, 2i, 2j. The running

time for both works is three minutes, but one writer has written four pages of script, while the second writer has written twelve pages of script.

What Kind Of Stories Work Interactively?

Most of us are familiar with interactive works in the form of games. Games have been popular from the earliest times, and before computers became ubiquitous, people played most of their games with simpler technologies like cards, boards and dice. Popular games like Monopoly have been loosely based on interactive story path — *I decided to become a real estate tycoon so I [roll the dice] [choose a card] [decide to buy a property] ... but it ended in disaster when I went bankrupt because I couldn't pay the rent and taxes.*

Some story formats that lend themselves to interactive treatment are:

1. *Single Story, Many Perspectives*

   The audience experiences the story through the eyes of different characters or from different locations. Example: *Tamara,* the theatrical work that takes place simultaneously in many rooms of a home. The audience gets to follow whichever characters they're interested in and constructs the story from these perspectives.

2. *Single Perspective, Many Stories*

   Follow a single character along a variety of story paths. Example: *Myst.*

3. *Adventure*

   A variety of obstacles are placed in the path of the lead character with different outcomes depending on how well the character overcomes them. Example: *Super-Mario.*

4. *Role Playing*

   A character's personality and attributes may be defined by the user. These affect the story path as the character interacts with situations and other characters. Example: *Dungeons and Dragons.*

Sharing Control With The Audience

A writer for interactive media must share creative control with the audience. In traditional media, the author is trained and rewarded for carefully crafting the emotional flow of a work. Whether it's building to a commercial break or untying the knot of a mystery, the successful writer controls the flow of events in order to bring the audience to satisfying levels of anticipation, interest and closure. In interactive works, the flow is controlled by the audience, and the process of creating multiple paths of satisfying user involvement is outside the experience of most writers. In the terminology of digital Infoways we say, "The consumer becomes a creator." In the writing community there is a clear feeling that the author's authority has been usurped by the untrained and unpredictable consumer.

Sharing Control In A Creative Team

Book authors have the most freedom and control of their works. Although they submit their texts to editors, they generally retain the final say over the finished manuscript and own the initial copyright to the work. In multimedia such as film, the screenwriter is subjected to many more editorial processes, working with producers, directors and picture editors who all contribute to the shape of the final work. In many countries including Canada, it's the producer, not the screenwriter, who gets the copyright to the screenplay.

Similarly, when you write for interactive multimedia, you will be part of a creative team. Generally the team includes the writer, the project manager, the lead designer and the lead programmer. The collaboration with these team-mates will likely be more intense because the writer will not be familiar with all of the complex technological issues that will affect the work. Marshall McLuhan said "the message is the medium," but he didn't foresee that the message might be in the authoring technology and the playback platform.

Each technical process — from wire frame modelling and photo-realistic rendering, through animation, QuickTime VR™, JPEG and MPEG coding, algorithmic modelling and so on — brings its own impact and influence to your story. Some systems allow for smooth real-time navigation of three-dimensional scenes, and an author would likely want to take advantage of this capability. Other systems have jerky motion, but allow the user to move objects and characters around in the scene. Even playback appliances have an impact on the creator's vision. In some instances the screenplay may end up being viewed on either a screen that can display only sixteen colours at low resolution, or a high-resolution screen with realistic colour capabilities. In the first case, images will look cartoony and digitized, while in the second, the same images will look more like a movie. The writer should be aware of these and other technical issues which will likely circumscribe the creative choices.

Modular Writing

The trend over the past five years in writing computer software has been towards the creation of reusable code modules. Each of these modules performs a simple specific function, like drawing a window on a screen or making a beeping sound. When strung together, they become a full-blown application like a word processor. Each module may be reused in other applications, or in many parts of the same application. Because writing for interactive media requires the creation of many branches, it is well suited to the modular approach. Story modules are multimedia objects that may be strung together as necessary, each performing a simple specific function. Modules with similar functions may be easily interchanged within the same story branch without losing coherence.

In this aspect, modular writing for multimedia is somewhat like writing a TV series. Each episode relates to its predecessor and successor, but an audience member may miss an episode or two without losing the gist of the story.

Frameworks For Interactivity

In creating the framework for interactive writing, it is necessary to modularize the story elements and connect them through a flowchart of interactivity. Following is a diagram of an interactive story framework. It is contrasted with a diagram of a linear story framework. The traditional dramatic arcs and pyramids, set-ups and resolutions are likely to be in different positions or altogether absent.

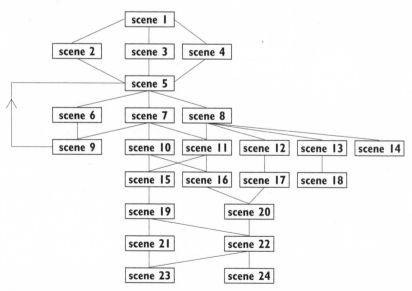

FIG. I. Interactive Story Framework

Can I Make Money Doing This?

Although writing for interactive media is in its infancy, the field is exploding with projects, some of them with significant funding from major players in the game, film, computer or telecommunications industries. Other projects may offer more interesting opportunities working with small start-ups with better concepts and more creative freedom. The most important benefit a writer will get in the short term from working on interactive projects may be the experience itself. In an emerging growth industry where no credible schools exist and few professionals have experience, the best way to position yourself for future income is to roll up your sleeves and go to it.

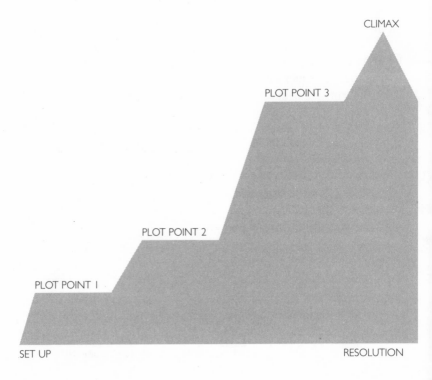

FIG. 2. Linear Story Framework

10

95 Secrets of Variety Writing

by Rick Green

R ick Green used his Bachelor of Science Degree while teaching at the Ontario Science Centre. After 2,000 performances Rick left to pursue a career in comedy. Seventeen years later, he is still pursuing it. He hopes to catch it soon. Rick, (or Rick to his friends), was a founding member of "The Frantics" comedy troupe, Writer/Host of TVO's Literacy program "Prisoners of Gravity" and currently co-writes, co-stars and directs "The New Red Green Show." He has written or co-written and performed in seven stage productions, over 150 episodes of radio and over 270 episodes of television. He is married and has the requisite number of cute kids.

The traditional variety television show which offered a fruit cocktail of songs, skits, guest stars, novelty acts, and musical interludes has vanished from the tube. But skit or sketch comedy is still going strong. Witness "The Royal Canadian Air Farce," "Double Exposure," "Kids in the Hall," "This Hour Has 22 Minutes" and even "The New Red Green Show."

What distinguishes this new breed of skit comedy from the old "Sonny and Cher" style of show is a distinct voice and comedic style. For example "SCTV" satirized television, "Air Farce" lampoons politics. As well, most contemporary skit shows have a regular format, a cast of returning characters, and regular features. And they usually feature a cast of writer-performers.

Today's skit shows have far more of an edge than most sitcoms, and perhaps surprisingly, more personal style than a lot of stand-up comedy.

Skit comedy has spun off dozens of memorable movie characters; from "The Blues Brothers" to the "Muppets." In fact, skit comedy, in the form of vaudeville, was the training ground for the first movie comedians, from

Charlie Chaplin, Stan Laurel and W. C. Fields to the Marx Brothers, Three Stooges and Abbot and Costello.

While stand-up comedy has become the hot route for comedians who aspire to star in their own "Seinfeld" sitcom, I think variety writing remains the best training ground for writers who want to branch out into sitcoms, movies, theatre, and/or song writing. Not to mention those who simply want to keep writing skits. The history of variety writing reads like a who's who of comedy: Moss Hart, Robert Benchley, George Kaufman, Ring Lardner, Herman Wouk, Neil Simon, Woody Allen, Steve Martin, Carl Reiner, Mel Brooks and the Zucker brothers, not to mention the alumni of "Monty Python," "Saturday Night Live," "In Living Color" and "SCTV."

Performers love variety because it allows them to show their range. Tracy Ullman, Lili Tomlin, Dan Ackroyd and Robin Williams all started in television variety.

OK, so enough of the sales pitch. What do you need to know to make it in variety? I don't know. No one knows. That's the remarkable thing about show business — no one *knows* anything.

But of course everyone *thinks* they know everything. And I'm no exception. So here, in no particular order, are 95 things about variety writing that I think are either true, important or at least useful.

Generating Ideas For Skits

1. The newspaper is a gold mine of ideas. Forget the world news, read "Dear Abby," "Miss Manners" and "The Doctor's Advice" columns.
2. Ride the public transit. Listen to how people talk in a singles' bar, a hockey rink, a cocktail party. A single turn of phrase can inspire a memorable character. Peter Sellers started fleshing out his characters by working on the voice, and mannerism. Start with the surface and work backwards.
3. A lot of writers find that two good places for generating ideas are in the shower and driving in a car. I have no idea why.
4. Watch commercials, infomercials and read advertisements.
5. Think about what annoys you. What strikes you as hypocritical.
6. When you're angry, stop and figure out what's bothering you, then turn it into a skit.
7. Think about your parents. Your teachers. Old lovers.
8. Think of a character. Make him or her outrageous.
9. Exaggerate small moments. John Cleese went into a shop to buy cheese

and his first five choices were out of stock. He exaggerated the situation into "Monty Python's" infamous "Cheese Shop" skit.

10. Play with words. "The Frantics," who write their own material, often draw up lists of silly names for imaginary scenes, and these names would inspire skits.

11. Focus on a theme. "This Hour Has 22 Minutes" spoofs Canadian culture. "The New Red Green Show" satirizes men's foibles. "Kids in the Hall" tears up middle-class social conventions. What strikes you as funny? What would you love to write about week after week?

12. Write something totally silly, rude or bizarre that will never see the light of day. It's more than a finger exercise; it gets your brain to break barriers and make silly connections.

13. Take a hackneyed dramatic situation and give it a weird twist. Some of "The Frantics" most bizarre skits started with, "Honey, I'm home."

What Are The Challenges Facing A Skit Writer?

14. Making a living at it.

15. Introducing characters quickly. In a two-hour movie, you can slowly reveal aspects of a character. In a three-minute skit, you hit only the highlights.

16. It's not only characters you have to reveal quickly — you also have to establish the time, place, situation, conflict, back story etc.

How Do You Introduce All These Elements Quickly?

17. You get to the point. Since skits are short and you have so little time, the first line of dialogue — in fact, every line — is crucial.

18. Get to the conflict right away, "Oh my God, it's my husband!"

19. Find a catch phrase that defines a character.
    "I crush your tiny head, I'm crushing you ..."
    "We are two wild and crazy Czechoslovakian brothers!"
    "Take off eh, ya hoser."
    "Use the Handyman's Secret Weapon, duct tape."

20. Clearly specify the character's look. Is he Mr. Canoehead, or Ed Grimley?

21. Create memorable "voices." Exaggerate unusual vocabulary, odd speech patterns, accents. The cast of "The Goon Show" were masters at this.

22. Avoid too many twists, too many ideas or too many characters in one skit.

23. Cut back on exposition and explanations — instead rely on costuming, blocking, sight gags and gestures to impart information to the audience.
24. Use stereotypes and clichés. For example, a man in a lab coat with a stethoscope faces a man who has his shirt off. The audience immediately understands the situation — patient and doctor. If the doctor is male and the patient is female, the audience will have different expectations. If the doctor is female and the patient is male, again, different possibilities, different expectations.

If You're Dealing In Stereotypes, Is Character Important?

25. Yes. Absolutely.
26. "SCTV," "In Living Color," "Saturday Night Live," "The Red Green Show" "Kids In the Hall," all hinge on character.
27. Create original character. Avoid impersonations. "Saturday Night Live" star Dana Carvey's character of the Church Lady will have a much longer life than his George Bush parody. Rich Little can impersonate more characters than Robin Williams, but he's never created one that made it in movies.
28. Give each character attitude when going into the scene — it emphasizes conflict, gets them talking and starts the sparks flying.
29. Monologues are a good format to use to define and round out characters.
30. A character can be developed over a number of skits. If a new character catches on with an audience, go back and write another scene for that character. When a character has a magical "something," then writing more scenes for him or her is a pleasure.
31. Develop memorable, well-rounded characters, and original scenes will flow out of them. Eventually they'll get their own movie deal.

What If A Scene Just Isn't Working?

32. Try making one aspect of the scene more outrageous. Monty Python's infamous "Dead Parrot" skit started out as a man returning a broken down car.
33. Increase the stakes. Give one character a secret want or desire.
34. Give several characters conflicting goals, wants or needs.
35. Give the "straight" character an attitude, a personal problem, an annoying habit or a crucial deadline.
36. Expand a character's complaint or insult into a big "rant."

37. Change the characters. Instead of two teenage girls mooning about the guys in their class, give the same dialogue to the president and vice-president of the United States, "Helmut Kohl, he is like soooo cute!"

38. Eliminate extraneous characters. Perhaps you've written a scene in which a medical researcher is describing his new breakthrough to a crowd of reporters. You realize the reporters are faceless. As characters they're interchangeable. Why not change the scene so the researcher is alone with one hapless patient, describing the procedure and trying to convince the poor slob to take it? Now you have two very distinct characters to work with, each with his or her own agenda. The stakes go up and the scene has more "heat." Go further. What happens if the patient's spouse is there too? Experiment.

39. Give each scene one twist. For example, Mr. Bean sleeps in late, so he gets dressed in his car as he drives to work. That's enough of a twist. Making him dress in women's clothes would be a twist on a twist. Having him steal his clothes from people along the way is probably a separate scene. Adding a passenger in the car would be a distraction. Give a scene one twist and then fully explore it.

40. Change the structure. Turn a romantic scene into a K-Tel commercial

41. Move the scene to a completely different location, or time period.

42. Turn a monologue into a dialogue, or vice versa.

43. Focus on what works. If it's just one very funny line, then throw out everything else and build a new scene around that gag.

44. Add sex.

45. And finally, my favourite trick; discard the scene and move on. It's often easier and faster to write a new scene than to hammer your head against something that doesn't work.

OK, But What About The Punchline?

46. Punchlines are the hardest part of skit writing. (Next to making sure you get paid.)

47. In a quick blackout the punchline is everything. If you have a great punchline, why not expand it? Lengthen it. Turn a blackout into a longer scene, knowing that you can sustain it because you have a great pay-off.

48. Decide which is the funniest gag in the scene, move it to the end and go out on your biggest laugh.

49. Give the scene a final twist or revelation. One "Frantics" blackout featured two fellows merrily handing each other gift packages, tearing

them open, and marvelling at the contents. "Here, this is for you." "Thanks ... Oh wow, a cuckoo clock!" Suddenly one fellow looked off, hissed, "Look out, it's the supervisor!" and the two of them started sorting the packages. "Overseas. Air mail. Insufficient postage on this one ..." It wasn't the most original scene in the world, but audiences roared.

50. Take a line from earlier in the scene and repeat it. Or go back and set up the final line in the body of the skit. For example, over the course of a seduction scene the woman insists, "I'm not that kind of girl," several times. The final blow might be the man blurting out, "Hey, I'm not that kind of boy!"

51. Bring the scene full circle to the first line.

52. Fade out on pandemonium.

How Do You Decide On The Genre Or Format Of The Scene?

53. Good question. Years ago I read an article in the *Toronto Star* about what each major religion believed the afterlife would be like and who would be admitted. It inspired a scene called "Heaven Is For Presbyterians," in which a good Catholic discovers he is going to hell for backing the wrong religion. I was satirizing the notion that anyone knows "the truth" about God, and I did it in a two-character scene. But I could have used ...

54. A movie parody: "Rocky 9: The Final Test."

55. A commercial parody: "So you've planned for your retirement, but what about afterwards?"

56. A speech: "Hello Presbyterians, welcome to Heaven ..."

57. A monologue: "Boy, was the Pope ever wrong ..."

58. A Song: "All Of You Are Going To Hell."

59. A Poem: "Twas the night before Christmas,
And a bus ran over my head,
Not a creature was stirring
I guess I was dead ..."

60. A Pantomime: A priest trying to sneak into heaven.

61. A Group Scene: A line-up at the Pearly Gates.

62. A TV Parody: "Next on the Real Estate Channel, Heaven ..."
Or: "Today on Oprah, People who chose the wrong religion."
Or: "Good evening, My guest today is St. Peter."
Or: "Welcome wrestling fans, tonight The Raging Rabbi battles The Punishing Priest!"

Or: "It's time to play, 'What's My Afterlife!'
Or: "This is Brenda Brown reporting live from the Pearly Gates where this mob of angry Methodists ..."
Or: ... you get the idea.

What About Improvisation?

63. Improvisation is great for generating new ideas and fresh situations.
64. If a scene is going nowhere, improvising can help to add conflict or action. It's a lively way to experiment.
65. But beware. Several people who have graduated from the Second City system told me that improvisation helped them develop a range of characters, and taught them to think fast on their feet, but not how to write. They didn't learn how to structure scenes. And they developed a bad habit of "breaking character" to get a laugh. Perhaps that's why improvisation has never worked on television. (And dozens of producers have tried to make it work in the hope that it would eliminate the need to pay for writers, rehearsals and expensive sets.) I believe classic comedy scenes cannot be improvised. They are carefully crafted. And one final thought — no television producer would dare improvise drama. Why should comedy be given less effort?

What Are The Advantages Of Writing Skit Comedy?

66. You can let your imagination run riot.
67. You don't have to agonize over plot, character development or story arcs. You're only writing one scene.
68. Since each new skit introduces it's own little world, you'll learn to consider all aspects of a scene; dialogue, accents, sight gags, physical humour, blocking, costume, props, special lighting, music, sound effects and soon.
69. Skit comedy teaches you to edit ruthlessly and compress every line to the bare minimum. Or should I say, "Skit comedy teaches you to edit, and compress every line." Or better still. "Edit and compress." Because skits are short. And besides, if you can say the same number of jokes using half the words, the audience thinks you're twice as funny!
70. You have the chance to write for a wide range of characters. It's perfect for writers with short attention spans.
71. It's a great place to develop characters. "The Simpsons," "Wayne's World" and many other TV and movie characters started out in skits.
72. Because skits are short, quick and cover a range, it's a great format in

which to experiment with other writers, and find collaborators.

73. If a skit doesn't work, you haven't poured a year of your life into it. At least I hope not.

What About Radio, Records And CDs?

74. From "Wayne and Shuster" to "Air Farce" and "The Frantics," a lot of radio comedians have gone on to do film and television. Radio allows writers to experiment more because costs are lower — no costumes to make, props to build or sets to construct.

75. Anything can happen on radio — use your imagination. The Pope can tap dance. A man can juggle live pigs. A kid can turn himself inside out. For a medium of pure sound, it's very visual.

76. Make each voice distinct and avoid too many characters in a scene or you'll confuse the listener.

77. Play with accents and affectations.

78. Build gags or scenes around sound effects. "The Goon Show" was famous for its bizarre and brilliant sound effects.

79. Radio teaches you the value of words. Listen to vocabulary of "The Firesign Theatre" or "Monty Python's" albums.

80. Radio allows wonderful word play. "The Goon Show" — "I walked into the room. The curtains were drawn, but the rest of the furniture was real."

81. Use silence and the dramatic pause. Listen to old Bob Newhart records.

82. Radio is a great forum for song parodies or original comedy songs.

83. If you can't write original music, write funny lyrics to a tune you know, then collaborate with a musician to create an original tune.

84. Write your lyrics for a completely in appropriate style of music. For example, a country and western song about Albert Einstein. A Gregorian chant about sex. A rock and roll song about senior citizens.

Any Suggestions For Putting A Skit Troupe Together?

85. Try to recruit writer-performers. It's easier to learn to act than to learn to write.

86. Try to recruit a variety of physical types.

87. Let each person in the troupe contribute where they can. Those who don't write may handle business, publicity, costumes, directing and so on.

Final Thoughts?

88. Learn all the rules of skit comedy. Then break them. Audiences have seen it all. Since "Monty Python," the rules have gone out the door.

89. But never break the reality of a scene or the audience will lose interest. No matter how outrageous the situation, your characters must believe in it. Think of the "Monty Python" scene in which the accountant desperately wants to be a lion tamer, while the guidance counsellor gently tries to talk him out of it. The conversation is played straight. The lunacy of wanting to be a lion tamer is never questioned. The concept is over the top, the performance isn't. Characters must really want their wants, and feel their feelings. You wouldn't break character in a sitcom or a drama, so don't do it in a skit.

90. Skits can be like a burlesque comedian's jokes, each one standing or falling on it's own merit. That's why the most successful stand-ups develop a unique "voice." Think of Louie Anderson, Sam Kinnison and Steven Wright — they simply couldn't do each other's material. In the same way, successful skit troupes also develop a personal style.

91. Avoid easy targets.

92. Make your performers work. Make them sweat.

93. Rewrite and rewrite and rewrite. If something new doesn't work, relax, you can change it back. If things suddenly go off on an irrelevant tangent, perhaps you've got a new scene in the making. "The Frantics" most popular character, Mr. Canoehead, started out as a minor character in another scene.

94. And finally, let the audience decide what's working and what's not.

One Last Question — Don't All These Rules Apply To Any Kind Of Comedy Writing?

95. Yes.

11

Writing Corporate Films

by Cal Coons

Writer-director Cal Coons' bread and butter work for the past several years has been producing, writing and directing music videos, commercials and corporate films for such clients as Volkswagen, North American Life, Bell and IBM. A graduate of Niagara College, he has had several feature film scripts in funded development and has also written and directed a number of television shows, including Missing Children *and* Cottage Life Television. *He is currently attending the Canadian Film Centre as a resident director in the feature film program.*

There is a general misconception that the world of corporate film-making is a stuffy suit-and-tie environment. In the last five years, I've never worn a jacket to a meeting. In fact, I've found corporate communications people happy to deal with a fresh perspective, a non-corporate viewpoint. I know other corporate writers who feel more comfortable in a suit and tie. It's whatever works.

Having entered corporate film-making from the production side, I worried that my lack of experience with corporate culture would be a problem. If anything, my lack of experience has been a bonus, giving me the naivety to ask the most basic of questions, questions that are often at the core of every communications problem we have been grappling with.

Every corporation is unique. Every writing assignment is different. For me, approaching things openly, honestly and personally has proven to be a simple, effective rule of thumb.

Definitions: Is It A Corporate Or An Industrial Film?
Defining a corporate film is difficult. The best definition I can come up

with is a film that has a sales component to it. Normally, you're working for a department or a facet of a business which has a communications objective that it needs to achieve; usually, that involves sales.

To give an example: I once wrote a documentary on the erection of SkyDome in Toronto. While the film was for public consumption, it was also very much a corporate film — a self-promoting sales tool garbed as a documentary.

People often confuse corporate films with industrial films. To me, an industrial film has a much more specific goal: to educate employees, clients or prospective clients about a product or a business. An industrial film tends to service the needs of a corporation far more directly than a corporate film.

To give   another example: I once did an industrial film for a San Francisco-based software company, Light Scape. Their product was a 3-D modelling/animation package. The audience the company wanted to address was diverse: industrial designers, architects, animators, video producers, special effects houses and major broadcasters. To help sell its product, the company thought a video should be produced. What we ended up creating was a boxed set of two videos. The first video used testimonials from users to promote the product. The second video — a pure industrial — was a step-by-step guide to using the software. While the vice-president of Development demonstrated the software on a computer, we simply filmed the screen. It sounds boring, but for the audience, it was the clearest and most effective way to illustrate the advantages of the product.

Somebody once described corporate film-making as nothing more than commercials without the money. While it's true that corporates are essentially advertisements, to my mind, that statement reflects an old way of thinking. In an age of 500 channels, advertisers simply must be more selective in how they advertise. They also realize that corporate films are not commercials. Averaging anywhere from five to 90 minutes in length, corporate films must sustain viewer interest in fundamentally different ways. Where a commercial might be able to sustain 30 seconds with image alone, a corporate film simply cannot — which is where corporate screenwriting comes in.

Corporate Screenwriting: How It Differs From Traditional Screenwriting And How It Is The Same

Let's start with the differences. Corporate films tend not to be character or even story-driven. Corporates are driven by product, message or whatever the client wants to say: the client is the one paying for the production. Normally the product is the star: I've done films featuring fire sprinkler heads, medical waste processors, you name it. Sometimes the employees themselves are the stars: I once worked on a film that likened selling oil to Olympic speed skating.

I am not recommending this approach (though the truth is that this approach often works, simply because the audience is either captive or inherently interested in the subject matter). In my experience, cornball rah-rah corporate films don't work. Invariably, viewers feel they're being forced to watch something akin to a film on hygiene in health and guidance class.

Audiences are sophisticated. This is where corporate screenwriting is the same as traditional screenwriting. Audiences don't suddenly become stupid just because they're watching a corporate film. Audiences expect to be entertained. The writer must come up with evocative turns of phrase. The images still have to be great.

In addition to having to fulfil similar audience expectations, corporate screenwriting techniques are often the same, too. Because of the length of many corporate films, plot devices are often needed to carry the film, "plot" being used loosely here. Quite often, the film will also use a thematic device to garb its message and give the audience members something with which they can relate.

I'll use the SkyDome documentary to illustrate. The client, Stadium Corporation of Ontario, decided that it wanted a historical record of the construction of SkyDome. At the same time, Stadium Corporation also wanted a film that could sell SkyDome to perspective consumers worldwide.

As with most corporate films, the product was the star. Given that the film's lead character was in this case a billion or so tons of concrete, the challenge was to create a story people could relate to. How could we humanize the story? How could the audience be given a way in? While the temptation was simply to shoot interesting visuals and string them together with narration, we knew from the outset that twenty minutes of even the most breathtaking construction footage would be mind-numbing.

As is often the case, we looked to the project's theme for an answer. Picking up on the concept of SkyDome as a "unique structure," we expanded the concept to include "the spirit of creativity": everyone involved with SkyDome, from labourer to executive, had the same basic desire — to build something of lasting value. As the concept was universal, it offered the audience a way into the film.

The plot of the film was pretty much self-evident: we would follow the construction process from beginning to end. Again, to help further draw the viewer in, we introduced a "sub-plot" based around the efforts of the architect and the engineer to create this huge structure.

The result was a plot, a sub-plot and a theme that all somehow hung together. Around these elements, we felt we could build some stunning visual sequences that had a real context and were not simply "eye candy." It worked pretty well. The film is the official souvenir video of SkyDome and has been seen by over 1.2 million people as part of the SkyDome tour.

Finding A Corporate Screenwriting Job

Corporate screenwriters tend to have a communications background. Many come from advertising. A lot of ex-agency people do this kind of work. Some are account executives who can bring a client to the table.

Typically a corporate screenwriter will work for a production company that specializes in business communications. That includes speech-writing, speaker-support material, videos, brochures, multimedia applications, that sort of thing. Occasionally, the screenwriter will work directly with the client. (Many times, because of budget limitations, writers also turn out to be the producer or the director of a project. The smaller the client, the more this will tend to occur.)

The Most Important Stage: Winning The Bid

Production companies will hear about jobs through any number of means. They'll beg, borrow, steal, call and harass, but mostly it comes down to hard work. As a corporate screenwriter, a big part of the job is actually helping production companies land the contract. Corporate film-making is a very competitive field. Often, the proposal you provide is the only thing that distinguishes your particular production company from the next. Your proposal must be excellent. That means clear, concise, well thought-out and original.

A writer's first step will likely be to meet with the client. That could be anyone from the president on down to a communications assistant. It may be a one-on-one meeting or the meeting may take place in a briefing room with several other production companies. Regardless, the writer will receive an overview of the job specifications and be given access to the pertinent research. The writer may also be allowed to scout the plant, meet the workers, see the environment and otherwise check out the situation. The bulk of the writer's time will likely be spent trying to get inside the communication problem itself: inside what the client's objective is.

The Pitch

Working with the production company, the writer will help prepare a proposal which will then be pitched back to the client. As a writer, it is very important to be able to read the client. If the client is adventurous, then thre is the opportunity to do some interesting things.

Next, you'll sit down with the production company and say, "Let's go with this approach. It's going to cost this much money." The client will probably have hinted that this is either a tight budget or that there's a fair amount of money to spend. This will have to be reflected in the creative. Even if the client likes the outer space idea, the budget may only permit shooting in their parking garage. The last thing anyone wants to do is disappoint the client. Even though the writer often has little to do with the budget, it is important to write with budget in mind (in general, this quality makes a writer a hero in a producer's eyes).

It is very important to understand the dynamic of the decision-making process. Large corporations usually have a tender list for video producers. It can start with twenty and get short-listed down until finally one production company is chosen. Many corporations have cut out this stage and have a list of four or five production companies who are preferred suppliers. As with anything else, relationships develop out of trust. Clients turn to producers whom clients believe in and enjoy working with. As a writer, it is very important to develop these same relationships: they'll be your lifeline in the years to come.

Dealing With The Client

Client tend to be reasonable. Nine times out of ten, they realize that audiences are smart enough to know when they're getting something shoved down their throat. Clients realize that they can't do that sort of thing anymore. Well, most do. Sometimes, however, client education becomes a large part of the job.

Communications people at companies tend to be very smart and well-educated people but generally they are not schooled in film. Still, a corporate film-maker must realize that the two things communications people know better than anything else are their respective businesses and their customers. Communications people are the experts in those particular fields. As an outsider, you can't go in there and try to write a script that says, "Well, your customers really want to know about this." That's an important part of writing for this market: accepting that the client knows things that the writer does not.

Often, the biggest part of a corporate film-maker's job is trying to figure out what a client's communication problem is. It is critical to be able to listen very carefully because sometimes clients are not able to state their objective clearly. Most of the time they know what the problem is, in a vague sort of way: discovering exactly what it is and deciding how to approach it is difficult.

Once You've Won The Bid

The first step will be to meet with the client again and find out what they *really* want to do. Do they buy all of the idea? What changes do they want to see? Typically, the writer will then complete the research, write an outline or a treatment, develop a shooting script and shoot it. In post-production there will probably be a rewrite. It's very similar to the documentary process in many ways.

Fees And Schedules

Corporate writing fees range from "experience" to 5 per cent of the budget which, again, is fairly comparable to a documentary. On average, a writer will spend two or three days researching and outlining, and two or three more scripting. Adding a polish day in post, the schedule will probably entail somewhere between five and seven days, including meetings. A writer can make a good living with corporates but he or she must be prepared to do a lot of work. A typical corporate budget is $30,000, maybe less. At 5 per cent, or $1,500 per, a writer probably needs to be averaging at least 30 projects a year.

However, a corporate screenwriter will probably find that they are not just going to write video. Often, they will produce speaker-support material and some speeches here and there. Since video is often unable to convey detailed information, ancillary print material is almost always needed. This is another employment opportunity for the corporate screenwriter.

The Future

The CD-ROM has revolutionized corporate communications. CD-ROMs carry enormous amounts of information and are extremely flexible in terms of sharing that information. Because CD-ROMs allow audience members to choose the information they are interested in, video and print materials can be used to satisfy far more specialized needs than has been possible in the past.

As a CD-ROM writer, the task, besides simply writing text or copy, is also to help audience members select information that is of value both to them and to the client. Often, the writer will end up creating huge flow charts that follow information down different paths of interest to various potential audiences. A great deal of time is spent creating an interface, the tool used to link the user with the data, that is both practical and interesting.

The CD-ROM is a big part of a corporate screenwriter's job now and will be even more so in the future.

The Upside, The Downside

The upside is that there is work in this area. For beginning writers, corporate films represent a great opportunity. Since companies always have to communicate, corporate films are always being made, even in the most dire of economic times. As a result, new people are always needed. Corporate production houses tend to be willing to take chances on new people. Writers who want experience can get it. Plus, the contacts made will be with you for life. There are a lot of talented people working in the corporate film world.

The downside is that corporate film-making can be quite mind-numbing sometimes. It's a different entity from dramas, documentaries and commercials. The skills a writer acquires are not necessarily transferable. The risk is, a writer will end up being very good at writing corporates and unable to write a drama, simply because he or she has never had to write something that was either character-driven or plot-driven.

Finally, corporate screenwriting can make a writer "safe." You reach a point where you're making a comfortable living and it's difficult to get out.

12

HOW TO SURVIVE AS A WRITER

by Richard Oleksiak and Tony Di Franco

R ichard Oleksiak tries hard to write good TV. He has been hired, fired and rehired by some of the best shows in Canada in a variety of capacities. He was educated in the United States, immigrated to Canada and found it a more meaningful experience. Starting in advertising, he has parlayed his obsession with words into something resembling a career. His writing credits include Diamonds in the Rough, Night Tracker, Fire and Ice. As executive story editor and writer he has worked on "Counterstrike, "E.N.G.," Neon Rider," "Top Cops," "Street Legal," "T & T," and "Edison Twins."

T ony Di Franco has worked throughout Canada and Europe as a writer, story editor and executive story editor. He has written a few hundred hours of television on series such as "Counterstrike," "Destiny Ridge," "Katts and Dog," "Sweating Bullets," "War of the Worlds" and "Inside Stories."

The Addiction

Advice to the would-be word junkie. There's still time to save yourself. Find something else to obsess on: men, women, cars, the stock market. Anything but this. Believe me, if you proceed much further, there will be nothing anyone can do for you. Before you know it you will be sacrificing everything you once considered sacred to maintain your habit. The words demand it. There are so many of them and just artfully arranging them delivers such satisfaction, such unbelievable personal gratification that you could sit there all day pushing them back and forth ... back and forth. Before you know it six, eight, ten hours will have passed. Night falls and your lover will pound on the door asking you if everything's all right, but you won't hear a thing because the words are dancing for you ... then again, maybe you won't hear a thing because the words have refused to dance for you.

For the addict just starting out, the only real question is how to support your habit. With a little searching around, you may soon discover that there are people who will actually pay to help you maintain your addiction. Furthermore, if you're willing to trade off just a little bit of your integrity, they're willing to make you rich, but we'll save that bit for later. These people that are willing to help you out usually wear pressed blue jeans and call themselves producers … television producers. Most of them will say that they are interested in your words, but they're not. Usually, they're interested in harnessing your addiction to their words, but that's a trade-off any good addict can live with. The best way to break into television is to write for a series. The reason is that series demand plenty of material, fodder. When they're doing 22 shows a season, even television's most highly paid word junkies can't think of them all, so they look for help. Generally, they look to other junkies they trust to deliver. Sometimes story editors owe other word junkies favours or they'd like to have other word junkies owe them a few. It's called survival. Word junkies hire other word junkies. It's a revolving door.

The trick is to get into the loop. The easiest way is to get a producer to go to bat for you. They do that for reasons of their own, many of them unfathomable and most of them you can't count on. It helps if you're related to them. Otherwise, it helps to be cool or good looking and sometimes it helps if you can write, but don't depend on that either. Although most producers read, the vast majority of them read within strictly proscribed boundaries of personal taste. If they're successful they generally like to read more and more of what they think made them so. If they aren't successful, why are you bothering with them? Let them figure it out first.

The first obligation of the word junkies is to know thyself. Despite what you think of yourself and your writing, you probably won't be equally good at everything. A few funny lines do not a comedy writer make. Likewise, being adept at writing a car chase does not make you a dramatist. To survive you must know what you've got to hock, then go out and hock it.

All of this presumes that you are addicted enough to have written a script. If you haven't, maybe now's the time you should seriously consider an alternative career, perhaps selling insurance. There are plenty of reasons why you shouldn't write something: it takes too long, you're not sure of the subject, you're not sure of your talent, you're not sure if it'll sell. All of these reasons are perfectly acceptable if you want to bail out of this profession.

There is only one reason to write ... the addiction. So, if you haven't written anything that you can show around, forget strategizing, and go write it.

Giving you the benefit of the doubt, let's say you've got three or four sample scripts to choose from. Of course they all stink — that's why you call them samples. But among those four, there must be one that you feel at least a little bit better about than the others. If not, throw them down the stairs and see which one goes the farthest. That's your sample script. That's the work you're going to stake your reputation as as word junkie on ... today.

Print up a nice clean copy of your sample script then sit down and watch some television and try to figure out which of the shows you see, best fits what you've written. If you've written a western, first try to find a western that's like yours. If there aren't any around, try to find a show that has about the same tone and sensibilities as the western you've written. That means if you've used a lot four-letter words, avoid shows that run in the family hours.

After you've targeted a show that seems appropriate, make contact. There are many ways to do this, but your objective is to make an impression on somebody who has something to say on the show you've selected. That is, someone who has the power to hire you. Producers are preferable to grips, gaffers or wardrobe mistresses.

Parties are always good because that's where producers surface looking for fresh meat. Introduce yourself to the producer but don't talk about yourself or your work. Listen to him or her to see what he's made of; it won't take long. Look for an appropriate place in the conversation to mention your addiction. If he's in the market for words, he'll probably bite. You can judge the degree of his or her desperation by just how quickly he makes his move. If he offers you his card immediately, watch out. This is a producer who has a crew booked for next week but doesn't have a script to shoot. Not very likely. More probably, a producer will listen to you spin out a few lines about your script before he tells you he needs a drink. Don't get discouraged. Producers get hit on more than lonely, busty blondes or hairy-chested hunks. They use their disinterest like armour. Furthermore, he's probably more interested in finding some way to forget his immediate problems than listening to your pitch. Don't get discouraged.

The well-practised word junkie can make a single idea last a long time, but like trout fishing, it's always wiser to have a few fresh flies tied. You never know what they're biting on that day.

Sometimes the producer will suggest that you talk to his story editor.

This is either a brush-off or an invitation to the dance, which is exactly where you want to be anyway. Story editors are the ultimate word junkies. They are people who are paid incredible amounts of money to sink into the swamp of a series up to their eyeballs. No matter what anybody tells you, a good story editor runs the show. The best story editors don't do it just for the money either. They do it because they love the words and in series television, words are power. To the story editor, a good script is like a bomb, ticking away secretly until it hits the floor where it explodes, knocking all those who doubted his words off their feet. That doesn't happen very often, but as a thoroughly hooked word junkie, the story editor will put up with a lot of duds in the hope of having one or two set-clearers per season.

Good story editors are always looking for good ideas or more accurately, ideas they can use and work with. Television series gobble up mountains of material but comparatively little of it makes the screen. Every week there are new parameters to be met: the star can't shoot for three days, the set's not ready, the budget has been chopped, the union needs a longer lunch to make turnaround or the actress the producer hired can't do a Russian accent but he thinks she can pass Transylvanian. All of these problems must be accounted for and explained away stylishly in the script. This is where the story editor earns his money, making the irrational process of series production into a cohesive seamless construct that will draw 'em into the tent once a week.

All this means that the story editor is more than willing to talk with anybody that can help him out. As we mentioned earlier, more than likely he will turn to people he's worked with before because the last thing he needs is a rookie in there when he's down two runs with two men on and two outs in the bottom of the ninth. This is the only game where the whole season is played like the bottom of the ninth.

If the producer has sent you to the story editor, you better be damn good or a relative. Generally the producer is slightly out of the loop when it comes to the story department. He has other priorities and his suggestions are usually taken with a large grain of salt. The other way to reach the story editor is by your own devices, but they better be good. The story editor's time is at a premium. He doesn't answer his phone messages quickly and doesn't see anyone unless they have an appointment scheduled well in advance. Even then he's usually late. To reach him you had better be damned determined and have some very snappy patter ready to catch his attention. If he calls back, hit him with your best shot, but remember he's looking for an idea he can use tomorrow. He doesn't care about your life history unless you can tell him something he doesn't already know and can use, like yesterday you won an Emmy or an Oscar.

Let's say you're lucky and based on your snappy patter the story editor wants to see your stuff. Send him down your best sample then hope and pray he likes it. If you send him a copy of a spec script you've written for his show, be prepared for the worst. No matter how closely you watch a show, chances are ten to one you can't write something he'll be interested in producing. There are two reasons for this. First, the story editor spends his waking and sleeping hours trying to dream up new ideas for next week's episode. That what he's paid for. Chances are he's either thought of your idea already and shot it or had it rejected. Second, a working television series is like a rain-gorged river. It's constantly slipping its banks and flooding everything in its path. It's unpredictable and anything you think you know about the show can be changed according to the producer or network's whim in a nanosecond. The point is, you can't really know a show from the outside. So your best shot for getting work is to hope that the story editor likes the way you write or, better, he likes the way you think. Good thinking is what he needs most. Good writing or more accurately rewriting is something he does every day.

If you have a script that demonstrates competent writing and good thinking regardless of its subject matter, chances are the sharp story editor will spot it and give you a call. If he asks to have a meeting with you, he probably wants to see if you have any ideas he hasn't thought of or if you can mesh with an idea he has thought of. Here's your shot. Don't blow it. The story editor will generally give you some time to do research on his show. You can gauge how desperate he is by how long he gives you. A week is normal. An hour means he's in big, big trouble.

After you agree on time, ask the story editor for a series bible. The bible is the ideal description of the show and the original concept for the characters. If nothing else, this question will show that you know something about the business. Don't be surprised if the story editor tells you that things have changed since the bible was written. Ask for cut-lines for previously produced shows. Cut-lines are two or three sentence descriptions written after the show's been shot and before it goes to air. In 25 words or less, the cut-lines will tell you what ideas have already been used. Study them carefully, then avoid them like the plague. The last thing a story editor wants to hear is an idea that's anything like one that he's already shot.

Now, sit down and think up a few ideas you can pitch to the story editor. Three are generally not enough. More than ten are probably too many.

Remember, at your meeting you'll probably be sitting in a grotty office with telephones ringing and people barging in to ask the story editor questions as you try to pitch him your ideas. So your first line is everything. Give him something he can see quickly and easily. If his eyes light up, follow it up and keep talking with all the animation and excitement you can muster until he butts in, then shut up. The objective is to try to engage the story editor in lively repartee. What you want most of all is to have him start to contribute ideas to your concept, then you have something. You have commitment, maybe. It's called sharing the blame. If he has a stake or perceives he has a stake in your idea, it means he might be able to sell it to his producer, which is good. Participation rarely happens with the first story you pitch. It's more likely that you'll have to go to a second or third idea. If you still don't have any signals from him after your fourth or fifth idea, pull out all the stops because at this point you have nothing to lose. After your sixth or seventh idea flop, you have two options: pluck something out of thin air and hope for the best or ask to use the washroom. Maybe you can think of something on the way there or back.

Let's say that you come up with something. Inevitably it will be a mish mash of your ideas and the story editor's. Don't try to determine who did what to whom. Just be grateful that you're walking out with something. The story editor will probably ask you to write it up. This means he wants one page that demonstrates that not only your ideas worked, but that his did too. Remember, the name of the game is share the blame. He wants something that he can sell and he probably knows better than you do exactly what that is. Besides, he's the one who is going to have to pitch this idea to the producer, so he'd better be comfortable with it. Listen to what he says and then do it. This isn't the time to ask for money. Be grateful for a shot. Think about the pleasurable hours you'll get to spend at the computer running the words back and forth across the screen. You're on your way to becoming a professional word junkie. God help you.

The Nuts And Bolts

The fundamental rule of survival for any writer is to write. If you're a professional screenwriter, the fundamental rule makes a further demand — write something that will sell and get produced. You can get a producer, a network or a studio excited about your idea, but at the end of the day, you have to sit down and write it. If you can't do that, you've got big trouble. You've made a promise you can't fulfil.

Which gets us back to the dilemma of the would-be word junkie. You *know* you can write, but you haven't got any real concrete proof for it. You haven't got a script to show anyone. You have great ideas but nothing down on paper. Not to worry. Everyone has to start somewhere. Maybe this book will give you the encouragement or the prod to turn those great ideas into a finished teleplay or screenplay.

While there's no guarantee that writing your screenplay is going to make you a successful writer, there's no real mystery to writing a screenplay. All it takes is an understanding of craft, a little talent, time and energy.

Craft is the nuts and bolts of writing. It's the know-how, the writer's equivalent of being a master carpenter. If you know craft, you know the techniques necessary to build your house. You know how to make a simple joint and you know how to create a structure that will support all your characters and your story. And you know how to do it with flair and style. Craft is something you can learn, and must learn if you hope to write a screenplay that's going to fly.

You can start learning about craft from a book, from reading and studying other screenplays, from writing courses — but most of all, craft is something you learn from practice. Simply, the best way to learn the craft of writing is to write.

John Keats, arguably the finest poet in the English language, set himself a goal to be as great a writer as Shakespeare. He consciously decided to aim for the top. Problem was, this being said, he had no idea how to do it. He had already written some poems and verses, but nothing yet that satisfied him, or allowed him to call himself a poet. So he sat down and wrote a long poem. The result was "Endymion." The poem is not perfect, but it does contain some of the finest and most memorable passages in the English language. Most important, however, is that by the time Keats finished writing the four thousand or so lines of "Endymion," he had not only learned a lot about the craft of writing poetry, he had also figured out his own style and was able to go on to write such magnificent poems as "Ode on Melancholy" and "La Belle Dame Sans Merci."

Of course, besides his craft, John Keats also happened to have a wonderful talent for writing. But without learning his craft, this talent would never have been realized. Raw talent is terrific; it's a great thing to have to impress your friends and relatives. But, raw talent alone will soon get tiresome. Challenge your talent, learn your craft and find your own style. In the end, the only true way to do this is to sit down and write.

A major hindrance to surviving as a writer is time. How many would-be writers have said that if only they had the time, they would sit down and write the great novel or the blockbuster movie of all time. Well, that may be the case, but it's not going to happen until and unless you actually sit down and chisel out a block of time which you are going to devote solely to writing your screenplay. If you need to, scribble your writing times on your calendar and check off each time slot that you sit chained to your keyboard. At the very least, you'll have an interesting looking calendar. Don't be afraid to use any trick you can think of that will keep you focused and writing for the allotted period of time. Until you can survive sitting at your keyboard, you're not going to survive as a writer.

You may have time, but if you have no energy, then you're back at square one. Writing is work. Treat it that way. Writing takes as much rigorous effort as any job, sometimes more. If you're going to be a professional writer, then you're going to have to find a way to dispel the million things that will sap your creative energy. Interestingly enough, one of the most effective ways a writer has to focus energy is simply to start writing down words. Words build on words and before you realize it, you've filled up a few pages. Characters that you create start using your words to talk to each other and pretty soon you might not be able to shut them up. You've forgotten about those million distractions and worries because the words are pushing them aside. The words are giving you energy. It's like exercising your body. You feel drained and the last thing you feel like doing is swimming 100 laps. But you force yourself into the water. The first lap is tiresome, but the water has woken you up a bit. A few laps later you have forgotten you didn't have any energy. By the time you're finished with your laps you have more energy than when you first dove in. And you feel a sense of accomplishment. Writing is like that. You've got to get into the habit of diving in and writing down words no matter how cold or drained you might feel. That's the job of writing. You've made the time; you've forced yourself to focus your energy. You're ready to exercise your craft and allow your talent to kick into gear.

The question now becomes what are you going to write about. The answer is that really it doesn't matter. Write anything that interests you. Just try to tell an interesting story about interesting characters. Start writing down the words until they fill up the right number of pages. Once you're finished and the script rolls off your printer page after page, you finally have concrete proof that you're a screenwriter. If the screenplay works, you've got a property you can put on the market. If it doesn't work, you go on to write your next screenplay, carrying with you lessons that you could only have learned by writing the first script. And remember, since you've survived writing your first script, chances are good you just might survive writing the next one.

If your most important concern at this point is to start working on your next screenplay, you've become the word junkie you always thought you were. You have a sample script. You have a sense of craft. Now you can go out and sell yourself, script in hand and new ideas in mind. You can call yourself a writer. Surviving as a professional writer simply means that you keep writing and you keep pitching your ideas and your work until somebody bites. There are no guarantees, but there never are when survival is at stake. All we can ever do is give it our best shot. Good luck.

13

SCREENWRITING RELATIONSHIPS: REFLECTIONS ON THE Collaborative Process

A Producer's Relationship to the Writer

by Peter O'Brian

Peter O'Brian is president of Independent Pictures Inc. He produced Phillip Borsos' The Grey Fox, which won the 1983 Genie for Best Picture and was nominated for a Golden Globe Award for Best Foreign film; Sandy Wilson's My American Cousin, which won the 1986 Genie for Best Picture and the 1985 International Critic's Award at the Toronto International Film Festival; Disney's One Magic Christmas by Philip Borsos; Gordon Pinsent's John and the Missus; Milk and Honey, John Palmer's Me, Rex Bromfield's Love at First Sight, Richard Benner's Outrageous! (Associate Producer), Paul Lynch's Blood and Guts and David Cronenberg's Fast Company. His most recent production was Phillip Borsos' last film Far From Home: The Adventures of Yellow Dog, which was released by Twentieth Century Fox in 1995. Peter O'Brian was a founding board member of the Canadian Film Centre and was executive director from 1988-1991. He is a member of the Board of Directors of the Centre's Feature Film Project and the Toronto International Film Festival/Cinemateque Ontario.

It may be obvious, but it's worth repeating: the screenplay is everything. The theatrical feature film audience experiences the film story through the actor's interpretations and the director's realization of the screenplay. The producer organizes and finances, packages and markets a film based on the rights to a story in the form of a screenplay.

An excellent screenplay is likely to get produced. The daunting statistics of one in a hundred produced should be ignored because quality is not taken into consideration. My estimate is that at least one in three top-quality screenplays makes it all the way to the screen. The other two that never get made may be perceived as too controversial, too dark, too expensive, too dated, too esoteric or simply "burned out," but these conditions are not necessarily permanent and a good screenplay is always valuable. The screenplay is first and foremost.

In a collaborative medium, involving both art and commerce, however, the writer of the screenplay cannot be first and foremost and does not necessarily carry into production the same importance as the screenplay itself. Cinema is the only situation in dramatic writing in which the work is not the final product. The screenwriter has a seat at the table with the director and the producer, but usually as the lesser of equals. The reason for this is that theatrical feature films are capitalized at huge cost. The producer and director must bring the product into being and deliver it to commercial interests. They are empowered and obligated to do so.

In my experience the screenplays that have made it to the screen and have worked out best as feature films, are those which were presented by a director and screenwriter team with an ongoing working relationship. Sometimes on the tundra of independent Canadian cinema such a partnership is a matter of practical necessity. At best, the director/writer team gets good films made; at the least, it gets more films made. First, the team approach is more powerful and appealing than the solo overture, and second, the business people get a much clearer idea of what the product will be. To make my point, in the last twenty years I have received from solo screenwriters about a thousand screenplays for review. Of these, none were made. Another thousand came to me from director/writer teams (or directors with their own scripts). In my opinion, over 30 of these screenplays were excellent and suitable for production. Eleven were subsequently produced — about one in three.

Also, the team has the potential for greater productivity. The screenwriter as the director's creative collaborator can make important contributions during preparation, production and editing. John Hunter did this for Phillip Borsos in *The Grey Fox*, and Don McKellar does it on Bruce McDonald's films, to name two examples. And while working together on a film, they discuss and prepare future projects.

My recommendation to screenwriters who write in the theatrical form is to connect with a compatible director and then approach producers with the project. Easier said than done? Definitely, but worth the struggle. In the end what is most important to screenwriters, and to all of us for that matter, is that their work gets on the screen where it can entertain and move an audience.

Canadian screenwriting can fall into a creative no-man's land which dooms it to the "unproduced" file. The powerful presence of the American cinema sometimes inspires our writers to either resist it to the extent of creating interior characters and passive stories, or to embrace it to the point of producing bogus facsimiles. In the first case I see our Canadian aversion to fictional heroes or the glorification of our historical characters as a limiting factor in achieving success in popular cinema. Nonetheless, our writers do their best work when they put aside the angst of deliberately inventing personal or national style and trust that the defining characteristics of style will naturally arise from their own talent and the contexts of their own lives.

The Importance of Understanding Story
by Christine Shipton

As vice-president, Creative Affairs (TV) for Alliance Communications, Christine supervises and coordinates creative development of Alliance television projects including co-productions for domestic and international markets and oversees all submissions and pitches. Christine was executive producer on The Diana Kilmury Story and Supervising Producer on Straight Up and Taking the Falls and is current executive on "Due South" and "North of 60." Prior to joining Alliance she was CBC executive in charge of production for TV Dramatic Series; she was the network liaison for all aspects of production and creative development of dramatic series such as "North of 60," "Street Legal," "Urban Angel," "Raccoons," and "Inside Stories." Christine also worked as executive story editor on "Street Legal," second season. During her first six years at CBC, she was casting director for TV Drama. Preceding her career in television, Christine had a ten-year background in theatre administration, production management and public relations.

I have the greatest respect for television writers and the work that they do. I also love working with them. I say this because I do not think that this is always the case with producers, network executives and even creative executives. We all know we need writers. "It all starts from a great script" is quoted endlessly. We recognize the process involved, but in terms of liking, or even accepting the actual time and patience it takes for the creative writing process? I wonder.

In television, there are times when we must work quickly. Network pickups and big money are usually at stake. Network executives have put their necks out with their bosses, producers only have a short window in the calendar year for financing and shooting, and creative executives are at their wit's end "communicating" with the writer. Meetings with writers can become the centre of this storm where all the tensions of all elements of production zero right in. Frustrations mount. Feelings of impatience rise. Thoughts such as "Why can't they just write it?!" and "It's so obvious!" surface. Respect and understanding get thrown out the window. Individual agendas from all parties start to surface. The focus is getting lost. The writer has by now decided that all these people and their notes have ruined his or her script. The story that everyone supposedly agreed upon has become blurred.

As a creative executive for a large production studio, I interact with each of these groups and often find myself caught in the middle. I find I need to wear different hats in all phases of development and throughout pre-production of a project. There are meetings when I must protect and speak on behalf of the writer and his vision. There are meetings when seemingly idiotic but necessary network notes must be addressed; and meetings when it is just me and the writer struggling through. I enjoy being in the middle, however. It challenges me to attempt to see that all the various needs are met without too much compromise on anyone's part. It can become a political nightmare at times, but well worth it if a true collaborative vision comes through at the end. Where it becomes difficult is when you are midway through the process and discover that different people (producer, director, writer, etc.) have different ideas about what is being made. I don't mean different ideas being contributed along the way to enhance the project (art direction, music, etc.) — I mean a fundamental difference in the tone or story. Differences about the story itself, its central idea. This can be a bit scary.

Let me use an example. The genre of romance is tricky because it can be very subjective — whether it be for television or feature film. Many of us have different ideas about what constitutes romance. Men and women approach it so differently. The telling of a romantic story can be easily swayed by attitudes and tone. I discovered this when working on a series of two-hour romance television scripts. We had female and male writers working on the scripts, and the difference was amazing. The language, the approach to character, the need for "action" versus "feelings" were very different. Added to all that was the input from executives who felt that romance meant sex. When all parties involved read the first drafts, their diametrically opposed notes started coming in to us. We arrived at a point where we needed to have a serious meeting of minds about the direction of these scripts. It wasn't enough to say they were romantic love stories. We had to look at who we were making them for, what the market was, and we had to ask ourselves, does romance equal sex? The writers of course got caught in the middle of all this. We realized, as we focused on these concerns, that as talented as some of the writers were, some were not right for the project.

In the case of the romance movies, the project was dictating which particular writer we'd go with. This often happens when dealing with properties or stories that require adaptation. These projects are market-driven, of course. Someone has decided that people want to watch this on TV. But there still exists the need for television that requires the writer's voice. Television has matured enough to allow the writer to now be a producer and this is giving us television that has a vision at its core. Even then, however, visions can get skewed. Projects can lose their focus.

A great idea, of course, starts with the writer. If I like the project that is being presented whether it be a series or a movie, I take a lot of time to ensure that my understanding is the same as the writer's. This is a critical stage and often skipped over. It is so easy to allow your brain to go off in one particular direction upon hearing an idea. I have suffered from it myself. A writer/producer once sent me a three-page series concept about a young female rookie cop in a tough downtown neighbourhood. I had been looking for something like this. I knew of a broadcaster who had said they wanted young female protagonists. The writer and I met. I raved about the possibilities for this concept — a woman in a man's world, tough urban issues, problems of promotions through the ranks, dating problems as a cop, family ghosts she was running from, etc. The writer looked at me blankly. This actually wasn't what he'd been thinking at all. In his mind she was a good cop who did tricky and in-depth detective work, and solved fascinating cases. Oops, different wavelength, different series. We talked more. "I guess I could take it more into what you're talking about" says he, "But I just wanted to do a series about good police work, how they catch those bad guys." This in itself is a credible concept to have, not perhaps one I would want to go to the wall for, but real and very direct.

I then needed to decide if I wanted to get behind this vision — not mine, his. Whether I did or not, was in fact irrelevant at this time. The key issue at this point was that we discovered our different expectations at this early stage.

This example could be applied to television movies as well. It is critical that right from the beginning I truly understand the story that the writer wants to tell. Right from the start I need to be clear about the writer's intention because it can so easily veer off a few degrees, and this blurring of focus will invariably come back to haunt us.

Let's say the executive comes back to the writer and says, "Great. The network wants to talk to you about your series. They love your idea. I knew your interest was in telling good police stories, so I knew you wouldn't mind making it two cops. More of a buddy series."

Is it at this point that the writer admits that besides the good police story angle, he really wanted to explore the loneliness of an individual detective struggling through the gory and dark puzzles of police work? Does the writer confess that the notion of the cop having no one to share her thoughts with drives a good portion of the subtext of his series? He'd better, or we would all be poised to travel down one messy road where viewpoint and intention become confused. And once again I say, that it will come back to haunt us all. Now, this doesn't mean that adjustments can't be made. We all want to work, right? But, unless this change in direction is clarified and agreed upon at the outset, we can't help each other.

Working with writers, for me, is about helping them tell their stories in the best possible way. It's about challenging them to work harder to dig deeper into their characters, to get the emotion on the page. It's also about standing behind what it is they want to say and to a certain degree keeping some of the cruelty of the business at bay. It's about keeping a clear path and alerting us all when we veer off that path.

Creative Collaboration at Work

by Daniel Petrie

Daniel Petrie *has directed more than 30 feature films and films for television. His features include* Lassie, Cocoon: The Return, Rocket Gibraltar, Square Dance, The Bay Boy, *for which he won six Genie Awards including Best Picture and Best Screenplay. He also directed* Fort Apache – The Bronx, Resurrection, The Spy with a Cold Nose, Lifeguard *and others. For* A Raisin in the Sun *he received a Special Award at the Cannes Film Festival. He received an Emmy nomination for Best Direction an Emmy Award and Cableace Award for Best Children's Program* "Mark Twain and Me", *received an Emmy nomination for* A Town Torn Apart *and* My Name is Bill W *and numerous other nominations and awards. Daniel Petrie is currently Chair of the Center for Advanced Film and Television Studies at the American Film Institute.*

The writer James Costigan and I had a very close collaboration on *Eleanor and Franklin*. But that doesn't mean we invaded each other's territory. He didn't direct, he wrote. I didn't write, I directed. He was on the set 75 per cent of the time. If the actors got the words wrong, he'd whisper into the ear of the script supervisor who'd then very diplomatically approach the actor and point out the *exact* phrasing. Once, when Costigan wasn't around, Ed Herrman juxtaposed two and when we rolled the dailies, James was upset. The line was, "You two *really are* a pair, aren't you?" Ed had said "You two *are really a* pair, aren't you?" "Oh come on, " I said to Costigan, "it's the same thing." "No" Costigan said, "*Really are* is more arch!" Even while exasperated at his hair-splitting, I nonetheless admired his precision — his insistence on *le mot juste*.

On another occasion we were setting up a ballroom scene. Teddy Roosevelt, Eleanor's uncle, had persuaded the sixteen-year-old Eleanor to come downstairs to where the dance was being held. The camera was to follow Teddy and Eleanor to the dance floor where they began to waltz. Mrs. Teddy R. noticed this and signalled the seventeen-year-old Franklin to join her — she whispered in his ear and pointed to her husband and young Eleanor. Franklin nods in agreement, crosses to the dance floor and taps Teddy on the shoulder. Teddy stops dancing, bows, and hands his niece over to Franklin. Franklin and Eleanor dance a few moments until Eleanor says, "Please, let's stop."

In other words, a fairly long scene without dialogue. All in dumb show. I went to Costigan. "Jimmy, I can pump up the music here but it seems unnatural that the usually garrulous Teddy says nothing, just bows, when Franklin cuts in. Can you come up with something?" Costigan thought a moment and said, "Can you give me fifteen minutes?" "Of course." I vamped, rehearsing the camera move, the placement of extras.

In less than fifteen, Costigan was back. At the point where Franklin, at the urging of Mrs. Teddy approached the dancers and taps Teddy on the shoulder, Costigan added this:

FRANKLIN
May I cut in?

TEDDY
(a broad smile)
Said the tailor to the morning coat!

FRANKLIN
And what did the morning coat say?

TEDDY
Cut away! Cut away!

FRANKLIN
(laughing)
I love it. (to Eleanor) Don't you love it!

AND HE SWEEPS HER UP AND DANCES AWAY.

It may not seem much but I was very pleased. It was funny, true to the period and a lovely evocation of Teddy's spirit.

It's a tiny example of the creative process of collaboration at work. In every step of the way from idea to finished screenplay, I continually challenge the writer to surprise, enthrall, delight me. Sometimes I have specific notions of just how they can improve the text, but at other times, my ideas are too subtle or unformed to articulate so I fall back on the letters, "CBB." That stands for Could be Better. You'd be surprised how effective that vague request can be.

Reflections on Working at Telefilm

Elke Town
Elke Town is creative head of Independent Productions for TV Ontario and is an active consultant and advisor in the film and television industry. Prior to joining TVO, she was manager of Creative Affairs for the Toronto office of Telefilm Canada. She was responsible for the creative evaluation of all production and development projects in both the Feature Film and Broadcast Funds. She moved to Telefilm Canada from a well-established career in the visual arts as a curator, critic, editor and arts consultant. Town has recently formed her own production, Carnelian Films.

I am recalling working at Telefilm in the first person. At Telefilm there is only "we" — everyone involved in making the decision about what films and television shows would get made. I was never alone. As an analyst, I went into the meetings with the head of the department; as the head of the Creative Affairs department, I was never without the analyst. We also had our coverage at hand, the "cold" read from a freelance reader who had no idea who was attached to the film or what was the anticipated budget. All we were looking for was a good script, a good team and a good deal. We wanted the comfort to make a leap of faith. The Creative Affairs department at Telefilm no longer exists although the work of analysing scripts continues.

I spent more than half of my time at Telefilm with scripts for feature films. Given that the Toronto office could finance only five or six features a year, the bulk of scripts were in one phase or another of development. I knew writers longed for their screenplay to be the next hot movie, the one that both critics and moviegoers would be talking about, the one that would also made a tidy — maybe even obscene — amount at the box office. I know I shared this common desire that may more accurately be described as a compelling fantasy. It lays bare the enduring gap between intention and realization, between script and movie, between what we want and what we get. Writers don't always get the movie they think they have written and investors do not always get the movie they imagined the script would make. Yet, this is a fantasy we can all secretly buy into, a fantasy in which everyone disregards the odds, ignores the hundreds of projects that languish in development, and forgets the many movies that die a quiet box office death, scorned by critics and the public alike.

The writer's relationship to Telefilm is once removed. More often than not, the writer is contracted to the production company to write screenplay X. Whatever the relationship of the writer to the producer and director — and in more than a few cases they are the same — the producer is the one who is trying to hoist screenplay X from the page to the screen by convincing not just Telefilm but any number of investors that they will see some return on their money. A good producer has many means of extracting money from investors but the principal one is the script. From very early on, everyone is asking: Is this a good idea for a movie? Can it be made for the proposed budget? Can it get financed? We have to assume that the producer likes the script and thinks it's both makeable and financeable. The budget question can be resolved by an analysis that balances the demands of the script against line items of the budget. In the triad of script, budget and financing, the writer and producer are at each other's mercy; both must have the ability to see the movie and the credibility to instill confidence. In the end it is the writer's job to help ease the producer into that special place where investors gladly part with their money.

I spent my happiest Telefilm days in a small office reading and analysing scripts. In the five and a half years I was there, I read hundreds of scripts in varying stages of development from outlines to production-ready drafts. My process of reading and analysis was pretty straightforward. I like to read scripts held together by one long brass-head fastener secured in the upper left-hand corner. Then, I need to know the precise length of the screenplay and, true to stereotype, I flip to the last page. It helps if the page numbers are in the upper right-hand corner. A length of somewhere around 100 pages bespeaks a potential economy of writing and knowledge of scriptwriting fundamentals. I approach screenplays that ran over 130 pages with dread. In the end, however, the page count matters little. It's just as easy in a short screenplay as in a long one to get stuck on page 30 with the horrible feeling of reading the same page over and over again with time at a dead standstill.

Occasionally after reading a script I felt like I had actually seen the movie that script would make. I was seduced into the unique world of the screenplay, I believed everything, I doubted nothing. The story worked, the characters lived and breathed and I felt something for them because I knew them. Mostly, however, I had to ask myself pretty ordinary questions like: What is this script about? Can this script make a movie that people will want to watch? Who are these characters and why are they behaving this way? Will anybody care about them? If they are intentional caricatures will the audience get it and find them funny? Sometimes I didn't know what I thought of a script until I was writing an analysis, until I had taken the bits apart and tried to make them fit back together again.

It goes without saying that it is the writer's job to establish a point of view and to seamlessly direct and redirect the reader's attention. In any script, the writer is intangibly present and is revealed on every page. The reader intuits this presence in a way that inextricably shapes the reader's response. What the writer knows, thinks and feels about the subject matter and the characters is there. Whether the writer believes in the story is there. One false move, one thinly disguised contrivance and the writer blows her cover. Cynicism and insincerity can be detected as easily as can genuine passion and empathy.

Next to reading the script, the most important part of the work was meetings with the writer and the producer. It wasn't always easy to tell what the writer had in mind, particularly if I had already been told by the writer or producer that the script would have the feel of such and such existing movie and the look of another. This referencing of other films is a double-edged sword. it indicates that the writer obviously has a good sense of what movies are all about and it can lead to a lively discussion about memorable scenes, great lines and fascinating characters. On the other hand, it can also be the give-away card that lets me know everyone is dreaming. It suggests the writer and producer have little sense of the value of the package on the table — usually a small film, often a first-time director, and a script that might never even make it to the next stage of development no matter what promising actor would play the lead.

I found these meetings terrifying. They are indeed a fragile construct. The screenplay had after all not written itself and hence ego and creative sensibilities were much at play. I know that writers must believe unconditionally that their scripts will make good movies — they have to. Yet, there is nothing more disconcerting than a meeting in which it appears that the key players have not spoken to each other in some time and in which the writer is as surprised as I am to hear the producer's version of the film. Under such circumstances, I often fluctuated between being a loyal fan and a hard-nosed professional with my allegiances shifting where they appeared to be most needed.

I was also always nervous about what kind of person the writer would be even thought I like talking to writers about their scripts. Usually I worried that I might have misread the script: I would therefore offend the writer as well as feel like a complete idiot. I worried I would be too inarticulate, resistant, impatient, obsequious, ungracious or hostile when, more often than not, I wanted simply to convey to the writer that I had read the script with great attention to all its details. I worried though that the writer might start speaking about the three-act structure of the script, a way of constructing and analysing scripts that I am simply unable, or unwilling, to grasp. Would the writer see my comments and criticism as helpful and constructive or as an attack, an affront? We, Telefilm, were after all the obstacle between the script and the first day of principal photography. This meeting was either Act One or curtains.

Sometimes, I had a genuine rapport with the writer. I then worked more closely with the writer and felt truly in my element. These meetings had more the nature of a dialogue in which the writer and I both knew and liked the subject under discussion. The writer was even more receptive to my comments if I was able to focus on precisely those places in the script where the writer was still in doubt. Likewise, the writer deepened my understanding of character and plot by directing my attention to the intricacies of the script's construction, to the careful positioning of scenes, to the resonance from one scene to the next. The writer let me take pleasure in the characters, in their motivation and story. Then, attentive and engaged in the task of fine-tuning, I was involved in the script's intellectual and emotional beats. I could feel the heat of the story beating and agree upon its manner of telling.

Some scripts improve through subsequent drafts; others go astray. More often than not I found the problems to be remarkably consistent, evident in script after script. Here is a random sampling of what can go wrong:

- the idea is not strong enough
- the characters are at the mercy of the plot
- the characters have attributes and personality but no depth and are hence interchangeable
- the characters are in the service of an idea or ideal
- the characters appear to come out of nowhere, having no history, no life before the script
- the writer is disdainful of the characters

Easy fixes are hard to come by and with problems such as these it is inevitable that in the translation of the script from the page to the screen the gap between intention and realization widens even further.

Equally problematic were the intensely detailed scripts written by remarkably literate writers who described every camera angle, every set, every costume, every facial nuance and every thought that went through the characters' minds. With such a script, what would be the role of the actors, the DOP, the art director, the costume designer and the director? Finally, there were the deeply flawed scripts which the writer and producer were convinced would be saved by brilliant directing and casting.

I learned many hard lessons repeatedly. Not the least of these was the mistake of reading a subtext into a script that I later learned was not there. I believed this subtext — character motivation and theme — would be revealed through the minutiae of the characters' actions. More often than not I found I had projected my own intentions and wishes for the characters on the script. Intentions and wishes, however, fade on the large screen where bold literalness generally takes precedence over the grammar of the interior life. Subtlety is not one of film's stellar qualities — nuance, looks and small actions pass without notice. An equally painful lesson was not trusting the writer's or my own instincts. Often first drafts were the best and no amount of refinement or nit-picking in the guise of helpful criticism could bring back the freshness of the first draft.

Inevitably, I suffered the condescension of writers and producers who believed in the superiority of their talent and passion, their unique vision and were immune to any criticism. I have also been with writers who became defensive if not showered with praise. Worst of all were writers who suffered being in the same room with others infinitely beneath them because it was the necessary evil for getting their brilliant work on the screen. They were usually accompanied by producers who believed that Telefilm investment was their due because it was the public purse. They saw me as a minion and wage slave, a wretched bureaucrat barely worthy of their contempt. I wished on them the fate that befalls the screenwriter in a short story I once heard Martin Amis read at Harbourfront. In Amis's story, fortune turns the tables on writers. The highest-paid, most sought-after and pampered writer in all the world is the poet. All of Hollywood is clamouring for his latest opus, "Sonnet." The impoverished screenwriter, on the other hand, is desperately attempting to get any one of his hundreds of screenplays published by ever less significant small presses and he spends all of his time in meetings with publishers in dingy cafes. I believe there are writers who would wish upon me an equally delicious fate.

Telefilm's creative affairs department's job was to make recommendations — yes or no — based primarily on the script, taking into account the budget, the team, the cast, the distribution plans, recoupment and so forth. Sometimes the recommendations of the creative department were adopted, sometimes not. I lost sleep over scripts I thought were hopeless that went ahead nonetheless. If a wonderfully engaging, critically successful movie emerged from a hopeless script, I was contrite, groveling and whimpering with praise. If the movie equaled the script in its ineptitude, I could feel a certain sense of "I told you so" coupled with the gloom of knowing that here was another Canadian movie that would fade mercilessly from view. Of course, I also lost sleep over scripts that I loved and championed that to my mortification became terrible movies.

In my second, sun-drenched Telefilm office with its panoramic vista of the Danforth, I often sat at a small round work table, a pile of scripts in varying stages of development at my elbow. A small cactus sat on the windowsill. This cactus seemed a fitting symbol of the scripts that never bloomed in spite of strong sunlight. Equally, it seemed a symbol of projects that thrived with only a modicum of nourishment. Whether the scripts became movies or not, my pleasure was in working to perfect the intricate details of narration, the nuances of character, and the apparently effortless suspension of disbelief.

The Writer and Me

Jana Veverka

As *a producer, writer and script consultant, Jana Veverka has over 200 hours of television drama to her credit, which cover a broad spectrum of subject matter and genres and include "Lonesome Dove — The Series," "Adventures of the Black Stallion," "Airwolf," "Bordertown," "Neon Rider," "Beachcombers," "The Campbells," and "Danger Bay." She has produced two Harlequin Romance moves of the week for CBS and is currently writing a feature film script based on the life of Emily Carr for Telescene, as well as developing her own projects.*

Early December. Morning. The phone rings …

ME
Uh …huh???

A.F.
(on phone)
Jana? Hi, how are you?
(long pause)
I hope it's not too early?

ANGLE ON BED

as I struggle through the layers of duvet and assorted covers to
sit up and pay attention.

ME
(brightly)
Of course not. How are you?

Husbands grunts something about crack of dawn and pads towards the
bathroom …another bright day dawning on the Wet Coast …

DISSOLVE TO:

A FEW MINUTES LATER

ME
Great. Mid-January, lots of time.
I'd love to do it. Sounds interesting … "The Writer in Me" … Good, ok.
Bye.

I hang up. I hope she didn't notice the slip ...

(I've been doing research for a feature film for the last few weeks and am preoccupied with the writer "in" me that unfortunately seems to be buried so deep I'm afraid it's in hibernation! This will give me an opportunity to reflect on the writing process and think about something else. Or so I hope.)

Like most writers I value a deadline. Mid-January, plenty of time, right?

I consider the following: I have spent as much time being a script consultant as I have a producer. I have written a number of scripts and know what it is like being on the receiving end of the producer's notes. Theoretically I should have a unique if not sensitive perspective on this topic ...piece of cake. I roll over.

FADE OUT:

AM I TALKING TO A WALL?

ACT ONE: Late December. I am starting to panic. It's after Christmas already! "The Writer *And* Me." Me — the producer. Is this even grammatically correct? *Fowler's Modern English Usage* informs me that it is.

Which writer? I start a list of the writers I have worked with over the years and when I get to 50 I take a rest. Are they Canadian? Okay, some of those I've worked with have been "non-Canadian Content" but most are "government agency" friendly. Most good, some bad; many more than once, a few never again. And then I think of the different relationship I have had with each and every one of them. I look up "relationship" in my handy dandy thesaurus; liaison, romance, intrigue; or rapport, communication, give-and-take; and even interdependence. Whew. I look longingly at my script.

The relationship between writer and producer is complicated and often turbulent. Part of the problem, it seems to me, stems from the fact that most writers rarely have the luxury of being able to pick and choose with whom they will work. A phone call will come out of the blue: "Would you like to pitch a story for 'West of Anywhere — The Series'? Experience with horses or guns preferable but not mandatory." Yesterday they were wondering if they'd ever work again, and today they're flipping through their parents' copies of Louis L'Amour paperbacks.

Except that it's not usually quite that serendipitous. Chances are more than good that I've either worked with that writer before, and therefore feel relatively confident that they will deliver a wonderful script for "West of Anywhere," or I've done my homework and read samples of the Unknown's work and checked references. The reverse isn't true though, is it? "Can you please tell me what your qualifications are for producing my script?" Well … that would be a first! In the hundreds of dramatic episodes I've commissioned, a writer has never turned down the job for any reason other than they are busy writing something else.

But it's still a tortuous dance that you engage in together. The writer occupies the moral high ground while the producer wields the power. It takes conscientious effort and a good character on either side not to take advantage. But then we're Canadians and generally pretty nice people. Yet even nice people have opposing points of view now and then. The difficulty is not so much in the choosing of the writer (or getting them approved if it's a network deal) but in the process of communicating to the writer the style and tone and humour that you'd like the story to convey. And then, having given the writer the go-ahead, their job is to somehow make the script their own.

Once that script is written the means of communicating suggestions and changes to the writer obviously vary with the personalities involved, but it's a general truism that everybody likes praise. Even producers. But even more than praise, writers need response. They stand alone against the onslaught of notes that arrive from the producer and story editor, they work alone, usually, and then they wait, alone. And while the script may be the single most important element of the movie or the series, it's not all the producer has to think about. And so this leads me to a rule I try to adhere to whenever possible: read the script as soon as you get it and then pick up the phone. As Frank Pierson, the author of *Cool Hand Luke* wrote: "Love me, hate me, kill me, anything. Just let me know it."

The second rule I've made for myself is to be as truthful as possible. As we all know, that's easier said than done, and so I add the qualifier "as possible." I recently chaired a panel called "Scenes From a Marriage: The relationship between the writer and the producer." The consensus of opinion of the panel, all writers and/or producers, was that indeed the relationship was like a marriage. Nothing good every comes from "lying' or cheatin'." And like any partnership, both members want to be treated as equals. And like adults. The writers on the panel couldn't understand why the producers had so much trouble giving them notes, while the producers wondered why the writers paid no attention to their notes in the first place.

Ultimately it comes down to trying to make your thoughts about the script as clear as possible, and the suggestions positive and as imaginative as you can. It's no good to ignore or prevaricate about the elements that don't work. Most of the time the writer will surprise you and you find that those things you didn't like, the writer wasn't happy with either. It should be a relationship which is sparked by creative intelligences, even though they are of different sorts.

Give and take. When to give the writer his head, when to push him into reaching deeper into himself, when to cajole, flatter, intimidate and threaten. Nicely of course. As I said, a turbulent relationship. And like the beginning of a love affair, it's treacherous ground. And like a good marriage, the rewards are usually worth it.

And what of all the other input that a producer has to sift through? Because of course I am not in this alone. There are always others who will have their say. The network. The executive producer. The director. The production executive. How much of their feedback should I pay attention to? How do I best interpret their notes to the writer? These notes vary from "make it better" to major structural changes to replacing a character for one reason or another. The producer is a conduit to the writer, and somehow has to make a coherency of the whole. If the network *really* wants to significantly modify the plot or change the lead character to a dog, whose job are you going to put on the line, yours or the writer's?

ACT TWO: Early January. I have an enormous amount of respect for writers; not the least because they have kept not only me, but thousands of industry workers employed. Over a martini lunch a few weeks ago (Do we need an excuse? It was Christmas!) I asked my friend, who also happens to be a writer (OK, I was doing a little research for this article) what epiphany-like moments we might have shared together. We reminisced for a few hours realizing that I probably had bought at least three-dozen scripts from him over the years. (A relationship worth preserving, I later thought.) His memory is better than mine, "Remember the time … " his eyes narrow as he looks at me, "when you called me at the last moment to rewrite a script saying you needed it the next morning? I happened to be in town for a meeting and didn't have my computer with me. The Selectric typewriter you so generously lent me broke and I had to borrow one from the hotel at two o'clock in the morning. The person in the next room pounded on the wall because of the noise the tapping keys made and so I typed that whole damned script on a pillow on my lap in bed!"

I never knew that. I did know that the script arrived in time and we shot it. However, what I also recall, were the "intense" discussions I had been having with the network about that script. It was the first of a two-parter which the network was adamantly set against. Ostensibly, their argument was that the episodes had to be able to be shown in any order which of course a two-parter precluded. The network wanted to be able to sell all their episodes irrespective of content and without regard to pre-emptions or other acts of fate. That of course is their prerogative. They were worried that audiences wouldn't hang around a week to find out what happened! A specious argument at best, and a total lack of regard for the audience at worst. But for the network it was only one episode out 105; for the writer it was the right and proper telling of the story, his story; for me it was the principle of the thing.

I've been known to dig my heels in and fight for what I believe in, but I think I also have a reputation for accommodating executives. In this instance I refused to give up and the network executive let it be known that it was on my head if the ratings dropped. They didn't. The episode was nominated for a Gemini. And my relationship with the writer as well as the network has continued.

Of the many crafts necessary for the creation of television and film, that of the screenwriter may be the most precarious and vulnerable. Everyone who can read the script usually has an opinion about it. And almost everyone who has an opinion thinks they could have done better. In their understandable desire to protect themselves, writers sometimes have a tendency to be isolationists. What they sometimes forget is that the script is ultimately meant to be seen, not read.

During one of the many episodes of horse dramas that I have produced I dragged a friend (another one) to the set. After watching the star struggling with a scene — he had to gallop up while delivering a particularly difficult line and then dismount — I called the director aside. Why not have the actor deliver the line after he dismounts? A relatively simple solution that we should have anticipated at script level. The scene was soon shot and the actor came over to where we were standing. He was obviously upset and no doubt embarrassed about his performance and the time it took to film. He proceeded to complain about the scene in particular and the story in general. My friend made a few astute remarks which surprisingly impressed the actor.

> ACTOR
> You're so right. That's exactly right. So, what do you do?

> FRIEND
> I'm …uhh, a writer, actually.

> ACTOR
> Then you know exactly what I'm talking about here. Jana, you should get this guy to write for us. (to friend) Do you ever write for series?

> FRIEND
> Actually, yes.

> ACTOR
> Damn. I wish you'd written this one.

> FRIEND
> I did.

The actor suddenly heard his cue and went back to work. My friend turned to me, "You should have told me that 'X' can't ride a horse and deliver dialogue at the same time. No wonder he's ruining the script. Can't you replace him?"

No I can't replace him, he's the star! But that was why I had brought the writer to the set. To see first-hand, what the process entailed. It does, after all, take two to tango. Or in the case of making movies, it takes many talents to put it all together. I had been trying to get the writer to understand why I had requested certain changes in the script. It's all too easy to look at the final cut, which is all a writer usually sees, and despair about the lack of fidelity to the script. Perhaps experiencing the knee-deep mud, lousy weather and unruly horses would change his perspective on long speeches. Or maybe not.

The story illustrates the fact that it is often incumbent upon the producer to make sure that the writer has as much information about the project as possible. The writer shouldn't just be part of the pre-production process, or development stage. Especially if you're working on a series and want to work with him or her again. It's not in anyone's best interest to keep the writer isolated from the production. The writer might have a good idea and be part of the solution.

After all, it's the script that brings everyone together on a project. The director, the actors, the art department the cameraperson are all interpreting various elements of the script. The script that the writer created. And even if all the words aren't his, or some of the characters have been rethought, or the director has changed the stage directions, it is the script that inspired all of this creative energy. Everyone wants to do their best. And it's this best that goes up on the screen. What most of us have come to realize of course is that this is the process of film-making, creative otherwise. And the final product, on the small or large screen, bears the mark of more than just the writer.

ACT THREE. The Deadline. I was recently in France where I happened to catch a number of old episodes of a series I produced which was a French co-production. In this one particular episode the French female lead was trying to talk the hero out of doing something foolish and he wasn't paying her any heed. She threw her hands into the air in a Gallic gesture and uttered the following line: "Am I talking to a wall?" It was obviously ad libbed. How could we have left a line like that in the script. I remember that we had killed ourselves laughing during dailies, and had intended to cut it. But I kept it in the various cuts and it ended up in the final.

It became a sort of shorthand during the rest of production, meaning …you're not listening to me, you stupid oaf! Well, there it was, on French TV, in French … translated literally. "Excuse me, is this a wall I'm addressing?" I laughed all over again. It sounded even funnier in French. I wondered what the French had made of it.

The trouble with this industry is that your sins as well as your successes follow you around for an awfully long time. It behooves us to play fair and do our best.

Over that same martini lunch before Christmas I regaled my friend with the story about the line, it had, after all, been his script. I laughed. He looked at me, a seriously dismayed expression on his face. "I wrote that line. If you happen to recall, the story was about illusion and reality and I rather thought the character should have an opportunity to express, unconsciously of course, her dilemma …"

I suddenly felt terrible. I took another quick sip of my drink, just in time to catch the twinkle in his eye. He grinned and ordered another round. And that's the beauty of it, the joy of working with writers. They always have another angle, another interpretation to give the story. I referred back to the list of relationships I had described a the beginning of this article — I had forgotten to include "surprising."

That's the way it is with writers … and producers.

FADE OUT

From the Market Places Of My Childhood

Danièle J. Suissa

Writer, director, producer, Danièle J. Suissa has substantial credits on the large and small screens. She has directed 32 plays in both French and English, a dozen features including Morning Man, No Blame, *and* Pocahontas: The Legend. *An expert in international co-productions she has produced over 28 films with France, England and Italy, and co-ventures with the United States. Ms. Suissa is on the Board of the Academy of Canadian Cinema and Television, Chair of Women in Film & Television — Toronto, past president of the Quebec Producers Association, and a workshop leader currently writing a hands-on manual on directing, "A Director Prepares." Her constant quest for new artistic challenges makes her a highly motivated member of our industry.*

Because of my Moroccan origins, I had my first mentor early on … The storyteller in the marketplaces of my childhood. He was the writer, the performer, he created his own sound effects and often he played his own music.

I was a very small child and I did not speak Arabic. But I laughed and cried and was mesmerized along with the others. Through the storyteller's emotions and the audience's reactions, the story reached us all, beyond words and language.

That was my first lesson. *The story is the star, and the magic of the story is the audience.* The audience is who I think and work for, who I write and direct for.

So, still today, the first time I read a script, it as an audience. I am not looking at the writer's style or craft … yet. "I came to marketplace" to be emotionally enthralled.

My second and most important lesson came when I decided, in Paris in 1959, that I wanted to become a director. I was lucky enough to meet a very old actor from the Comédie-Française, who looked at my nineteen years of age and laughed. He told me, "Live, love and learn. Suffer, cry, learn some more and, in the meantime, try to go to the Conservatory. Work as an actor in order to understand what actors need. Work with, and assist as many directors as possible and, *maybe*, when you are 30, you can start directing." I directed my first play, *Butterflies are Free*, when was I was 31.

In the meantime I had learned ... learned to trust, respect and support the actors in their responsibility to carry the story ...

As a director and or a producer, I motivate writers, actors, technicians, and all those involved in the process, to go to the extreme limits of their talent ... to tell the story. The same story that I first read and loved as an audience, I loved to the point of wanting to direct or produce. The stronger my reactions were on the first read, the more able I am to retain the emotional impact of the story when working with the writer. Using our craft to test our instincts, we hone these emotions for our audience; we choose and create the motivations that we will all adhere to in order to tell the same story.

So how do we tell the same story? Some call it the "heart" of the story. It is what the story is about ... it is the common denominator. I call it the "thrust."

Why thrust? Because it has a movement to it. Because it is a word that propels my imagination and therefore my desire to act. So, what is the thrust of the story? What is the thrust of each character in every scene?

I once directed a young actor in his very first play. He was so nervous that he started to panic ten days before opening night. On opening night, he was a basket case. The audience was there, and in the audience was the boy's uncle, a famous actor himself.

This young actor was carrying on in the wings, convinced that he would forget every line, that he would never be able to walk on stage, and so on and so on. I said nothing but I tailed him until the very last minute. Just before his cue to enter, I grabbed him and motivated him "Your father is leaving now. You need the keys to his car. You want his car. Go for the keys!"

He ran on-stage, charmed his father, remembered all his lines, came off-stage with the keys and, only then, realized he had made his debut. All he needed was the thrust of the moment.

When I directed Donald Martin's first script, *No Blame*, we had developed a good friendship and a camaraderie of peers, trusting each other's talent. So, I invited Donald to participate in my director's "homework." Together, we did what I call my director's cards.

On individual little cards for each scene, I determined the thrust of each and every scene and the thrust of each and every character in each of their beats, always making sure it tied to and led us to the thrust of the story. It is a long and thorough process but the result is worth the effort.

Donald, who also studied theatre, was not unfamiliar with this approach. But, I think he had not consciously imagined adopting it as a writer. The result was astounding.

Every time I asked, "But why is she or he saying that? What is her or his thrust?" we would inevitably discover more layers in the script and Donald was prompt to see what had to happen. Sometime it even meant going back to a much earlier scene, because that was where we had started to manipulate the characters' truths.

My love for actors and the need to respect their work is the best I have to offer to my writers. And, as a result, I love and respect the writers too, those who leave their ego at the doorstep of the story and Donald certainly does.

I cannot and will not say to any writer, "This is bad," or "This is stupid," "Do this," or "Do that," and expect results. But I know my actors' needs; so I say to a writer:

Me: Are you sure this is what the character should say (or do?)

Writer: Don't you think it's a great line … isn't it a scary moment?

Me: Yes, but I doubt I can justify it to the actor. In fact, I am convinced this will unnecessarily confuse him. So, please justify it for me.

Sometimes the writer can justify it and I am grateful for it. Now, I have the answer if my actor does get confused.

But, often, for the sake of a good line, an unconscious manipulation of the story or an effect for the audience, a writer might betray the thrust of the character and maybe of the story itself. Usually going back to the fundamental question: "Is that what the character really wants or needs at this very minute?" is enough to trigger for the writer the right dialogue, the right action. Only, because now, the dialogue and the action stem from the primary need of the character at this particular moment … as in life.

In life, I go to get a glass of water because I am thirsty, or because I need to take some time before I answer a question or face a situation. It is *my need* that makes me leave the room. I cannot manipulate the story of my life. I cannot be aware that my husband needs that time to confess to my best friend that he loves her. I am leaving the room not to help him betray me, but to carry on with my own personal need; to quench my thirst or to get my kid to school! It must be the same for a character and an actor.

Yes, to me, writers must use the same process as the actors to layer the actions and feelings of their characters. And, when a writer has not received this kind of training, it is the director's responsibility to take him through the process and the writer's responsibility to respect the process.

Because, for me "Telling It" is laughing, crying, suffering and laughing again.

Telling It is recreating the needs and wants of a given set of characters until it creates interactions that become situations that achieve the thrust of the story.

14

High-Tech Screenwriting

by Peter Mohan

P eter Mohan is a Toronto-based writer-producer. His episodic television credits as a producer or executive story editor include "Due South," "Taking the
Falls," "Secret Service," "Sweating Bullets," "Diamonds" and "Night Heat." He
received a Gemini Award for an episode of "Night Heat" and was nominated for
a Cable Ace Award as a co-writer of the television movie, Race to Freedom: The
Underground Railroad. Mohan has also served two terms as a delegate to the
National Forum of the Writers' Guild of Canada.

Sure, Aristophanes, Molière, Shakespeare and Shaw did OK for a bunch of
guys who had nothing more sophisticated to write with than pen, ink ...
OK, and an ability to craft human conflict into compelling drama. But in
this day and age, when even your coffee-maker is driven by high-tech
computer processors, the temptation to use computers as tools for screenwriting is almost irresistible. The trick is to decide which programs will
really help improve the quality of your work (and of your working conditions), and which are novelties which will be used a couple of times and
then set aside.

The first step towards choosing screenwriting software is to decide what
you want and need the software to do for you. If you're writing a feature
film without a production order, you might simply require a program to
format the script with proper margins and print it for you. If you're working on a television series or on a finished feature screenplay that's about to
be produced, you might need an all-in dedicated script processor that will
provide automatic formatting and production breakdowns. If you're still
struggling with your script at the story stage, you might want a program
which will help to aid in character and plot development. Or you might
simply plan to use your computer to do research on the history, location

and setting of your story through databases or the Internet. Programs and services for all of these purposes are available.

Screenwriting software falls into four main categories. (1) add-on script processors which turn popular word processing programs like Word or WordPerfect into script processors; (2) stand-alone script processors like ScriptThing and Scriptware, designed specifically to write format and provide breakdowns for scripts; (3) story structure programs which help to analyse and construct stories; and (4) reference programs and services which help find background information which will lend richness to the world you create in your story.

Macro Magic

Clearly, the most important piece of software a writer can own is the text editor used to capture their dialogue and action and present it in script format. While any of the major word processors such as Word or WordPerfect can be set up to enter and format scripts to industry standard (i.e., the correct margins for blocks of scene description, dialogue, scene headers and the correct positioning of character names, scene numbers and parenthetical dialogue descriptions), these word processors are not ideal for what happens to the script after it's input. When one wants to number or renumber the scenes in a draft, lock the page numbers so that future partial drafts will integrate into the current script, create new scenes which fit between existing scenes while still retaining the previously locked scene numbers, omit scenes while maintaining the continuity of scene numbering or any of the other things one might be called on to do to their masterpiece once they're ready to put it into production, there are often many hours of work required to correct and maintain the script's formatting.

Enter add-on script processors. Programs like Script Wizard and ScriptWright are complicated sets of macros that turn Word for Windows into full-featured script processors. They add powerful tools like single key margin settings, auto-capitalization of scene headings and character names above dialogue blocks, fast and easy functions for scene/act/dialogue breaks, automatic scene numbering and much more. For those who love the power of their current word processor and the convenience of only using one program, these are ideal. Because the add-ons are only macros which integrate with their current word processor, the writer has access to the onboard spell checker, thesaurus of their current program and the ability to use all of the editing commands they're already familiar with.

The downside of add-on script processors is that, although these programs can be quite powerful, one is constantly reminded that you're still only fooling the word processor into working as a script processor. There's still a bit of tweaking necessary to keep page breaks and scene/page numbering consistent. Still, for the freelance writer who doesn't worry about the demands of maintaining production scripts where elements of the scripts change day by day at a sometimes dizzying pace, these programs should be more than sufficient.

Another word processor add-on is the hoary classic, Scriptor. Once the industry standard, Scriptor has the disadvantage of operating independently from the word processor. One must convert the script file into raw text (i.e., stripping the embedded control codes each word processor attaches to the files to let it know how to format them), exit the word processor, then load Scriptor and "scriptorize" the raw text file. Whew! To re-edit the file, one must once again reload their word processor, edit the file and scriptorize it again afterwards. Double whew! This is all fine if one is working exclusively on completed drafts, but if you're endlessly revising dialogue or circulating limited drafts which change by the hour (as is often the case in TV production), it makes for far too much work. On the plus side, Scriptor is produced by the same company that manufactures Movie Magic Scheduling and Breakdown, which are programs used by producers and assistant directors in budgeting and the planning of shooting schedules for film and television productions. Because Scriptor is part of the same "family," it has been designed to share information with the other programs. Scriptorized files can be imported into Movie Magic to create detailed breakdowns of cast, locations and props as well as helping to create the production "boards" which are used to juggle actor availability, location availability and time allotted to shoot the production into a workable plan. While not being as friendly to the screenwriter as some of the screenwriting systems, Scriptor is guaranteed to make friends around the production office.

I Want The Works

The next generation of screenplay software are the stand-alone script processors. Some of the most powerful of these include, ScriptThing, Scriptware and Movie Master for DOS, and Final Draft for the Macintosh. The advantage of these programs is that all they do is write and format scripts.

They all support automatic formatting of margins, character names, scene headers and automatic scene numbering. All can also be set to automatically mark revisions as a script goes through the rewrite process. Other features of the stand-alone script processors are: onboard spell checkers and thesaurus, the ability to add hidden script notes, "index card" scene shuffling, outline modes, the ability to break down scripts for production and sophisticated search functions that allow the writer to fly from scene to scene or to a specific page or line of dialogue. The stand-alone script processors also have intelligent import functions to convert scripts from DOS text files or any of the major word processors into script files, and the ability to generate production breakdowns of the script by character and by location. ScriptThing and Scriptware have even issued slick Windows versions. ScriptThing's supports feature film, two TV sitcom formats, stage play, two-column audio-visual scripts and interactive multimedia scripts, as well as the ability to export scene breakdowns to Movie Magic.

Just think of what this would mean to Shakespeare if he were still working ... After writing his masterwork, *Romeo and Juliet* in ScriptThing, with just a few keystrokes, he could reformat it as a movie of the week or even a pilot for a wacky sitcom.

Character Name   6:36 pm   Num: 281640

Juliet
Sweet, so would I; Yet I should
thee with much cherishing. Go
good-night! Parting is such sweet
sorrow That I shall say good-night
till it be morrow.

She exits above.

Sleep dwell upon thine eyes,
thy breast! Would I were sleep
peace, so sweet to rest! Hence
I to my ghostly father's cell, His
help to crave, and my dear hap to tell.

He exits.
2 INT. FRIAR LAURENCE'S CELL — NIGHT

Enter Friar Laurence with a basket.

Names
FRIAR JOHN
FRIAR LAURENCE
JULIET
MERCUTIO
MONTAGUE
PARIS
PETER
ROMEO
TYBALT

2X11

Doc: 3   Pg: 1 of 2   Line: 36   Pos: 37

A Screen from the ScriptThing production of Romeo and Juliet

As you can see, script processors are definitely a boon to the freelance writer. In the hectic world of TV series production, they are invaluable. Once pages are edited, the revised pages can be printed and on their way to the production floor in seconds. Previously, one would have to spend another hour or two (usually at three in the morning when you were least prepared to spend the time) making sure page breaks and scene numbers were correct.

The great advantage to the stand-alone script processors is that they make the physical process of writing effortless. The less brain power you have to invest in thinking about fonts, tabs, margins and formatting, the more time you can spend focused on breathing life into your exciting, dynamic characters.

The Plot's The Thing

Another advantage of the computer age is in the area of story structure programs. In the old days, Shaw would have had to spend many lonely hours fretting out the plot and story for a *Major Barbara* or a *Pygmalion*. If he was working today, he might have opted for recent arrivals on the software landscape like Collaborator, Dramatica and Storyline Pro to help in the process.

The intention of these programs is to analyse your story and to hone the elements of character, setting, plot, complication and crisis. This analysis helps to focus your work and to create a powerful climax and resolution. All employ classic dramatic theory as well as comparison to proven successful films' structures to help examine and shape your story.

Although you might be tempted to write off the concept of story structure programs as novelties to amuse you during protracted bouts of writer's block, there's a lot more to them than that. Each program works to force the writer to answer hundreds of questions about who their characters are, what they care about and how each will resolve their conflicts and obstacles to achieve their goals. Too often, this basic groundwork is never done in the process of writing a script and the work suffers for it.

The story analysis engines in these programs are quite sophisticated and, rather than turning out dull, mechanical, computer-generated stories, they help the writer weave theme, plot, genre, character and crisis, integrated in a way that could only happen in this specific story. It's still the writer who makes the choices; just that they suddenly have a tireless writing partner doggedly asking deeper and more specific questions about the story and synthesizing the answers into a cohesive structure. The thing to understand about story structure programs is that they're no substitute for your own creativity and instincts for expressing *your* story in a way which only *you* can tell it. The best they can do is allow you to look at the story in different and deeper ways.

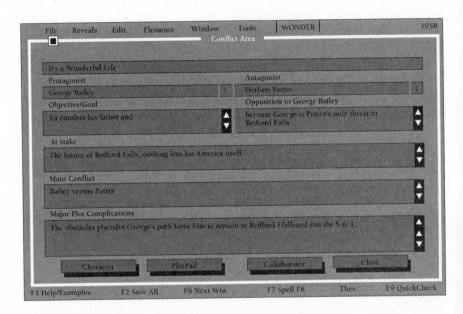

A Screen from the Collaborator Demo Analysis of It's A Wonderful Life

The story structure programs discussed above presuppose you're already having a concept for the story. If you haven't made it that far yet, Ideafisher might be the program for you. Termed an "idea generator," Ideafisher asks you to describe your task, then it provides a rich selection of questions and free associations to help break through creative blocks. As you make choices from the words and concepts the program offers, you begin to focus your idea and, by association, the program suggests surprising aspects of the idea and startling directions it could develop into.

Another computerized aid to structuring a story are the Outline programs, three by five (for the Mac) and Writer's Blocks (for Windows). Much like the process of structuring a story on three-by-five index cards, these outlining programs allow the writer the flexibility to throw down ideas, scenes, images, characters and anything else that pertains to the story, then shuffle the cards, grouping and connecting them to produce a structured story. Sure you accomplish the same thing using real index cards, but then how would you rationalize buying yourself the new Pentium?

What's "Water" In Inuit?

The final area where technology can come to the aid of screenwriters is Reference. If you're lucky enough to have a CD-ROM drive, there are hundreds of reference works which can sit in the background of your desktop, ready to be accessed whenever you need them; everything from full-featured multimedia encyclopedias like Microsoft Encarta to atlases and even compendiums of famous works of literature. All of these sources help supply the detail and solid factual foundation that will help make your screenplay come alive. For example, Molière might have found new afflictions with which to bedevil his *Imaginary Invalid* if he were able to consult the *Mayo Clinic Family Health Book* CD-ROM.

Another reference gold mine for the screenwriter is the Internet. Surely no writer can resist being plugged into an endless sea of information. For any area of study or interest, no matter how obscure, there's a Web Site or a Usenet Newsgroup which exists to draw together its followers and inform the unenlightened. Not only is information available on thousands of topics, but it is also possible to connect directly to experts in hundreds of fields, many of whom are immensely generous in sharing their information.

A writer I know recently posted a query on the Usenet screenwriters' conference about acquiring rights to real-life stories and received over a hundred replies from people who'd had experience with negotiating this kind of deal. Perhaps the best clearing house for information on the art and the business of screenwriting is the "Screenwriters' and Playwrights' Home Page" (http:// www.teleport,com/~cdeemer). The host, Charles Deemer has assembled a huge array of links to screenwriting sites on the web, from script databases, to TV networks, to studios, to reference sites, to writers software stores and hundreds of other resources. An important caveat is that the "Screenwriters' and Playwrights" Page is guaranteed to eat up many hours of what might otherwise have been productive writing time.

So which of these programs do you really need to write your first magnum opus? OK, I should have been honest with you up front. You don't really *need* any of them. Some of the best writers I know still write longhand or two-finger type their work on antiquated manual typewriters. But all of these programs have the potential to make your life easier and to make your work better.

Demonstration versions of many of the programs I have discussed (as well as many others) are available for download from the screenwriting areas of CompuServe, America Online and FTPs sites on the Internet. Also, some writers' software stores will provide demos and/or money-back guarantees if you're not satisfied with what the software is doing for you. When you've figured out what you want the programs to do, test-drive a few until you've found one you're really comfortable with. Who knows, maybe they could help you write the next *Chinatown* … and you wouldn't even have to share the credit.

15

Do You Need a Lawyer or an Agent?

by Charles Northcote

*C*harles Northcote *brings a unique perspective to his career as a literary agent. Over the course of his more than twenty years in the entertainment industry, he has been an actor, theatrical director, stage manager, acting coach, teacher, writer, story editor, casting director and anything else that has kept him from getting a "real" job. He is a founding partner of* The Core Group Talent Agency Inc. *and finds the role of literary agent to be the ideal synthesis of all of his skills.*

"I've got a great idea for a movie!"

"I've written six episodes of a great new series … and I want to direct the pilot."

"I've written an episode of 'X Files' and they tell me it has to come through an agent."

"I've written a feature for Robin Williams to star in and I want to get it to him."

Serious concerns? For those people who call my office with increasing frequency …absolutely! The difficulty is that these concerns, on closer scrutiny, are also somewhat misguided.

Anyone with just a nodding interest in the entertainment industry has heard about agents. *Premiere Magazine, Entertainment Tonight* and all of the other purveyors of mass culture which are so readily available, talk about the agent and how important that person is and can be, in the professional life of a creative artist. Michael Ovitz and CAA have become synonymous with power. In the United States! This book, however, is dealing with a Canadian perspective, and the reality here is quite different.

What is an agent? What does he do? How did he learn to do what he does? How do you know when you need an agent? Where do you find one? What can you expect an agent to do for you? Do you even need an agent? I'll address all of these questions, and in doing so, will doubtless be diverted into other areas which pertain to launching your career as a professional screenwriter.

Let me preface all of this with some comments about writers and writing in general. I believe that screenwriting is a highly skilled profession. It is a craft of which the rudimentary basics can be taught and learned. The practice and refinement of those basics, and the constant striving to be better at your craft is what I recognize as *talent*. Sometimes that talent can produce a work that transcends the craft to become a work of art. Anyone can take a few pieces of wood and knock them together into something approximating a table. The difference between a couple of sawhorses holding a slab of plywood, and a finely carved, gleaming rosewood dining table is obvious. The ability to commit oneself totally to the pursuit of improving the skills which have been acquired, and the constant self-criticism that goes with the practice, are essential ingredients for a writer to have.

Too many people attempt to enter the profession for the wrong reasons. Some actually think that it's an easy way to make a buck. How hard can it be, right? After all, most of us write every day — grocery lists, letters, memos and so on. One of the most skillful and talented writers whom I represent has called her company (with tongue ironically planted in cheek) "Twenty-six Letters." With only that many letters in the alphabet, how hard can it be to write something for the screen? We are also living in the age of the self-help book and writing gurus who encourage the "wannabe" writer to believe that writing for television and film is as easy as learning a recipe for banana bread. It just isn't true. These books and concurrent seminars and lectures serve a purpose but it should not be considered "Instant-writer-in-a-can." Just spray and poof, we have a screenplay ready to be filmed.

Writing for a living is not something to be considered lightly. It isn't a part-time pursuit. Nor is it a hobby. Notice that I'm not saying that writing cannot be a hobby, but "writing for a living" cannot. If you have written an "X Files" episode — great! Just don't expect an agent to drop everything and get out there to sell it. The same holds true for the single spec script that you've been toiling over the for past two years. Hopefully the reasons why will become apparent as we proceed.

In my experience, the best writers are natural storytellers with something to say, who love language and what it can do, and above all, feel compelled to share — to communicate. Nine times out of ten when I ask a young writer seeking representation what his or her screenplay is about, they'll reply, "Well … it's about these two guys who rob a bank and then they …." I'll stop them and say, "No. No. What is it *about?*" and they just can't answer. They're telling a story but what isn't evident is why they felt compelled to tell it, and what they are trying to communicate to the audience about themselves and about their view of the world. Characters should speak as "real" individuals that have been keenly observed and captured by the writer, not as pale copies of characters that exist in the "reality" of film or television. What is missing is what I have come to call the writer's "voice."

An agent is always on the lookout for new, unique, individual voices that he can present to the world. Recently I've been inundated with Quentin-Tarantino-esque scripts from emerging writers. The reason that everyone responded to Tarantino in the first place was because of the uniqueness of his own voice. Now everyone is trying to be him. It's not possible. Rather than send an agent something filtered through a sensibility other than your own, try writing something that celebrates and shouts out in your voice. The cliché, "Write about what you know" is, in fact, a truism.

What Is An Agent?

In simplest terms, an agent is a creative artist's advocate. A go-between for the artist and the professional world. A friendly ear. A cheerleader. A critic. A negotiator. A record-keeper. A protector. A promoter. A collection agent. A long-term strategist. A dime-store psychologist. An employee. A creative partner … and so on. And ultimately, the goal of the agent is to let the writer do what the writer does best — write! To give the writer the freedom to write and not worry about complicated or time-consuming negotiations, tracking down that overdue payment or where the next job is coming from.

The relationship between the writer and agent should be just that — a relationship. Mutual and long-term. It is a creative marriage that should be based on trust, respect and open communication. The relationship should be constantly growing with the two parties working together to achieve common goals. Contrary to the stereotypical, money-grubbing, "love ya babe" image that is a product of the Hollywood myth, the Canadian literary agent, at least in my experience, is far more mindful of the long-term investment rather than the short-term gain. We want to work with our clients to build careers that have staying power. Agents are not merely script brokers, but are professionals who genuinely care about what they do and who they do it with.

The agent attempts to keep in as regular touch as possible with producers, production companies, distributors and networks to find out what is being looked for. These days, most productions come about because of a deal that has been struck. Hence, the term "deal-driven." The nature of the deal determines the nature of the people who are asked to be a part of the production. If it's an American network deal and the writer hasn't been produced by that network previously, chances are the writer won't be considered. The agent will try to get a new writer read and considered either through the relationship he has built up with the producer over the years, or by getting one of his writers, who has been produced by the network, into a staff position on the show. This way, a possibility opens up for the new writer to be presented for consideration. Remember always that the people paying the bills are the ones making the decisions and no matter how good a writer you are, if they don't get to read your material, you won't get entrée. That's where the agents comes in — he'll try to get your material read and considered.

In order to do that, the agent needs the "ammunition" from the writer. If the writer doesn't have the appropriate writing samples for a specific show, he won't get considered by the producers. A single half-hour spec script written for "The Simpsons" won't get looked at if a one-hour drama series is being produced. The same holds true for long-form writing. An agent will get a call from a producer saying that he is looking for a writer for a romantic comedy. Your suspense-thriller script is all that you've got. The agent can't use that as a sample, so you don't get considered. It's that simple. If you are looking for an agent to represent you, and you only have that one script, regardless of how good it is, an agent might not be interested in you. You just aren't able to provide enough ammunition for the agent to do what he has to do.

How Do You Know When You Need An Agent?

The best time to approach an agent is when you've accumulated a body of work. This becomes the ammunition that the agent uses to get you considered for the work that's available. The scripts that you have been writing may not get produced immediately, but they may become the perfect sample that lands you an assignment. You then get produced as a writer, and in turn, you gain credibility, and that may eventually lead to your own scripts being produced. Another time to approach an agent is when you've managed on your own, to get a producer interested in your work. If the producer wants to strike a deal, you gain instant credibility, and that will surely get an agent's attention.

You will have noticed that the notion of "credibility" has crept into these pages a couple of times. For me, it is an important concept. The agent, since the beginning of his own career, has fought for credibility in an increasingly competitive marketplace. He is known for the manner in which he does business. Fairness. Negotiating skills. Ethics. Personality. And so on. First and foremost, however, what gives the agent credibility is the nature of the client which he has been able to attract and how the client is represented. I once had a production executive tell me, "We like doing business with you because when we ask for oranges, you give us oranges. You don't give us fruit salad and make us pick out the oranges." What I take that to mean is, be specific and don't waste people's time. Why use a shotgun approach when the possibility exists to be specific?

It's the agent's credibility that you, the writer, will want to tap into, and whether you like it or not, we are all known not only for our achievements, but also for the company we keep, so the agent will look for a few attributes from the writer as well. If you've studied your craft at a reputable film school; if you've had student films produced; if you've apprenticed with a film production company; if you've been personally recommended by another client or reputable production person; all of these, plus a body of work with a unique voice, will provide you with the credibility that an agent requires in order to consider you for representation. Once you have your agent, the hard part begins — establishing your own professional credibility. Now, however, you've got someone working with you who can help you reach that goal.

Where Do You Find An Agent?

The best place to find an agent is by asking around. Ask at the Writers Guild of Canada. They have a list of reputable agents. Ask other writers. If you know producers, production people, development types — ask them! Do your homework. Then, once you've identified your prey and before you pounce, do some more research. Call the agency and ask for the agent or the agent's assistant, or at the very least, the receptionist. Find out whether or not the agent is even looking for clients. A lot of the time he's not looking, so you can save the time, trouble and expense of inundating the agent with your material. If the agent is looking, find out the procedure for submitting to that agency. It does vary. I, for example, will ask for a résumé along with brief synopses of available material. Based on that, I'll make my decision about what I want to read. You can also make this enquiry in writing by either fax or by mail. Find out the proper address, spelling and pronunciation of the agent in question. And yes, spelling does count in your material as well. And grammar.

Be persistent without being pushy and learn to take "no" for an answer. Ask if you can call back in a couple of months. Situations do change. Be positive and upbeat. Be yourself! Be the professional that you are or want to be.

What Can You Expect An Agent To Do For You?

First of all, is the agent going to sign you? In other words, are you going to sign a legal contract with the agent specifying what the agent will and will not do and what the terms and conditions of this relationship will be? Think of the contract as a kind of prenuptial agreement. Until recently, many agents, myself included, did not have anything other than a handshake with our clients while some agencies had *power of attorney* over theirs. This situation is changing and one of the prime reasons for the change is an organization called T.A.M.A.C.

The acronym above stands for Talent Agents and Managers Association of Canada and constitutes a group of over 40 member agencies from Vancouver to Montreal (with more to come). These agents and managers represent actors, writers, directors, craftspeople and other professions within the entertainment industry.

As you may or may not be aware, Los Angeles (i.e., Hollywood) based agencies are licensed by the State of California and they are regulated not only by that state but also by the various unions and their collective-bargaining agreements. There is a very strict adherence to rules and regulations. In Canada, an agent does not require a license and this can lead to abuse. You've all seen ads in newspapers from so-called agencies all too willing to exploit the gullibility (and wallets) of a star-struck public. (Note: Never go with an agent or so-called producer who asks for money to represent you or read your work. They are not legitimate!) These types of agencies tarnish the whole profession. T.A.M.A.C.. developed a mandate to become a self-regulating body to identify and eliminate unethical business practices within the profession. It has established a Code of Standards, Ethics and Business Procedures to ensure the legitimacy of member agencies. T.A.M.A.C.., as part of all this, has had a standardized contract designed (which can be modified for individual concerns with additional clauses) that clearly defines what is expected from both parties entering into the relationship. This contract is soon to become standard practice so don't let it worry you. It's to protect you as well as the agent. Ask whether the agency you're approaching is a T.A.M.A.C. member.

Is There A Difference Between An Agent And A Manager?

The truth is that in Canada we, in essence, are agent/managers. The delineation is a lot sharper south of the border. Agents can, by law only perform certain functions and the same for managers. Agents in the United States tend to more cut and dried and business-oriented, while the manager looks after the more personal side of the artist's life. But even that is getting fuzzy around the edges in Los Angeles. Suffice it to say that if you are a new writer, you don't need to be paying commissions to two people at this point in your career. Wait until you've got producers backed up around the block waiting to work with you before you even consider a manager. You'll know when the time is right.

The agent makes his living through commissions. The rate of commissions varies between 10 per cent and 15 per cent, depending on the agency. Ask first. And please don't think of the commission as some kind of performance bonus that you are bestowing on the agent for landing you a job. All agents at some time or other have heard the refrain, "Why should I pay 10 per cent to you? The producer came to me directly and there was no negotiation involved." Well, the commissions you pay on all work are part of the ongoing relationship between the two of you. The agent is continuing to work on your behalf on a regular, consistent basis even when you are not receiving money for your work. Remember if you aren't being paid, neither is he. Part of the responsibilities of maintaining the relationship therefore, is paying commission on all work. Agents keep clients on their rosters because they believe in the "voice" of that writer. It isn't uncommon for an agent to invest at least a year in "grooming" that writer before the first paying job happens and credibility is established. Always think long-term and "big picture."

Elsewhere in this book you will find information on the Writers' Guild of Canada (W.G.C.). Membership in this union is yet another one of those credibility bridges that the agent will try to help the emerging writer to cross. Membership is important and helps to guarantee that you will be treated in a professional manner. The I.P.A. (Independent Production Agreement) is the collective-bargaining agreement between the Guild and the various producers' associations and it forms the basis for all contract negotiations. While not a perfect document, it is invaluable and your agent should know it backwards and forwards and maintain a good relationship with the Guild. The I.P.A., when you become a member, protects you, and your agent also protects you. Together they make a strong team. As long as you are not a member of the Guild, you and your work are vulnerable to being exploited by producers.

Do You Need A Lawyer?

Many successful writers don't have an agent after a certain point in their careers. Work is coming to them regularly and all they need is scrutiny and advice regarding contracts. The obvious choice for them is a lawyer. This lawyer should be schooled in, and familiar with entertainment law and have a knowledge of the current I.P.A. or other pertinent collective-bargaining agreements. In other words, he needs to be up-to-date with the business as it currently exists. Most agencies have their own lawyers to protect their interests. Personally, I feel that the new or emerging writer's interest is better served by an agent. When you have reached a stage of credibility which allows you the opportunity to afford an entourage of lawyers and managers, then you become legitimately entitled to use that pretentious Hollywood-created phrase, "Have your people call my people."

The mention of Hollywood brings me back to the most frequently asked question that I get from young writers. This question gives me the opportunity to debunk a large myth along with providing me a tidy way of wrapping up these ramblings. The question is, "Do you have a way of getting my stuff to the States? I've written an action-adventure film for X (fill in the name of your favourite box-office star) and want to get it to them."

Most established Canadian agencies have some sort of access to the American and other international markets. The marketplace is becoming increasingly global and it makes sense to try to expand the potential for the clients as well as the agents by gaining whatever direct access is possible. Some agencies have affiliates with whom they work closely and in fact, share clients. Others access the Los Angeles producers, networks and so on, personally and directly. For many it is some form of combination of the two or other variations, but access to information is the goal.

If you have not been produced in your home market, it is hopelessly naive to believe that you will be produced in Hollywood. Even if your script is stunningly original, the simple fact is that they just don't need you! There are thousands of writers in the United States. Those thousands have millions of ideas and generate thousands of spec scripts. A depressing statistic I heard a couple of years ago had 40,000 spec scripts being registered with the Los Angeles Offices of the W.G.A. (Writers' Guild of America). Of those 40,000 something like 1,000 had some money invested in them (usually nominal options) and, of those, 100 were actually made. Now here's the kicker; of the 100 that were made, two were action-adventure films! The odds are definitely not in your favour.

If you do just a modicum of research, you'll notice that established producers, directors and stars tend to work with established writers with whom they have worked before. There already exists a sense of trust and "comfortability." There exists a professional relationship. If by any wild stretch of the imagination, an unsolicited spec script does make its way through the various traps and obstacles and lands on the desk of the wonderfully talent Mr., Miss, or Ms. X and gets read and enjoyed, that's when the fun begins. Nine times out of ten, if that miracle occurs, then the script will be optioned and the first thing that will happen is that Mr., Miss, or Ms. X will then turn it over to one of their writers to do a rewrite. Since the W.G.A. agreements specify that for a writer to receive credit for the rewrite, more than 33 percent of the existing script has to be reworked, you, the writer of the original script, can kiss at least one-third of your script away! It's not personal. It's business. Did you ever notice the five or six names that appear as writing credits on those Hollywood movies? Now you know why.

If you want your work considered in the Hollywood market, go to Los Angeles and live there. Make the rounds. Get an agent. Take the pitch meetings. Do lunch. Just don't expect to access the market from Wawa, Ontario, through your Toronto-based agent. In a business that values time as much as money, it just doesn't make any practical sense. That doesn't mean that Canadian writers' work isn't being looked at and done in Los Angeles. It is happening more and more but it's happening for writers who have established a track record for themselves in Canada first. They have been produced. They have climbed the ladder of credibility. They have won ratings. They have won awards. Their work has been seen in the United States either through US sales or distribution deals. They have travelled back and forth to Los Angeles on a semi-regular basis. To coin a cliché "They have paid their dues."

Take the time; pay our own personal dues. Don't settle for the plywood sawhorse table when you know that with a little more care and attention to the details of your craft, you could be polishing that rosewood table for all the world to enjoy.

16

Copyright Law and the Screenwriter

by Lesley Ellen Harris

L esley Ellen Harris is a copyright and new media lawyer and consultant who works on Canadian, US and international legal issues in publishing, entertainment, computers and the Internet. Ms. Harris began her career in copyright in 1984 working with a lobbying group interested in revising Canada's copyright laws. From 1987–1991, Ms. Harris was senior copyright officer with the Canadian government where she helped revised the country's copyright laws. Her articles and papers are published internationally and she is the author of the book, Canadian Copyright Law (McGraw-Hill Ryerson) now in its second edition — see http://www.mcgrawhill.ca/copyrightlaw. Ms Harris has spoken at conferences on copyright law in Canada, the United States and Mexico. She can be reached by e-mail at copylaw@interlog.com.

There's an often heard expression, "You never escape death and taxes." And, for writers, one should add "copyright." Copyright is the underlying basis of rights in the film industry and the starting point of any film — the literary property. Although it's a convoluted and complicated issue, writers who understand the basics of copyright will understand the rights they own in a literary property, the basis upon which negotiations are undertaken and payment for their work is made, as well as the control they have over their work. This chapter discusses the basics of copyright law from the screenwriter's perspective, the meaning of electronic rights and rights stemming from new media and the Internet, rights relating to the integrity of one's work, the differences between Canadian and US copyright laws, and international aspects of copyright law.

What Is Copyright?

Literally, copyright means the "right to copy." The Canadian Copyright Act grants copyright owners the sole and exclusive right to reproduce, perform, adapt, publish and broadcast a work. These rights give copyright holders control over the use of their works. Writers generally license some or all of their rights to film and TV producers, book publishers and multimedia developers and get paid lump sums and/or royalties for these licenses. The Copyright Act sets out the rights of creators and then it is up to the creators to negotiate the use of their rights for an agreed upon price. In addition, copyright protects the reputation of creators.

IS COPYRIGHT THE SAME THINGS AS "INTELLECTUAL PROPERTY"?

Yes, copyright law is one area of a larger body of law called "intellectual property." The word "intellectual" is used to distinguish it from "physical" property. Intellectual property law refers to and protects the intangible or "intellectual" nature of an object, whereas physical property law refers to and protects the tangible or physical aspect of an object.

For example, there is both an intellectual and physical property component to a book or washing machine. The physical component of the book or washing machine is the object itself, the book which you can hold in your hand, or the washing machine whose door you can open and close. The intellectual component of the book is the words which appear on the page and the *expression* of any ideas contained in those words. The intellectual component of the washing machine is the material that led to its creation such as sketches containing its design or plans for its motor, and even the name of the washing machine.

The physical and intellectual components of any creations are separate. By owning the physical or intellectual property in a creation, you do not necessarily own the other type of property in it. This means that purchasing or owning a book does not give you the copyright in that book. You cannot make any uses of the book which only the copyright owner may do.

Your scripts, treatments and outlines are all considered intellectual property. Specifically, these creations are protected as copyright works under the Copyright Act.

WHAT ARE THE OTHER AREAS OF INTELLECTUAL PROPERTY?

In addition to copyright, intellectual property includes patents, trade marks, industrial designs, confidential information and trade secrets and semiconductor chip protection.

APPLYING COPYRIGHT LAW TO SCREENWRITERS

This chapter is organized to examine and highlight your concerns about copyright law during the various stages of writing a script, from the idea to the outline, treatment and script to the film, TV program and CD-ROM. In some cases, the information below will answer your questions. In other cases, it will raise issues of which you should be aware.

This chapter is not intended to be a treatise about copyright law nor is it intended to substitute for legal advice. The purpose of this chapter is to inform you about valuable property rights in your work. Use it as a primer and as a guide to raise your antennae as to when you should read more comprehensive information in this area and/or seek legal advice.

The Idea

IS AN IDEA PROTECTED BY COPYRIGHT LAW?

Screenwriter James Dearden knew his copyright law when he wrote the lines for Michael Douglas' character in the film *Fatal Attraction*, "As you know, you can't copyright an idea."

Ideas, facts or factual information (for example, historical details) are not protected by copyright law. What is protected is the *expression* of an idea or fact, creation or thought. For example, there may be copyright protection in a book setting out the history of the film industry in Canada. However, there is no copyright protection in the facts concerning the film industry in Canada which are set out in the book; there is merely copyright protection in the expression of those facts.

SO HOW DO YOU PROTECT AN IDEA?

Write it down, tape it or save the words expressing it on your computer hard drive or on a disk. You still won't have protection in your idea, but you will have copyright protection in the words chosen to express your ideas.

HOW DO YOU PITCH AN UNPROTECTED IDEA?

Because ideas are not protected under copyright law, writers are vulnerable to their ideas being "stolen." There are precautions you can take when pitching ideas. For example, don't tell everyone you know about your idea, just those who are in a position to help you. Pitch your ideas to reputable film and TV producers. If you're concerned about a producer claiming your idea as his or her own, think about whether this is a producer with whom you really want to work. Record your pitch meetings. Take your agent, co-writer or another person to a pitch meeting. Present your pitch in writing during or after a meeting. Make it clear to producers that you are presenting your idea on a confidential basis. These are all suggestions and not fool-proof methods of protecting your ideas.

Obviously, you believe in your ideas and feel that they are worth spending the hundreds and millions of dollars it takes to turn them into a TV project or film. But you should also be reasonable about your ideas. They may not be as original as you think. Debra Hodgson, an attorney who specializes in the representation of entertainment insurance companies in errors and omissions underwriting and claims and a former entertainment litigator in Los Angeles, says "Writers often truly believe their ideas are stolen but in fact very few ideas are stolen in this business." Ms. Hodgson advises writers "not to sue every producer who develops an idea close to the one you pitched them. Writers normally lose these lawsuits, often because other writers have also pitched similar ideas to the producers."

On the other hand, a recent US lawsuit left Sandy Veith with $7.3 million US in damages for the concept for the TV series *Northern Exposure* which was lifted from Veith's script *Coletta* about a New York doctor paying off his tuition in a small town.

Is Your Idea Based On A Real-Life Event?

With the popularity of reality-based television shows and docudrama movies, the issue of obtaining rights from the people involved in these real-life events has become the focus of much discussion. Like facts and information, real-life events are not per se protected by copyright.

However, if you are writing a docudrama and there is an article or book about the real-life event, obtaining permission from the author of the article or book would insure that the author does not later make a claim of copyright infringement against you. Also, the author may have valuable research materials you can use. In addition, writers and producers of projects based on real-life events often obtain releases or rights to the stories from involved people to protect themselves against other legal claims such as defamation, privacy and publicity. Further, having exclusive rights to a story from the people involved can give the writer an advantage over other writers basing a project on the same story.

Is Your Idea Based On An Existing Work?

If your idea is based on an existing work, you will need the rights to adapt that work before you write a script based on it. For example, you will need the rights of an author before adapting a book, or the rights of a playwright before adapting a play.

The Outline, Treatment and Script

SETTING YOUR IDEA IN WRITING (OR ON DISK, ETC.)

Once your idea is in some tangible form, you have copyright protection in the *expression* of your ideas though not in the ideas themselves. The protection is automatic by virtue of creating the outline, treatment, script or other document.

WHAT DOES AUTOMATIC COPYRIGHT PROTECTION MEAN?

It means you do not have to register your work, mail a copy to yourself, mark it with the copyright symbol or deposit it with a deposit registry. However, doing one or more of these formalities may help you enforce your rights. For example, marking your work with the copyright notice, © Jane Doe 1996, reminds people that copyright exists in the work. Also, it may help people who want to use the work to locate the copyright owner to obtain permission before using it.

SHOULD YOU REGISTER YOUR WORK WITH THE CANADIAN COPYRIGHT OFFICE?

Registering a work with the Canadian Copyright Office gives you certain advantages in a copyright violation lawsuit. To register, send $35 with the completed one-page form available from the Copyright Office. Do not send a copy of your work. The Canadian Copyright Office is not a depository and any copies of your work will be sent back to you. Copyright Office, Place du Portage, Phase I, 50 Victoria Street, Hull, Quebec K1A 0C9. Tel. (819) 997-1725 Fax (819) 953-6977.

Some copyright owners use other methods of "registering" or "depositing" their works either as the sole method of registration or in conjunction with the Canadian government registration system. Although these alternatives may provide some proof in a courtroom, a copyright owner would not be entitled to the advantages which benefit copyright owners who register their works with the Copyright Office. On the other hand, using an alternative method in conjunction with the Canadian government registration system may provide additional proof to that obtained from merely using the Canadian registration system.

SHOULD YOU MAIL A COPY TO YOURSELF

Mailing a copy to yourself is one simple and inexpensive way to "register/deposit" a work. Put your manuscript in an envelope and mail it to yourself by registered mail. When you receive the envelope/package, put the registered mail slip and envelope/package in your files (or safety deposit box or give it to your lawyer). Do not open it under any circumstances, unless and until you are before a court of law. Once opened before a judge, the envelope and its contents will act as evidence in establishing a date of creation, and ownership of copyright, in that work.

SHOULD YOU REGISTER IN THE UNITED STATES?

Other depositories for copyright works include the US Copyright Office. As a Canadian, you have automatic protection in the United States but you may register and deposit your work in the United States by contacting the US Copyright Office, Publications Section, LM-455, Library of Congress, Washington, D.C. 20559 USA tel. (202) 707-3000 Tel. (202) 707-9100 (Forms hotline — 24 hours) Fax (202) 707-6859.

WHAT ABOUT THE WRITERS' GUILD DEPOSITORY?

Further, if you are a television or film writer, you can deposit your work for $20 (nonmember) or $10 (member) with the Writers' Guild of Canada, 35 McCaul Street, Suite 300, Toronto, Ontario M5 1V7. Tel. (416) 979-7907 or 1-800-567-9974. Fax (416) 979-9273.

The Writers' Guild of America, West (in Los Angeles) and East (in New York) offer similar depositories to the one administered by the Writers' Guild of Canada.

HOW DO I OBTAIN COPYRIGHT PROTECTION IN OTHER COUNTRIES?

If you have copyright in Canada, you are automatically protected in over 100 countries according to the laws where that work is used. For example, you have protection in the United States under US copyright laws. Similarly, Americans have copyright protection in Canada under Canadian copyright law.

WHO OWNS THE COPYRIGHT IN A TREATMENT, OUTLINE OR SCRIPT?

The person who first puts the work in some tangible form, for example, on paper, owns the copyright. To illustrate this point, if a producer tells you a story for a treatment or script (without any treatment, etc., written by the producer) and you prepare a treatment, outline or script, you own the copyright in the treatment, outline or script. But remember, the ideas are not protected by copyright, only the expression of them.

HOW LONG DOES COPYRIGHT PROTECTION LAST?

Subject to various exceptions, copyright protection automatically lasts for 50 years after the author's death. For example, an author who dies on February 1, 1950, has copyright protection in her works until December 31, 2000.

WHAT DOES IT MEAN TO OWN COPYRIGHT?

The owner of the copyright has the sole and exclusive control over the use of the work. For instance, if you own copyright in a script, only you can license that right to a film producer or CD-ROM developer. The Canadian Copyright Act provides copyright owners with a number of rights including the right to reproduce, adapt, translate, broadcast and publicly perform a work.

DOES OWNERSHIP MEAN CREATIVE CONTROL?

Ownership of a script means that you have control over the use of the script. However, once you license that script, for example, to a film producer, you license the right to make a film based on your script in the circumstances upon which you agree. At that point, the creative control you have in the project is generally dependent upon the relationship and/or contractual arrangement you have with the producer. (Also see the discussion below on moral rights.)

WHAT ARE ELECTRONIC RIGHTS?

Like other rights in copyright, electronic rights are a "bundle" of rights over which the rights holder has exclusive control. Each right is separate and distinct from the other rights and can be separately exploited in exchange for monetary compensation. Electronic rights include reproduction, enhancement and manipulation of text. Electronic rights also refers to formats which embody your work such as CD-ROM, CD-I, digital tape, laser disk and magnetic drive. It further refers to the mode of distribution, like sale of hard copies in stores and over the Internet.

WHO OWNS ELECTRONIC RIGHTS?

If you own a work, you own the electronic rights in it unless you have given them away. By assigning or licensing other rights such as the right to make a film based on your script, you do not automatically assign or license your electronic rights. In fact, writers are regularly advised to retain their electronic rights and negotiate them at a later time for additional compensation.

Of course, if you're writing scripts for CD-ROMs, you will have to license some of your electronic rights to a CD-ROM developer, but you do not have to license all of your rights for all media whatsoever, whether they exist now or in the future.

WHO OWNS THE RIGHTS IN AN OPTIONED WORK?

In simple terms, an option is a right (usually an exclusive right) a writer gives to a producer generally in exchange for money, for a specified period of time to represent that work in order to obtain financing and further interest to produce the work. An option does not convey any rights. The original copyright holder, the writer, continues to retain copyright in the script during the option period.

WHO OWNS THE RIGHTS IN A COMMISSIONED TREATMENT, OUTLINE OR SCRIPT?

The author of a commissioned treatment, outline or script owns the rights in it. This is true unless there is an agreement stating otherwise.

WHO OWNS COPYRIGHT WHEN A WRITER IS AN EMPLOYEE?

If you are employed by a film, TV or CD-ROM company as an employee and not as a freelancer, your employer owns the copyright in all of the works you create during the course of employment. However if, for example, you are writing a script in the evenings on your own time, that is not part of your employee duties, you will own copyright in that script.

ARE YOU WORKING IN THE UNITED STATES OR FOR A US COMPANY?

If you are working in the United States or for a US individual or company, be aware that the United States has different laws and industry standards than Canada for works created in the course of employment and for commissioned works. Also, in certain industries in the United States, you may automatically be asked to assign, as oppose to license, your copyrights as a precondition of employment. For instance, US movie and TV producers may require an assignment of the publishing rights to a musical score. Similarly, if you write a spec script for a film, you will initially own the copyright in the script; however if you sell the script to a US production company or studio, they will require an assignment of the copyright. Even if the assignment of rights is not obvious, be on guard for US contracts which automatically vest copyright ownership in the party specially ordering or commissioning certain types of works, such as collections and audio-visual works, including motion pictures and certain computer software. Also keep in mind that contractual arrangements can override the statutory law and you may be able to negotiate better terms in a contract than those initially offered to you.

WHO OWNS COPYRIGHT IN A SCRIPT WRITTEN BY MORE THAN ONE WRITER

Co-writers jointly own copyright in a treatment, outline or script. There is only one copyright in the case of works of joint authorship. Co-authors of "works of joint authorship" are co-owners of the work. They must jointly exercise their rights in the specific copyright work. Neither author is an exclusive owner of the copyright in the work and neither author can authorize the use of his or her work without the other author's approval. For example, neither co-writer of a screenplay can license the right to a producer to produce the screenplay without the permission of the other co-writer.

If you are writing with a partner, it is a good idea to always have a written agreement clearly setting out the rights and obligations of each writing partner.

WHO OWNS COPYRIGHT IN "NOTES"?

Notes given on a script are not necessarily protected by copyright unless those notes are in a tangible form, that is, written down. When a writer incorporates notes in a treatment or script, those notes are interpreted by the writer as ideas and are appropriately incorporated into the treatment or script which is the property of the writer.

WHO OWNS RIGHTS IN A FICTIONAL CHARACTER?
Fictional characters, such as Bart Simpson or Garfield (the cat), are not, by themselves, protected by copyright, but may have some components which are subject to copyright protection. The different elements of fictional characters must be examined on their own. The name of a character is not protected by copyright as a copyright does not protect names. A physical portrayal of a character may attain some copyright protection. For instance, if the character is represented in a drawing in a comic strip, the drawing may be protected as an artistic work. If a copyright work contains a character as a substantial part of it, and includes highly distinctive characteristics of the character, the character may be subject to copyright protection (for example, if copied accurately and in detail, it might constitute a violation of copyright).

In any legal suit dealing with the violation of copyright of a fictional character, a successful defence must show: a similarity in the *expression* of the idea of the character in the original and copied versions of the character; the character has significant importance to the original work; the character possesses original and distinctive characteristics; and the character has a certain popularity, including one in the eyes of the violator that entices a deliberate appropriation of the character.

HOW DOES THE LAW WORK WITH AMENDMENTS TO THE ORIGINAL SCRIPT?
Writing for film and TV, unlike writing books, is a collaborative process which begins with an original script written by a sole writer or jointly written by more than one writer. It is not uncommon (especially in the United States) for other writers who were not involved in the original or subsequent drafts of the script to be hired to write a further draft or drafts of the script. Also, it is not uncommon for others involved (like producers, directors and actors) in the film or TV project to provide input into the script. These situations can result in the original script being changed in manners in which the original scriptwriter(s) does not agree. Where this occurs, the original writer may have protected his or her interests by providing for them in a written contract with the film or TV producer prior to the

beginning of the project. Also, in some situations the writer may be protected by a Writers' Guild of Canada collective production agreement. Whether or not the writer is otherwise protected by an agreement, the writer may have some recourse under the Canadian copyright law. Where a script in which copyright belongs to the writer has been amended, the writer may, under certain circumstances, claim that the right of adaptation has been violated. In addition, the writer may claim a violation of his or her moral rights.

WHAT ARE MORAL RIGHTS?

Moral rights are part of the Canadian copyright legislation (as well as copyright legislations of many other countries). In Canada, moral rights provide the following protection to all creators including writers, even if they no longer hold copyright in their work.

1. *Right of paternity:* This right allows an author to have his or her name appear on his work and allows an author to remain anonymous or to use a pseudonym.

2. *Right of integrity:* This right allows an author to prevent the distortion of his or her work where the distortion is prejudicial to his or her honour or reputation.

3. *Right of association:* This right allows an author to prevent the use of his or her work in association with a product, service, cause or institution where it is prejudicial to his or her honour or reputation.

HOW DO MORAL RIGHTS PROTECT A SCREENWRITER VIS-À-VIS SCRIPT REVISIONS?

In one moral rights case, playwright Sharon Pollock was awarded an interlocutory injunction in a Canadian court on April 29, 1983, to ban the broadcast of a television version of her play, "Blood Relations," which she felt distorted the play's interpretation of the life of accused Massachusetts axe-murderer Lizzie Borden. In this case, Ms. Pollock asserted her right to integrity to prevent a distortion of her work which could be prejudicial to her honour and reputation.

Another method of dealing with script revisions is to exercise your right to remove your name from a script. Joy Fielding, a Canadian fiction writer, recently wrote the first draft of a script for a TV movie. A subsequent draft of the script was written by another writer and then discarded and ultimately it was the producer and director who revised the script in a manner which Ms. Fielding claimed was not hers. In the end, Ms. Fielding felt that the final script wasn't the one she originally wrote and she had to decide whether to ask for her name to be removed based on her belief, stated in her own words, "I couldn't put my name on something I didn't write." This is an example of the type of protection moral rights provides. In this case, Ms. Fielding could assert her right of paternity to ensure that her name was removed from a script with which she chose to no longer be associated.

The Film, TV Program And CD-ROM

DO YOU SELL YOUR COPYRIGHT IN ORDER FOR YOUR WORK TO BECOME A FILM, TV PROGRAM OR CD-ROM?
No, never sell your copyright. As the current Independent Production Agreement of the Writers' Guild of Canada states, "All rights negotiated under this Agreement or in any individual contract between a Writer and a Producer shall be in the form of a license from the Writer to the Producer for a specific use during a specified term of whatever right is in question. The Writer's copyright shall not be assigned."

An assignment is equal to a sale and a licence is like a rental. By licensing your work, each time it is used in the copyright sense, that is, photocopied, translated, performed in public or made into a film or play, you, as the copyright owner are the only one entitled to authorize such uses of your work and to be paid for them. Always license your copyright for a specific use and explicitly retain all other rights (for example, electronic rights).

DOES A WRITER OWN COPYRIGHT IN A FILM, TV PROGRAM OR CD-ROM BASED ON HIS OR HER SCRIPT?
Generally speaking, the writer of the underlying work — the script — is not the owner of the copyright in the film, TV program or CD-ROM. This is possible because there is more than one copyright work in a film, TV program or CD-ROM. For example, some of the copyright works in a film may be a literary work, musical work and artistic work. These underlying works continue to have copyright protection in them as does the film itself enjoy a separate copyright protection.

Other Legal Issues

This chapter deals with one area of the law of concern to writers. Other areas of the law to be aware of include privacy, publicity and personality rights, libel and trade mark.

REVISION OF COPYRIGHT LAWS

This chapter sets out the principles of copyright laws in Canada. Long-awaited changes to our copyright laws are pending. For the most part, any revisions will build upon the principles of copyright law as set out in this chapter. Also, the Canadian and US governments, as well as other governments, have recently released recommendations for revising their copyright laws to take into account new rights issues due to the Information Highway. As writers, these changes are important to you and can affect how you make your living. Because of the prominence of copyright issues on the Information Highway, "copyright news" is more comprehensively covered in traditional media and on the Internet. The more you are aware of your rights, the easier it will be for you to protect them and earn a living from them.

* Copyright law reform Bill C-32 was introduced into the House of Commons on April 25, 1996. For up-to-the-moment news on this bill and other proposed copyright legislation and amendments to Canada's copyright laws, see http://www.mcgrawhill.ca/copyrightlaw.

17

The Writers' Guild: Rules and Protection

by Maureen Parker and Sarah Dearing

Maureen Parker is the executive director of the Writers' Guild of Canada. she joined the Writers' Guild in 1989 to head the Industrial Relations Department responsible for the Independent Production Agreement. Prior to her appointment, she was contract administrator with Skyld/Spectrafilm.

Sarah Dearing is the former director of Membership and Information Services at the Writers' Guild of Canada.

Why The Writers' Guild Of Canada Is Necessary

The entertainment industry is big business. Several Canadian production companies now trade on the Toronto Stock Exchange. Many maintain their own distribution companies and some have offices in the United States and throughout the world. In 1994, writers contracted under the Writers' Guild of Canada's collective agreement, the Independent Production Agreement (IPA), earned $13,346,006, and in 1995, they earned $15,051,679. Under the CBC agreement in 1995, writers combined earnings totaled $4,709,168. During the years 1992 to 1995, 129 English-language feature films were written under the IPA and 25 were produced. For the same period, 45 one-hour television series, and 73 half-hour series were produced, with each cycle of a series running from thirteen to 26 episodes. Produced television movies (MOWs) numbered 26.

Within this busy industry, the writer's interests can get lost in the shuffle. A million things can go wrong between the time you begin writing and the first day of principal photography. Financing falls through, visions change and not every producer out there is able to keep it all together. Writers must be knowledgeable about the business and their rights, and be prepared for any number of problems. You may not be paid as promised or not credited for your work. The producer may wish to rewrite your material himself, or ask you for an unreasonable number of rewrites without additional compensation.

The Writers' Guild of Canada was established to further the professional creative and economic rights and interests of writers in radio, television, film, video and all recorded media. It represents all persons eligible for membership in the Guild, whether they decide to join or not, and promotes and maintains high professional standards among its 1,200 members.

On a day-to-day basis, the practical mandate of the WGC is the negotiation and enforcement of its collective agreements which set forth minimum terms and conditions of employment. This sets the Guild apart from other organizations, such as the novelists' Writers' Union, which do not have collective agreements defining minimum terms.

The WGC meets its mandate through collective action; it accomplishes collectively what cannot be accomplished individually. It exists to champion the rights of writers by protecting their interests and speaking on their behalf.

Currently, the Guild has four collective agreements: the Writers Independent Production Agreement (IPA) between the WGC, the Canadian Film and Television Production Association (CFTPA), and the Association des Producteurs de Film et de Television du Quebec (APFTQ); the CBC Television Writers Agreement; CBC Radio Writers Agreement; and the OECA/OAAE Agreement (the TVO Agreement).

The Guild office is administered by a staff of twelve, headed by an executive director. A seven-person council of writer members, elected biannually from across the country, oversees the affairs of the Guild, establishes priorities, policies and rules and regulations of membership.

A national forum of fifteen representatives is elected at the same time to meet yearly and function as a think-tank where matters of craft, the collective agreements, and general policy such as training initiatives, are discussed.

How The Guild Was Created

The Writers' Guild of Canada evolved from within the Alliance of Canadian Television and Radio Artists, which represented performers, journalists and writers of drama, variety and documentaries. The first collective agreement governing writers was between ACTRA and the CBC in 1961. The agreement for the independent sector followed in 1967.

Writers have their own unique set of creative issues, and as a result, with the growth and increased complexity of the industry, a self-governing, independent organization was required to focus on writer-specific problems. In April, 1991, members of the ACTRA Writers' Guild voted to establish an autonomous organization within the Alliance — The Writers' Guild of Canada — mirroring the structure of their colleagues in the International Affiliation of Writers' Guilds. The WGC formally separated from ACTRA in 1995.

The collective agreements are improved upon each time they are renegotiated, but there are always new issues arising for the screenwriter, issues requiring resolution through collective action. The need for a Writers' Guild continually increases. Some of the most common problems are in the areas of copyright, financial compensation and credits.

Copyright And Moral Rights

Whether a script is based on a true story, best-selling novel, stage play or an original idea from the producer, the *screenwriter* puts the ideas into motion and begins the process that will result in a film or television program. A director, performer or producer with an idea will still require a writer. In order to claim ownership of a work, a writer must create more than an idea. Copyright doesn't extend to ideas. It is possible that more than one person could come up with the same idea for a motion picture, particularly when there are tried and tested formulas for box-office success. In Canada, copyright belongs to the person who actually sits down and puts pen to paper: the creator.

Under all of the WGC agreements, writers are prohibited from assigning their copyright. Rather producers purchase a *licence* for specific uses of the script for a certain period of time, but copyright in the script remains with the writer.

The right to maintain the integrity of a work and protection from any distortion or misuse are moral rights the writer may assert and are also protected within the WGC collective agreements. Provisions require a producer to consult with the writer of a script regarding any changes, additions or deletions which substantially affect the meaning, theme, characterization or plot development. Unless the original writer is not available, the agreements require the original writer be asked to make any changes. The WGC collective agreements also ensure that writers receive an on-screen writing credit and it is also their right to request a pseudonym if they wish to use one.

In the United States, screenwriters assign their copyright to a production company. This system has existed since the "studio" days when writers were hired by a single company to sit in a small dark room churning out scripts. Canada has never had a studio system and the act of creation is self-directed.

Script Registration And Release Forms

Even though writers own the copyright in their material through the act of creation, it is wise to protect your intellectual property. For a nominal fee, members or nonmembers may forward material to the Guild's Script Registration Service. This system records the date of completion of a work, the author and assigns an official registration number. In the event that registered material is plagiarized or any other problem arises, the Guild can supply evidence as to when the material was completed, but does not represent the author in any legal action.

When material is filed with the Guild, the author receives a letter listing the registration number. It is suggested that writers forward this letter with a copy of their script each time it is submitted to a producer, as it serves to remind the producer who owns what. Before reviewing material, a production company may require the writer to sign a form releasing the producer from all liability should any material inadvertently appear in another production. While the Guild does not advise its members to sign such release forms, it is a common request, and writer may protect themselves by attaching a copy of their registration letter to the release form.

Resource Material

The WGC will provide lists of resource materials so a novice writer can become familiar with projects in production, Canadian producers and contact names. It also maintains a list of writer agents and entertainment lawyers. The Guild has a very limited role at this stage, for it does not assist writers in finding work, but rather represents their interests once they are working. The WGC is a professional association for working writers, operating in the same fashion as a traditional trade union: negotiating, administering and enforcing collective agreements containing basic minimum working conditions, rules and rates.

Compensation

As writers are copyright holders in their script, they must receive financial compensation for any use. Writers with completed scripts may option their material under the Independent Production Agreement to a producer for a fee, based on the option period, type and length of the program.

Screenwriters contracted under a WGC agreement receive a fee for writing the script — the script fee. The script fee is paid in installments upon delivery of material and upon payment of the full fee. The producer thereby acquires a licence to produce the script.

Under the IPA, the writer receives a further payment on the first day of principal photography, called the production fee. This additional payment is a percentage of the total production costs (above and below the line-budget items). Under the IPA, both the script fee and the production fee are paid as an advance on future royalties. When 4 per cent of the total receipts for a production (including all presales and licences) exceed the amounts previously paid to a writer, the writer is entitled to an additional 4 per cent in royalty payments.

Under the CBC and TVO agreements, the compensation system works differently. Writers receive either residuals (fees based on a percentage of the script fee), or a royalty (a percentage of producers' receipts). Further, the writer receives an additional payment called a reclearance fee when the licensed rights expire after a predefined period.

Credits

Credits are sacrosanct to a writer. Not only do they build a professional reputation recognized internationally, credits also determine payment. The form, size and placement of credits are all governed by the WGC's collective agreements. Incorrect placement or size of credits is dealt with through the collective agreements' grievance procedures. Disputes about who receives credit, however, require an arbitration process to ensure a fair and unbiased resolution.

All writers engaged on the same script are entitled to receive notification from the producer stating the credits given to each writer. Should any writer disagree with the proposed credits upon receipt of the notice, he or she may contact the Guild office, which immediately contacts the production office to inform them of the problem. A request is made for a copy of the final shooting script. This is then sent to the writer for review.

If a writer disagrees with the credits, or is not completely satisfied with the final script, he or she can replace his or her own name with a pseudonym. Complete removal of credit, however, is not an option.

If a dispute cannot be resolved the credit arbitration process is initiated. Copies of all script material are forwarded to the Guild office, where names are removed before being forwarded to three experienced writer volunteers. The volunteers also remain anonymous so as to remain immune to peer pressure or any consequences. They review the material using the arbitration manual, collective agreement and common sense as a guide. The arbitrators individually make a decision and the majority ruling constitutes a final, binding decision with respect to the credits.

Story editors can also be writers or hyphenate writers (story editors/-writers). They provide creative input, analysis, consultation and rewrite services. Series story editors also develop the story lines and characters on which an episode or program is based. Almost all series story editors provide some rewrite functions so as to ensure continuity from one script to another. Series story editors contracted under the IPA who provide rewrite services are not eligible for a writing credit under any circumstance. This is a recent change to the collective agreement, as previously story editors could receive a credit, but only as the result of a credit arbitration. Story editors generally receive a salary for their services and if they were to share a credit, the compensation of the freelance writer would be diminished. They may receive a variety of credits such as: Story Editor; Creative Consultant; Associate Producer; Executive Producer; Creative Producer; Story Consultant.

While there are internationally recognized credits and credit arbitration procedures, there are differences. For example, hyphenate writers working under the Writers' Guild of America's Minimum Basic Agreement (MBA) may receive a writing credit as a result of a credit arbitration; however it is generally an unspoken rule that they do not seek it.

The International Affiliation Of Writers' Guilds

Common credits and credit arbitration procedures exist between member guilds of the International Affiliation of Writers' Guilds (IAWG). The IAWG consists of: The Writers' Guild of Canada; Writers' Guild of America West; Writers' Guild of America East; Australian Writers' Guild; Writers' Guild of Great Britain; New Zealand Writers' Guild; and Société des Auteurs, Recherchistes, Documentalistes et Compositeurs. These seven member guilds are party to the IAWG agreement which contains credit arbitration procedures where the collective agreements of any two such guilds may be involved. Members of the IAWG also strive to ensure that credits are of the same value in all member guilds. After all, credits make a writer's reputation.

It is quite common for writers from different guilds to work on the same project in light of the increase in coproductions and coventures. For this reason alone, international cooperation is essential among writers and writer organizations.

Other countries, such as France, are not members of the IAWG and have not established any sort of credit arbitration procedures. This is particularly problematic in this country as France is Canada's most frequent co-production partner. Treaty co-production agreements have provisions regarding contracting and crediting resident writers in each country. One country's writer may be afforded a credit indicating a substantial contribution to a script; however, the other writer may consider the changes to be merely cosmetic and not deserving of a screen credit. When such a dispute arises between writers from two different countries, a lack of common credit rules and procedures makes resolution difficult.

The IAWG meets annually in a different member country, with delegates and staff from each guild exchanging information, and discussing issues of craft, trade and membership. Observers from other countries also attend. Recently, the IAWG formed a subgroup which focuses on policy and research issues and reports back to the annual meeting. Founded in 1962, the IAWG has become of greater importance in light of the globalization of the entertainment industry.

Much is to be gained from the sharing of information, human resources and experience in collective bargaining. Most important is the support member guilds provide one another during labour disputes such as strikes. During the 1988 WGA strike, the WGC supported its sister guild by refusing to allow American producers to engage Canadian writers, in essence, strike-breakers.

The IAWG works to ensure better protections and basic economic and moral rights for all writers. It also facilitates the free movement of writers in and between countries. If a writer from one guild works in the jurisdiction of another member guild, he or she is required to join that organization; however, all members of the IAWG have agreed to waive initiation fees. The rates for basic and working dues vary from guild to guild.

Jurisdiction
Working rules, or by-laws, have been developed by each guild to ensure the continued protection and advancement of writers. Unity of action by members is required to ensure working conditions do not deteriorate in one country. It is detrimental to all writers to have individuals undercutting one another, as producers could shop around for the best deal.

The WGC has jurisdiction over all writers and series story editors working for adhering producers (a producer who is a signatory to one of the guild's collective agreements) within Canada. As well as the other members of the IAWG, the WGC has its own set of by-laws and working rules. WGC members are required to work only for adhering engagers within Canada, or when working in foreign territories, producers signatory to that country's guild agreement.

Each member guild of the IAWG has a different geographic jurisdiction; however, there is often overlap particularly with the WGA. The WGA's constitution sets forth working rule number 8 which states "No member shall accept employment with or sell literary material to any person firm or corporation who is not signatory to the applicable MBA." The WGA has developed an internal procedure to enable their members to accept work in foreign countries without violating their working rule number 8. WGA members may request an official waiver of the working rule. The waiver itself sets forth additional terms which must be met by foreign producers, should they wish to employ a WGA member.

Benefits Of Being A Member

No writer is obligated to join the Writers' Guild of Canada, but all writers who work for signatory producers are covered by the terms of the collective agreements. Should a person choose not to join, they are still accorded the protection of the agreements, but are charged a nonmember fee of 5 per cent or 6 per cent.

The decision to join the WGC should be made with the knowledge that once you become a member, you can no longer write nonunion scripts. When a member accepts a nonunion engagement, they are undercutting the minimum terms of the collective agreements, thereby worsening work conditions for fellow writers by making it more difficult for the Guild to maintain the same minimum levels of protection. Members who do accept below minimum levels of compensation may be subject to fines and disciplinary proceedings.

Once you join, however, you receive benefits not available to nonmembers. The collective agreements require producers to contribute to an Insurance and Retirement Plan set up for each member. The insurance coverage you receive is based on your annual level of earnings. Dental care, eyeglasses, chiropractic services and extended health care are a few of the provisions in the plan. You also contribute to a Registered Retirement Savings Plan, which the producer also must pay into. These services are administered by an arms-length organization called the ACTRA Fraternal Benefit Society.

A WGC member is considered to be a professional writer. An annual directory listing credits and areas of experience is distributed to all signatory producers to assist their search for talent. The *WGC News* is published quarterly and distributed free of charge to all members. A favourite feature is the "Marketplace," listing projects in development and contact information.

Writing is a solitary endeavour, and members enjoy the opportunity to be able to get together and talk about their craft, who's hiring and who's not, or who's difficult to work for and who's the best. The Guild has a substructure of local forums whose goal it is to organize opportunities for discussion, networking and socializing.

Professional development for writers is essential in order to ensure continuing work opportunities in Canada. The WGC is working with organizations such as Praxis, TFI and the Canadian Film Centre to establish writer-specific training programs. Additionally, the Guild has organized screenwriting seminars, inviting prominent Canadian screenwriters to discuss their bodies of work.

The Guild presents writers' concerns to government and other administrative bodies, such as the CRTC, in order to establish policies which benefit the writer. The Guild has been active in ensuring copyright protection and supporting funding agencies, as ultimately they enable Canadians to tell their own stories. It is also an advocate of free speech, opposed to all forms of censorship. The WGC is working in conjunction with other artists' groups to pass Status of the Artist Legislation, which will recognize the right of artists to organize collectively.

The Writers' Guild of Canada exists to promote and protect the economic, creative, moral and professional rights of writers. This can best be accomplished through collective action and unity of purpose. Alone, it is very difficult to affect change and ensure minimum protections, but with the voice of many, writers can attain fair compensation and treatment.

18

WHERE TO STUDY IT

by Cindy Lewis

C indy Lewis is project manager of the Canadian Film and Television Production Association's National Training Programme. She was instrumental in setting up the program, which was created in 1995 and focuses on mentorship/on-the-job training. She was responsible for initiating and developing the CFTPA Professional Development/Educational Database, which will be made available in 1996. A native of Prince Edward Island, she has worked in the film and television industry as a publicist, production manager and research assistant since graduating from the Cinema Studies program at Laval University in Quebec City in 1987. She currently serves on the Cultural Human Resources Council's Audio-Visual Committee and the National Film & Television Professional Development Co-ordinating Committee.

"In the beginning is the word ... and the idea."

The film and television industry in Canada has grown and developed at a steady pace over the past twenty years. The need for writers has also increased and this has placed more emphasis on training and the development of writing skills.

Aspiring screenwriters have the option of learning their craft within the settings of universities and colleges leading to graduate and postgraduate degrees or diplomas. More recently, professional development organizations have sprung up to provide additional opportunities for mastering screenwriting skills through workshops and seminars. New approaches to growing screenwriters are constantly being developed.

Mentoring, although not a new invention, is becoming an ever popular method in professional development and it provides an effective means of training writers. One way to do this, for example, is by offering "trainee" positions within story departments of current television productions.

Writers are increasingly able to receive support from other, more established writers through on-line communication. Partnering of institutions is also a growing trend where resources are pooled and programs developed that can extend to smaller regions or be designed to meet specific needs.

This chapter is intended to provide for both the novice writer and the advanced writer an overview of organizations that offer the professional skills and expertise necessary for the further development of film and television writing. Selections were made based on those professional development institutions that provide screenwriting courses, workshops and mentoring programs, and that range from professional training institutions, to women's organizations, to regional film-cooperatives to ethnocentric programs.

For each of the professional development organizations listed, you will find a short description of its program(s). Arranged alphabetically by province, a second list includes the address, telephone numbers, fax numbers and in some cases, an e-mail address or website address for each organization discussed. A third listing includes all Canadian universities offering screenwriting as part of an undergraduate or graduate degree program.

Please note that the programs selected for entry in this chapter are not fully representative of all professional development writing programs offered in Canada at this time. It is a selected list based on organizations that have both a national representation and in some cases, a regional representation, and where the history of the individual program indicates a foreseen longevity. In no way is it suggested that these are the only professional development programs available. Each entry is listed in the language of instruction offered at that particular institution.

If you would like more detailed information on a particular program, please contact the organization directly. The CFTPA Professional Development/Educational Database will also be made available in 1996 and will provide annual detailed listings of both the professional development programs and accredited courses available to screenwriters in Canada among other film and television categories.

Professional Development Organizations

BRITISH COLUMBIA

Academy of Canadian Cinema and Television (see Ontario for detail)
Académie canadienne du cinéma et de la télévision

Capilano College — Extension Program (Vancouver)
Capilano College offers a Certificate Program in Film and Television Studies, which has been developed specifically to meet the industry's training needs, through consultation with unions, professional organizations and college faculty. The program combines a broad-based overview of the industry with studies in screenwriting, productions, cinematography and other areas of interest. Individual courses are also offered in screenwriting.

Praxis Film Development Workshop (Vancouver)
A screenwriters' resource centre which serves to support and stimulate the production of innovative independent Canadian feature films through screenplay development. A program of Simon Fraser University's School for the Contemporary Arts, Praxis is planning to expand beyond the feature film format to include writing for television and new technologies such as CD-ROM and other interactive media. A homepage on the Internet provides information about programs, links to other screenwriting resources and promotional materials including synopses of Praxis scripts available for option. Writing programs include: (i) Lectures/Workshops/Courses: Public readings of four feature film scripts; "After the First Draft" Workshop; The Pitch; and a screenwriting course with writers with completed first drafts. (ii) Screenwriting Competitions; and (iii) Script Analysis Program for Canadian Screenwriters. Occasionally workshops are conducted in other Canadian cities and towns, usually in conjunction with a local organization.

Vancouver Film School (VFS) (Vancouver)

This private trade school is dedicated to providing intensive, hands-on, immersion programs in disciplines associated with film, television and multimedia production. VFS is registered with the Private Post-Secondary Education Commission and the Ministry of Skills, Training and Labour for the Province of British Columbia. Writing programs include: Scriptwriting: The Basic Tools (eight weeks); Scriptwriting Workshop: Developing Your Script (twelve weeks). Three part-time sessions per year. Part-time courses range in duration from one day workshops to twelve week sessions.

ALBERTA

Academy of Canadian Cinema and Television (see Ontario for detail)
Académie canadienne du cinéma et de la télévision

Banff Centre for the Arts (Alberta)

The Banff Centre for the Arts is a place for cultural industry, producers and artists and is dedicated to lifelong learning, training and professional career development in the arts. The Centre acts as a catalyst for creative activity and experience. The Banff Centre hosts a number of programs geared towards screenwriters, as well as to producers, directors, multimedia producers, website developers and media intensive workshops at the professional level, and work study programs.

National Screen Institute (NSI) (Edmonton)

NSI offers a professional development program that encompasses hands-on workshops, mentorships, production, exhibition and marketing for emerging Canadian writers, directors and producers of film and television dramas: (i) NSI Drama Prize: applications accepted only from teams of writer, director, producers of two or more people and offers a professional development opportunity for emerging film-makers already working in the industry; (ii) Professional Development Workshops: Practical, relevant, hands-on workshops tailor-made for the needs of emerging writers, producers and directors in Canadian film and television drama.

Southern Alberta Institute of Technology (Calgary)

Continuing Education, Communication Arts Department: Academic courses include: Scriptwriting — Fact-Based Films and Videos; and Scriptwriting — Fundamentals.

Television and Film Institute for Screenwriters (TFI) (Edmonton)

To encourage and assist Canadian writers in developing screenplays for the global market by providing programs for education, promotion and networking. Since 1979, the TFI has provided educational programs for all levels of screenwriters, from the novice to the professional. Programs include: Annual Alberta Screenwriting Competition; Annual Seminar; Screenwriting Courses; Wednesday Workshops. TFI's Writers' Resource Centre is available to all TFI members and boasts a growing collection of feature film and television scripts among its resources.

SASKATCHEWAN

Saskatchewan Film Pool (Regina)

An artist-run centre which supports and encourages independent visionary film-making in Saskatchewan. As part of its mandate it provides professional development opportunities in motion picture production. The objective of the Workshop and Special Projects Program is to provide members access to information and professional development/skill enhancing opportunities.

Saskatchewan Motion Picture Association (SMPIA) (Regina)

A nonprofit organization representing the interests of the film and video community in Saskatchewan. The SMPIA Programs Committee plans programming yearly designed to meet the diverse and ongoing needs of professionals and emerging professionals in the film and video community. Programs are planned in consultation with the SMPIA membership and organizations with like concerns. They include professional development workshops, seminars, mentorship programs and individual assistance. Examples of SMPIA programming include a Documentary Writing/Film-making Workshop, an ongoing Screenwriter Mentor Program and a Story Editor/Agent Workshop.

MANITOBA

Winnipeg Film Group (Winnipeg)

An artist-run centre, the Film Group provides training at basic and advanced levels for individuals interested in learning about film-making. Writing programs have included: Advanced Workshop in Scriptwriting; and Intermediate Workshops which provide opportunities for film-makers with limited experience to create a more ambitious project by collaboratively writing a script and sampling each technical position on the crew during filming and post-production.

NORTHWEST TERRITORIES

Inuit Broadcasting Corporation (IBC) (Iqaluit/Ottawa)

IBC has been operating an Inuit television network in the Eastern and Central Arctic since 1982. IBC provides Inuktitut television programming to 30,000 Inuit in 48 communities in the Northwest Territories, Arctic Quebec and northern Labrador. The principle objectives of the organization are the promotion of the Inuit culture and language, and the improvement of communications for and among Inuit. IBC's main production centre and network uplink facility is located in Iqaluit. Programs in 1995/96 included: TV Drama Apprenticeship; TV Documentary Apprenticeship; Takuginal Versioning; Documentary Production; Drama Production; Takuginal Production. Writing programs in 1996/97 include multimedia CD-ROM; drama; intermediate television production and Women in Film and Television apprentice program.

ONTARIO

Academy of Canadian Cinema and Television (ACCT) (Toronto)
Académie canadienne du cinéma et de la télévision

A national professional association comprised of over 2,500 film and television craftspeople and artists, the Academy of Canadian Cinema and Television was founded in 1979 to stimulate, recognize and promote achievement in Canadian film and television. In addition to producing the annual Genie, Gemini and Gemeaux Awards for achievement in Canadian film and English- and French-language productions, as well as various professional development programs and publications, the

Academy offers two programs for screenwriters. First is the Understanding Story Workshop, a hands-on workshop about story, the process of communicating story from concept to script, from analysis to pitch. The workshop travels across the country. The second program is the National Story Editor Training Program and is a three-phase hands-on professional development program to train writes as qualified story editors for Canadian television series, long-form drama and feature film. The inaugural workshop took place in Toronto in 1993. This is not an annual program.

Algonquin College of Applied Arts and Technology (Ottawa)

Algonquin College is the only college program in Canada offering a Dramatic Scriptwriting program. This is a one year, post-diploma program, concentrating on writing dramatic scripts for feature films, movies of the week, television series, comedy shows and miniseries. The program is 32 weeks in duration.

Black Film and Video Network (Toronto)

A nonprofit organization of professional film and video makers actively supporting and promoting the development of film and video by Black Canadians. Writing programs include the Artists' Triad Workshop of weekend workshops for scriptwriters, directors and actors extending over three months culminating in one-day video shoots. The Internship Program provides an opportunity to apprentice with a production company or an individual professional in the film and video community.

Canadian Broadcasting Corporation (CBC) (Toronto)
Société Radio-Canada (SRC)

CBC Training and Development is a national service for the people who contribute to CBC broadcasting. It consults, trains, manages resources and supports professional development in the pursuit of programming and management excellence. It began with basic courses and crossover workshops to bring experienced writers to television. Specialized and advanced courses were developed from dramatic series, MOWs and children's television. Building on this experience, CBC now provides story workshops for story editors, producers and executives. A lot of this work continues to take place in cooperation with other organizations, and these programs are often open to independent professionals who contribute to Arts and Entertainment programming. Other initiatives include a Drama Project that combines training and real production experience for writers, directors, actors and all crafts. Writing programs included: Understanding Story (Halifax and Vancouver); Internships in Dramatic Series Writing, Variety and Comedy Writing, and a Master Writer's Workshop.

Canadian Film Centre (CFC) (Toronto)
Centre canadien du film

As a national organization which began operations in 1988, the Centre's mission is to advance the artistic and technical skills of writers, directors and producers in support of a dynamic industry, and to increase the awareness and appreciation of Canadian film and television. The TV Drama Programme was established in 1993 for participants who have one or more credits as a television writer or producer and who come to the Programme with a dramatic project in development. During the four-week workshop in early spring, these projects undergo intensive development with experts in the broadcast industry. Open to screenwriters with a proven commitment and mastery of the art and craft of screenwriting, the Centre's Professional Screenwriting Programme transforms the aspiring writer into a working professional in a unique twelve-week, industry-immersion workshop. In The Resident Programme, Writer and Director Residents are provided with the opportunity to develop their creative skills through a series of workshops and film-making exercises. Through their participation in a series of story editing workshops, each resident completes a fully developed draft screenplay.

Canadian Screen Training Centre (CSTC) (Ottawa/Sudbury)
Réseau d'ateliers cinématographiques canadiens

The Canadian Screen Training Centre is a nonprofit organization that has been training screen professionals since 1981. The CSTC offers screenwriting workshops for all levels in both English and French. The Summer Institute of Film & Television, the CSTC holds its largest event every June for five days, where there are over twelve screenwriting workshops from which to choose, taught by some of the best in the business. The workshop experience is enriched by learning from working with successful professionals. Moreover, there are screenings, panels, discussions, networking, social events and more to supplement the classroom dialogue.

CTV Television Network (Toronto)
CTV Production Apprentice Program: supports and develops talent in key areas of production such as writing (producing, directing and editing). This program is implemented in conjunction with independent Canadian producers and applies to television series, miniseries, made for television movies and specials.

Directing, Acting and Writing For Camera Workshop (DAWC) (Toronto)
DAWC is a nonprofit corporation involved in training professionals in film and television. This Workshop is designed for directors, writers and actors to master their work for the screen. This is achieved by giving writers and directors training and experience of direct work with actors in the production of original dramas, written specifically for the team. Each semester-long workshop, one in the spring and one in the fall, consists of 150 contact hours. Classes are held evenings and shooting is done on the weekends. Five hundred young professionals have graduated from this Workshop and over 100 short original dramas have been produced.

Independent Filmmakers Cooperative of Ottawa (IFCO) (Ottawa)
Founded in 1991 to provide Ottawa-area film-makers with the facilities and funds to make independent films. The co-op offers a series of ongoing workshops including Basic Screenwriting, Screenwriting & Storyboarding for Low-Budget Films, Advanced Scriptwriting and Hands on Film. Three blocks are offered through the year and each participant will have worked on his or her own film by the end of the session.

Queen's University (Kingston)
Part-time Studies: Special topics course in Screenwriting offered at Brockville campus, one evening per week.

Ryerson Polytechnic University (Toronto)
Professional Development Workshop Series & Continuing Education, School of Radio and Television Arts.
More than 100 workshops are offered between May and July each year that examine various aspects of media production in a very practical and hands-on manner. Specific workshops are offered in writing for television

and radio broadcast, writing drama for television, writing for interactive multimedia, writing creative copy for media and critical analysis of television scripts. RTA also offers several writing courses in its continuing education program (such as Elements of Style in Media Writing and Writing for the Electronic Media). From time to time, RTA also offers additional seminars and "master writing workshops" which are open to the public.

Continuing Education, Department of Film and Photography
Offers year-round courses in scriptwriting within its film-making program through Continuing Education.

Script Lab (Toronto)

In its sixth season, Script Lab is mandated to provide developmental, informational and resource services for Canadian writers of new works for the stage, screen or radio. Programs include: Extended Development Workshops, which put together new works on a project-by-project basis; Lecture Series, a series of informational lectures, mini-workshops and panel discussions designed to be of interest to Canadian writers; a Script Analysis Service; and Writers Intensive (for writers and actors). A Reading Evening Series is at the heart of the Script Lab mandate with its goal of providing writers with the opportunity to hear their early draft scripts read out loud by professional actors and to receive constructive feedback from a facilitated audience discussion period. In the first five sessions, over 100 scripts have been presented in this manner.

Women in Film and Television — Toronto (WIFT-T) (Toronto)

Founded in 1984, WIFT-T's mission is to enhance the opportunities for women in the industry nationally and internationally, to provide leadership and to celebrate the accomplishments of women in film and television. The WIFT-T Mentor Program provides an opportunity for women at various levels of the film and television industry to gain experience and knowledge under the guidance of more senior industry professionals who generously agree to serve as their mentors. The WIFT Studio is a permanent weekly professional lab where writers, directors, actors, camera operators and producers "workshop" scenes with their peers, and constantly hone their talent and crafts.

Writers' Guild of Canada (WGC) (Toronto)

A national association representing more than 1,200 professional free-lance writers working on English-language film, television, corporate, multimedia, educational and radio production in Canada. The WGC established a training committee in spring 1995 to initiate professional development opportunities for its members. To date, the WGC has co-sponsored a multimedia seminar at the 1995 Vancouver Film Festival trade forum, and has contributed to a workshop for advanced TV writing in October 1995. As well, it co-sponsored a TFI 13-day workshop on writing for series television in January 1996.

QUEBEC — THESE PROGRAMS ARE AVAILABLE IN FRENCH ONLY

Academy of Canadian Cinema and Television (ACCT)
Académie canadienne du cinéma et de la télévision

Bande vidéo et film de Québec (La) (Québec)

Fondé en 1977, la Bande vidéo et film de Québec se définissait comme un centre d'accès technique et de formation audio-vidéo. La Bande vidéo et film de Québec est un organisme sans but lucratif. Les ateliers de formation (1993-95): scénarisation de fiction; scénarisation de documentaire; et scripte.

Institut national de l'image et du son (INIS) (Montreal)

L'INIS c'est un institut de formation professionelle en cinéma et télévision dont la mission est de former des scénaristes (des réalisateurs et des producteurs). L'INIS c'est enfin le privilège d'apprendre un métier de création grâce à un corps professoral composé uniquement de professionnels actifs dans les milieux cinematographique et télévisuel. Bref, l'INIS est le seul institut de formation professionnelle francophone en Amérique du Nord qui offre un programme d'une durée de trois ans en cinéma et en télévision.

The objective of INIS is to train qualified people in the creative fields of scriptwriting (directing and producing) in order to ensure the cultural vitality and development of the audio-visual industry; and to develop multimedia expertise in order to foster the professional integration of tomorrow's specialists in the fields of film, video and television in scriptwriting, directing and producing.

Parlimage (Montreal)

Depuis plus de 18 ans, Parlimage, le plus important centre de formation en audiovisuel, a pour objectif de former les futurs professionels du cinéma et de la télévision. (Deux fois par année.) Parlimage propose les ateliers d'écriture suivants: Scénarisation Fiction *Long Métrage* — Cet atelier d'écriture qui se déroule sur trois mois, a pour objectif de vous permettre de maîtriser les techniques propres à l'écritue ciné-matographique. A l'aide d'exercices pratiques vous aurez la possibilité de travailler au développement d'un sujet personnel sous la supervision d'un(e) scénariste de métier.

Scénarisation Série Télévision — Ponctué de visionnements, d'analyse de scénarios existants et d'exercices pratiques, ce stage intensif de cinq jours vous permettre d'acquérir les techniques propres de la scénarisa-tion télévisuelle et ainsi de découvrir les subtilités, les exigences et les contraintes inhérentes à ce médium.

Spirafilm (Quebec City)

Spirafilm est une coopérative de cinéastes-vidéastes indépendants. Ateliers de formation en production cinématographique: Les ateliers qu'offre Spirafilm ont pour but de former les participants dans les dif-férentes disciplines rattacheés à la production cinématographique indépendante. Ateliers offerts: Pré-production: Scénarisation (6 heures). Spirafilm possède un plus grand choix de matériel cinématographique que les autres organismes (commerciaux ou éducatifs) de la region de la ville de Québec. Spirafilm est le seul organisme local où les méthodes de production font usage fréquent de la cinématographie.

NEW BRUNSWICK

New Brunswick Filmmakers' Co-operative (NBFCO) Fredericton

A nonprofit group of independent film-makers involved in the produc-tion of 16-mm motion pictures. Ongoing workshops are offered in the-oretical and practical film-making skills such as writing (directing, acting, editing, etc.). The 1994/95 short (two-day) workshops included: "In the Beginning ... Writing the Great Canadian Film." The 1995/96 writing workshops include Scriptwriting and Storyboarding.

NOVA SCOTIA

Academy of Canadian Cinema and Television (see Ontario for detail)
Académie canadienne du cinéma et de la télévision

Atlantic Filmmakers' Co-operative (AFCOOP) (Halifax)
Incorporated as a nonprofit film production centre in 1974, AFCOOP functions as an independent production centre and as a film training and professional development centre and a funding agency. It aims to maintain a suitably encouraging environment for beginning and advanced film-makers to create skilled and confident film professionals. AFCOOP programs include their Five Minute Film Series, Intermediate Training Program and the Nova Scotia School of Art and Design/AFCOOP Filmmaking Courses.

Centre for Art Tapes (Halifax)
A community-based, nonprofit artist-run video, audio and computer access centre founded in 1978. Main activities include: production facilities, programming, workshops, an artist-in-residence program and scholarships for video, audio and computer. Workshops: Script Writing (among others).

PRINCE EDWARD ISLAND

Academy of Canadian Cinema and Television (see Ontario for detail)
Académie canadienne du cinéma et de la télévision

Island Media Arts Co-op (Charlottetown)
Since 1982, IMAC has provided its members with resources, facilities and support for 16-mm film production. IMAC devotes time to workshops, training and exhibitions. Weekend workshops in writing are usually taught by senior members.

NEWFOUNDLAND

Newfoundland Independent Filmmakers Co-operative (NIFCO) (St. John's)
Incorporated in 1975, this association of independent filmmakers originate and execute film projects using Co-op equipment and facilities. Their Introductory Film Course offers, as part of the overview of the first part of the course, an exercise in developing a script for a five-minute film. They also provide Professional Development Workshops in conjunction with the Writers' Alliance of Newfoundland Labrador and organize week-long workshops on adaptation.

How to Contact

BRITISH COLUMBIA

Academy of Canadian Cinema and Television (ACCT)
Académie canadienne du cinéma et de la télévision

Vancouver Office
1385 Homer Street
Vancouver, British Columbia V6B 5M9
Telephone   (604) 684-4528
Fax   (604) 684-4574

Capilano College Extension Programs
2055 Purcell Way
North Vancouver, British Columbia V7J 3H5
Telephone   (604) 984-4901
Fax   (604) 983-7545

Praxis Film Development Workshop
#200-1140 Homer Street
Vancouver, British Columbia V6B 2X6
Telephone   (604) 682-3100
Fax   (604) 682-7909

Vancouver Film School (VFS)
Part-Time Courses
400-1168 Hamilton Street
Vancouver, British Columbia V6B 2S2
Telephone   (604) 685-5808
Fax   (604) 685-5803
E-Mail   queryl@griffin.multimedia.edu
Website   http://www.multimedia.edu

ALBERTA

Banff Centre for the Arts
Box 1020, Station 28
Banff, Alberta T0L 0C0
Telephone   (403) 762-6180
Fax   (403) 762-6345
E-Mail   Arts Info@BanffCentre.ab.ca
Website: WWW.BanffCentre.Ad.CA

National Screen Institute (NSI)
3rd Floor, 10022-103 Street
Edmonton, Alberta T5J 0X2
Telephone   (403) 421-4084
Toll-free   1-800-480-4084
Fax (403)   425-8098
E-Mail   deb-nsi@Supernet.ab.ca

Southern Alberta Institute of Technology (SAIT)
Continuing Education, Communication Arts Department
1301 16 Avenue North West
Calgary, Alberta T2M 0L4
Telephone   (403) 282-6184
Fax   (403) 284-7112

Television and Film Institute for Screenwriters (TFI)
Room 441, 10045-156 Street
Edmonton, Alberta T5P 2P7
Telephone   (403) 497-4304
BBS   (403) 487-7089
Fax   (403) 497-4330

SASKATCHEWAN

Saskatchewan Film Pool
1100 Broad Street
Regina, Saskatchewan S4R 1X8
Telephone   (306) 757-8818
Fax   (306) 757-3622
E-Mail   filmpool@ucomnet.unibase.com

Saskatchewan Motion Picture Association (SMPIA)
2431 8th Avenue
Regina, Saskatchewan S4R 5J7
Telephone   (306) 525-9899
Fax   (306) 569-1818

MANITOBA

Winnipeg Film Group
304-100 Arthur Street
Winnipeg, Manitoba R3B 1H3
Telephone   (204) 942-6795
Fax   (204) 942-6799

NORTHWEST TERRITORIES

Inuit Broadcasting Corporation (IBC)
P.O. Box 700
Iqualuit, Northwest Territories
X0A 0H0
Telephone   (819) 979-6231
Fax   (819) 979-5853

ONTARIO

Academy of Canadian Cinema and Television (ACCT)
Académie canadienne du cinéma et de la télévision
158 Pearl Street
Toronto, Ontario M5H 1L3
Telephone   (416) 591-2040
Fax   (416) 591-2157

Algonquin College of Applied Arts and Technology
Woodroffe Campus, 1385 Woodroffe Avenue
Nepean, Ontario K2G 1V8
Telephone   (613) 727-0002
Toll Free   1-800-565-4723
Fax   (613) 727-7632

Black Film and Video Network
24 Ryerson Avenue, Suite 307
Toronto, Ontario M5T 2P3
Telephone   (416) 504-1442
Fax   (416) 504-1478

Canadian Broadcasting Corporation (CBC)
Société Radio-Canada (SRC)
CBC Training and Development
P.O. Box 500, Station A
Toronto, Ontario M5W 1E6
Telephone   (416) 205-3323
Fax   (416) 205-3756

Canadian Film Centre (CFC)
Centre canadien du film
Windfields, 2489 Bayview Avenue
North York, Ontario M2L 1A8
Telephone   (416) 445-1446
Fax   (416) 445-9481

Canadian Screen Training Centre (cstc)
Réseau d'atiliers cinématographiques canadiens
61A rue York Street
Ottawa, Ontario K1N 5T2
Telephone   (613) 789-4720
Toll Free   1-800-742-6016
Fax   (613) 789-4724

CTV Television Network Ltd.
250 Yonge Street, Suite 1800
Toronto, Ontario M5B 2N8
Telephone   (416) 595-4100
Fax   (416) 595-1203

Directing, Acting and Writing For Camera Workshop (dawc)
50 Prince Arthur Avenue, Suite 1407
Toronto, Ontario M5R 1B5
Telephone   (416) 922-5378

Independent Filmmakers Cooperative of Ottawa (ifco)
Arts Court, 2 Daly Avenue, Suite 100
Ottawa, Ontario K1N 6E2
Telephone   (613) 569-1789
Fax   (613) 564-4428
E-Mail   bil61@freenet.carleton.ca

Inuit Broadcasting Corporation (IBC)
251 Laurier Avenue West, Suite 703
Ottawa, Ontario K1P 5J6
Telephone   (613) 235-1892
Fax   (613) 230-8824
E-Mail   ibcicsl@sonetis.com

Queen's University
Part-Time Studies
Kingston, Ontario K7L 3N6
Telephone   (613) 545-2471
Fax   (613) 545-6805

Ryerson Polytechnic University
350 Victoria Street
Toronto, Ontario M5B 2K3

Continuing Education, Film Studies and Media Arts, Film and Photography Department
Telephone   (416) 979-5035
Fax   (416) 979-5277

Continuing Education & Professional Development Workshop Series, School of Radio & Television Arts (in conjunction with Rogers Communications Centre)
Telephone   (416) 979-5107
Fax   (416) 979-5246
E-Mail   czamria@acs.ryerson.ca
Website   http://www.rcc.ryerson.ca/learn.htm

Script Lab
52 Strathcona Avenue
Toronto, Ontario M4J 1G8
Telephone   (416) 465-6071/(416) 964-8566
Fax   (416) 465-9024
E-Mail   sgreen@interlog.com

Women in Film and Television — Toronto (WIFT-T)
20 Eglinton Avenue West, Suite 902, Box 2009
Toronto, Ontario M4R 1K8
Telephone   (416) 322-3430
Hotline   (416) 322-3648
Fax   (416) 322-3703

Writers' Guild of Canada (WGC)
35 McCaul Street, Suite 300
Toronto, Ontario M5T 1V7
Telephone   (416) 979-7907
Toll-free   1-800-567-9974
Fax   (416) 979-9273
E-Mail   WGC@io.org (aski format)

QUÉBEC

Academy of Canadian Cinema and Television (ACCT)
Académie canadienne du cinéma et de la télévision
Montreal Branch Office
3575 boul. St.-Laurent, bureau 709
Montréal, (Québec) H2X 2T7
Telephone   (514) 849-7448
Fax   (514) 849-5069

Bande vidéo et film de Québec (La)
541, St-Vallier Est, B.P. 2
Québec (Québec) G1K 2V6
Telephone   (418) 522-5561
Fax   (418) 525-4041

Institut national de l'image et du son (INIS)
1301, rue Sherbrooke Est, Edifice Lafontaine, bureau 1208
Montréal (Quebec) H2L 1M3
Telephone   (514) 525-6361
Fax   (514) 525-6364

Parlimage
4398, boulevard St-Laurent, bureau 103
Montréal (Québec) H2W 1Z5
Telephone   (514) 288-1400
Fax   (514) 288-2989

Spirafilm
541, Saint-Vallier Est, B.P. # 1,
Québec (Québec) G1K 3P9
Telephone   (418) 523-1275
Fax   (418) 523-0135
E-Mail   spira@qbc.Clic.Net

NEW BRUNSWICK

New Brunswick Filmmakers' Cooperative (NBFCO)
P.O. Box 1537, Station A, 51 York Street
Fredericton, New Brunswick E3B 4Y1
Telephone (506) 455-132
Fax   (506) 457-2006

NOVA SCOTIA

Academy of Canadian Cinema and Television (ACCT)
Académie canadienne du cinéma et de la télévision
Halifax Branch Office
1652 Barrington Street
Halifax, Nova Scotia B3J 2A2
Telephone (902) 425-0489
Fax   (902) 425-8851

Atlantic Filmmakers' Co-operative (AFCOOP)
P.O. Box 2043, Station 'M'
Halifax, Nova Scotia B3J 2Z1
Telephone (902) 423-8833
Fax   (902) 492-2678

Centre for Art Tapes
5663 Cornwallis Street, Suite 104
Halifax, Nova Scotia B3K 1B6
Telephone (902) 429-6399
Fax (902)   429-7299

PRINCE EDWARD ISLAND

Island Media Arts Co-op (IMAC)
P.O. Box 2726
Charlottetown, Prince Edward Island C1A 8C3
Telephone (902) 892-3131
Fax   (902) 682-2019

NEWFOUNDLAND

Newfoundland Independent Filmmakers' Co-operative (NIFCO)
40 Kings Road
St. John's, Newfoundland A1C 3P5
Telephone   (709) 753-6121
Fax   (709) 753-5366

Universities

The following is a listing of graduate and postgraduate programs offering screenwriting as part of a degree program in cinematography and television.

Alberta (Edmonton, AB)
Department of Modern Languages and Comparative Studies: BA
Tel: 403-492-3111

Brock (St. Catharines, ON)
Department of Film Studies, Dramatic and Visual Arts: BA
Tel: 905-688-5550

Carleton (Ottawa, ON)
School of Studies in Art and Culture: BA
Tel: 613-788-7400

Concordia (Montreal, PQ)
Department of Cinema: BFA, MFA
Tel: 514-848-4600

Laval (Quebec City, PQ)
Faculté des lettres: certificat
Tel: 418-656-2131

Manitoba (Winnipeg, MB)
Film Studies (program): BA
Tel: 204-474-8880

Montréal (Montréal, PQ)
Département d'histoire de l'art: BA, diplôme, MA
Tel: 514-343-6111

Queen's (Kingston, ON)
Department of Film Studies: BA
Stage and Screen Studies (program): BA
Tel: 613-545-2000

Regina (Regina, SK)
Department of Film and Video: BA, BFA
Tel: 306-585-4111

*Ryerson Polytechnic (Toronto, ON)
Department of Film and Photography: BAA
Department of Radio and Television Arts: BAA
Tel: 416-979-5000

Simon Fraser (Burnaby, BC)
School of Contemporary Arts: BFA
Tel: 604-291-3111

Toronto (Toronto, ON)
Department of Classics: BA
Tel: 416-978-2011
Innis College: BA
Tel: 416-978-7023

University of British Columbia (Vancouver, BC)
Department of Creative Writing: MFA
Department of Theatre and Film: BA, diploma, MA, MFA
Tel: 604-822-2211

Université du Québec à Chicoutimi (Chicoutimi, PQ)
Module des arts: BA, certificat
Tel: 418-454-5011

Université du Québec à Montréal (Montréal, PQ)
Module d'études littéraires: certificat
Tel: 514-987-3000

University of Western Ontario (London, ON)
Department of English: BA
Tel: 519-679-2111

Victoria (Victoria, BC)
Film Studies (Program): BA
Tel: 604-721-7211

Wilfrid Laurier University (Waterloo, ON)
Film Studies (program): BA
Tel: 519-884-1970

Waterloo (Waterloo, ON)
Department of Fine Arts: BA
Tel: 519-885-1211

*York (Toronto, ON)
Department of Film and Video: BA, BFA, MFA
Department of Fine Arts (Atkinson College): BA
Tel: 416-736-2100

*must call to confirm screenwriting courses

Glossary

Ad slick The proof of an advertisement created for newspapers.

Advance Money obtained up front in anticipation of profits. A portion of the advance may be refunded if the film does not perform in the marketplace, unlike a guarantee, which is not refundable.

Art film Synonymous with *specialty film*, a film made by an independent filmmaker, often on a modest production budget and without stars, and distributed as a genre film.

Avid A regular filmgoer, someone who sees more than 20 theatrical films a year.

B-roll Informal footage of filmmaking activity, usually included in the EPK. *See also* EPK.

Box office Colloquial term that stands for box office grosses, all the money taken in at theatres for ticket sales.

Break The publication of a story about a film in a major newspaper or magazine.

Contra deal A financing arrangement whereby suppliers provide services to the film production or marketing campaign, in return for prominent placement of their products in the production or a promotional listing in the credits and marketing materials.

Demographics The categorization of consumers/audience according to their vital statistics such as age, sex, social status, income, etc.

Distributor A person or company holding the right to market and distribute films or videos to such markets as theatrical, free TV, pay TV, video clubs, airlines, etc.

Electronic press kit (EPK) A video package distributed to news media to publicize a theatrical feature film. It usually contains interviews with stars and director, movie clips, sound bites, and behind-the-scenes footage edited to be easily adapted to TV formats.

Errors and omissions (e&o) Insurance for a film covering the producer's legal liability for alleged unauthorized use of titles, ideas, characters, plots; invasion of privacy; libel; slander; defamation of character; etc.

Free tv Television service broadcast without charge to viewers; includes commercial (advertiser-supported) tv and public (mainly government-supported) tv. Also known as *conventional tv*.

Genre film A category or type of film distinguished by subject or technique; examples include thrillers, westerns, family films, and science fiction films.

Give-away An item created for publicity purposes and handed out free of charge to potential moviegoers. T-shirts, coffee mugs, and pens are common give-aways.

Gross deal A type of distribution deal in which the gross receipts are shared between the distribuor and the producer from first dollar, with no deductions other than the producer's advance, if there has been one. *See also* **Net deal.**

Gross rating point A basis for estimating the percentage of households or target audience exposed to a broadcast commercial or published advertisement.

Guarantee A sum of money that is payable regardless of a film's performance in the marketplace. The minimum amount of revenue offered for the right to exploit a movie. Guarantees can be paid in advance, on signing a contract, or at a specific date thereafter.

Internegative A duplicate negative derived from the interpositive and from which release prints are struck.

Interpositive An intermediate step between the cut negative (after the answer print is approved) and the internegative.

Key art The design concept used to identify a film or television program for packaging and marketing purposes, including such items as script cover design, advertising and promotional material, company logo, and title design.

Mainstream audience The broad, general audience sought for most films in commercial release.

Marketing The process of producing and selling at a profit products, including films, that people want.

Marketing plan A written plan describing the activities involved in achieving a marketing objective.

Marquee casting The selection of actors based on their potential as stars to attract audiences.

Mass marketing A commercial advertising method that provides high visibility for a film in all media and in many theatres.

Net deal A type of distribution deal in which the gross receipts are shared between distributor and producer after deduction of distributor's fee, agreed-upon distribution expenses, and advances to the producer, if any. *See also* **Gross deal**.

Niche marketing All of the steps involved in marketing a production to a discrete and identifiable segment of consumers.

One-sheet The film poster.

Output deal A type of distribution deal whereby a distributor contracts the right to exploit the entire output of a foreign producer or seller for a given period of time.

Package A compilation of elements about a film in development used to attract financing for it. The package usually includes the script, names of key cast and filmmakers, a description of the target market, and revenue projections.

"Pay or play" A "pay or play" obligation is a contractual commitment to use (and pay for) the services of an individual, or to pay for those services even in the event that you do not use them.

Pay TV A TV service paid for by viewers and carried on a cable network.

Pitch The term stands for *sales pitch*, an attempt to sell or win approval for a proposal.

Platform release A release method whereby a film is opened in one theatre in one city at a time to build public and critical awareness and positive word of mouth.

PosiTioNiNq A segmentation technique, as well as an advertising style, that attempts to position a product in a consumer's mind often by comparing an unknown quantity to a known one. Includes creating an effective first impression of the title and subject of a production.

Press kit A package of materials designed for the media and prepared under the supervision of the unit publicist. The kit contains photos, plot synopsis, bios of feature players, producer, director, and screenwriter, column notes, and feature stories.

Press screeNiNq A private screening for journalists before the release of a production, intended to enable them to prepare reviews of it.

PriNcipal phoToqraphy The shooting of all scenes requiring the main body of the crew and any of the leading performers.

PriNts aNd adverTsiNq (P&A) The total cost of releasing a film, based on the costs of making prints and of advertising and publicity.

Producer The person with overall responsibility for the production, who exercises control over financing, hiring, spending, the selection of key creative personnel, commercial exploitation, and so forth.

ProducTioN charTs Lists of projects in production published weekly or monthly by trade publications.

ProducTioN stills Photographs taken by the set photographer during the course of shooting of a film or television program.

Publicist A specialist in coordinating and presenting information about a client in such a way that media attention is directed toward the client. *See also* **Unit publicist**.

Sales aqeNt Sales person who represents a producer or production company and its productions, usually on a commission basis.

SpecialTy film *See* **Art film**.

Spot TV or radio advertisments for a feature film.

STaNdee Point-of-purchase advertising in the form of a stand-up display placed in theatre lobbies or other locations likely to attract the attention of potential filmgoers. Also known as a *stand-up*.

Star Performer who is sufficiently well known that he or she is perceived to bring an economic benefit to any production in which he or she appears in a leading role.

Target audience/market The audience to which marketing, selling, or advertising is aimed. This audience is determined by demographic or psychological segmentation techniques. *See also* **Demographics.**

Teaser Also called a pre-trailer; a short (30- to 45-second) promotion for a film placed in theatres about six months before the release date. *See also* **Trailer**.

Test marketing A method of testing a marketing plan on a limited scale to gain an indication of the likely acceptance by consumers of the product.

Theatrical release The process of advertising, promoting, and distributing films to theatres.

Tie-in A method of extending the promotion of a film by finding co-sponsors and creating cross-promotional advertising.

Title treatment The distinctive logo of a film's title used consistently in an advertising campaign.

Trailer A commercial for a film exhibited in movie theatres before or during the run of a film. Most trailers include scenes from the coming attraction edited to create the greatest interest in it.

Unit publicist The person responsible for co-ordinating and disseminating to the media information about a film in production.

Wide release A release method whereby a film is opened in more than one theatre in key markets. In Canada, a wide release implies opening on over 45 screens in Toronto, Montreal, Vancouver, Ottawa, Calgary, Edmonton, and Halifax as well as the smaller markets of London, Kitchener, Saskatoon, Regina, and Victoria. In the United States, a blockbuster film may be opened on over 2000 screens in key markets.

"Window" A period of time during which a purchasor of rights (e.g., theatrical, free TV, pay TV) receives the exclusive right to exhibit the production.

Word of mouth The negative or positive opinions about a film that viewers disseminate.

Bibliography

Academy of Canadian Cinema and Television. Barbara Hehner and Andra Sheffer, eds. *Making It*. Doubleday: Toronto, 1995.

— Joan Irving, ed. *Selling It*. Doubleday: Toronto, 1995.

Brady, Ben. *The Understructure of Writing for Film & Television*. Austin, Texas: University of Texas Press, 1988.

Brenner, Alfred. *TV Scriptwriter's handbook: Dramatic Writing for Television and Film*. Los Angeles: Silman-James Press, 1992.

Callan, K. *The Script is finished, Now what do I do?* California, K. Callan, 1993.

Cooper, Pat, and Ken Dancyger. *Writing the Short Film*. Boston: Focal Press, 1994.

Ergri, Lajos. *Art of Dramatic Writing*. New York: Simon & Schuster, 1972.

Field, Syd. *Screenplay*. New York: Dell Publishing, 1984.

— *Four Screenplays: Studies in the American Screenplay*. New York: Dell Trade Paperback, 1994.

— *The Screenwriter's Workbook*. New York: Dell Publishing, 1988.

Goldberg, Natalie. *Writing Down the Bones*. Boston: Shambhala Publications, 1986.

Goldman, William. *Adventures in the Screen Trade*. New York: Warner Books, 1983.

Harris, Lesley Ellen. *Canadian Copyright Law, 2nd ed.* Toronto: McGraw-Hill Ryerson, 1995.

Hunter, Lew. *Lew Hunter's Screenwriting 434.* New York: Perigree Books, 1993.

King, Viki. *How to Write a Movie in Twenty-one Days.* New York: Harper & Row, 1988.

Posner, Michael. *Canadian Dreams: The Making and Marketing of Independent Films.* Vancouver/Toronto: Douglas & McIntrye, 1993.

Rosenthal, Alan. *Writing Docudrama: Dramatizing Reality for Film and TV.* Boston: Focal Press, 1995.

Seger, Linda. *The Art of Adaptation: Turning Fact and Fiction into Film.* New York: Henry Holt, 1992.

— *Creating Unforgettable Characters.* New York: Henry Holt, 1990.

— *Making a Good Script Great.* Hollywood: Samuel French, 1987.

Trottier, David. *The Screenwriter's Bible: A Complete Guide to Writing, Formatting, and Selling your Script. (rev. ed.).* Los Angeles: Silman-James Press, 1995.

Vogler, Christopher. *The Writer's Journey: Mythic Structure for Storytellers and Screenwriters.* Los Angeles: Michael Wiese Film & Video Book, 1993.

Walters, Richard. *Screenwriting: The Art, Craft and Business of Film & Television Writing.* New York: Penguin, A Plume Book, 1988.

Index